George Stewart

The Story of the Great Fire in St. John, N.B.

June 20th, 1877

George Stewart

The Story of the Great Fire in St. John, N.B.
June 20th, 1877

ISBN/EAN: 9783337249748

Printed in Europe, USA, Canada, Australia, Japan

Cover: Foto ©ninafisch / pixelio.de

More available books at **www.hansebooks.com**

RUINS OF THE GERMAIN ST. BAPTIST CHURCH BY MOONLIGHT.

THE STORY

OF THE

Great Fire in St. John, N.B.

JUNE 20TH, 1877.

BY

GEORGE STEWART, JR.,
OF ST. JOHN, N.B.

Toronto:
BELFORD BROTHERS, PUBLISHERS.
ST. JOHN, N.B.: R. A. H. MORROW; MONTREAL, P. Q.:
DAWSON BROS.; TORONTO, ONT.: JAS. CLARKE &
CO.; DETROIT, MICH.: CRAIG & TAYLOR;
BOSTON: LOCKWOOD, BROOKS & CO.

Entered according to the Act of the Parliament of Canada, in the year one thousand eight hundred and seventy-seven, by BELFORD BROTHERS, in the office of the Minister of Agriculture.

HUNTER, ROSE & CO.,
PRINTERS AND BINDERS,
TORONTO.

TO

GILBERT MURDOCH, C. E.,

MY FIRST FRIEND,

I DEDICATE THIS VOLUME.

The Author.

CONTENTS.

CHAPTER I.

                                                                                            PAGE

The Great Fire—Its Extent—Its Terrible Rapidity—A Glance Backward—What the People Passed Through—The First Fire—Protective Movements—The People who Lent the City Money—Minor Fires—Fire of 1823—The Great Fire of 1837—The Calamity of 1839—The Trials of 1831—The King Street Fire,................ 9

CHAPTER II.

The Late Fire—Its Origin—Bravery of the Firemen—The High Wind—The Fire's Career—Fighting the Flames—Almost Lost—The Escape from the Burning Building—Destruction of Dock Street—Smyth Street in Flames—The Wharves—Demolition of Market Square—Something about the Business Houses there—The Banks—Fire Checked at North Street...................................... 19

CHAPTER III.

The Fire in King Street—Recollections—The Old Coffee House Corner—The Stores in King Street—The Old Masonic Hall—The St. John Hotel—Its Early Days—The Bell Tower—King Square—A Night of Horror—The Vultures at Work—Plundering the Destitute...... 27

CHAPTER IV.

The Fire in Germain Street—The First Brick House in St. John—Old Trinity—The Loyalists—Curious Ideas about Insurance—The Rectors of Trinity—The Clock—The Royal Arms..................... 36

CONTENTS. v

PAGE

CHAPTER V.

The Old Curiosity Shop on Germain Street—A Quaint Old Palace—
"Rubbish Shot Here"—Notman's Studio—The Mother of Methodism—Destruction of the Germain Street Methodist Church—Burning of the Academy of Music—The Old Grammar School—Presbyterians among the Loyalists—The "Auld Kirk"—Saint Andrews—The Grants of Land—Legislation—The Building of the Kirk—Ministers—The "Victoria" in Flames—Fascination of the Fire—The "Victoria" in Ruins—What might have saved it 48

CHAPTER VI.

The Odd Fellows' Hall—The Fire in Horsfield Street—The sweep along Germain Street—The Old Baptist Church—Some Early Ministers—Two Fiery Ordeals—The Brick Church—The Ruins—The Bay View Hotel—An Old Landmark Gone—The Blazing Barracks—St. James's—The Hazen House—St. Malachi's Chapel—The First Roman Catholic Church... 65

CHAPTER VII.

A Hard-Working Manager—The Dramatic Lyceum—The Temperance Hall—The Water-Works Building—A Hard Fight—Another Rush of the Homeless—The Weary March of the Unfortunates—History of the Water Supply—Early Struggles—Changes—The Old Way—The St. John Water Company—Placed in Commission—The Company to-day 76

CHAPTER VIII.

Burning of the Leinster Street Baptist Church—The Varley School—Centenary Chapel—The Gas Works—$17,000 worth of Coal burned in Ten Days—The Tall Sentinel—St. David's Kirk—The Reformed Presbyterian Church—The Victoria School—Gigantic Ruins—An Accident—Sketch of the School-house............................. 90

CHAPTER IX.

Queen Square—Incidents in the Burning—The Old Pitcher—" God is burning up the World, and He won't make another"—Saved from the Flames—Overtaken by Fire Three Times—The Night of Terror on Queen Square—Alone amidst Perils—The Lone House on the Square—Three People under a Table—The Sailor—" If I die to-night, sir, hunt them up"—The Escape—The Deserted Streets—An Anomaly—The Marine Hospital—What a few Buckets of Water did—The Wiggins Orphan Asylum—The Block in Canterbury Street—The *News* Office—Savings Bank 101

CHAPTER X.

Incidents—An Old Corner Burned Down—The Lenders and Borrowers—" Twenty per Cent"—The Shylocks of the Curbstone—The Human Barometers—The Vultures of Commerce—Chubbe's Corner—The Old Commercial Bank—The *Telegraph* Office—The Bank of New Brunswick—A Hard Worked Cashier—The Post Office—Not a Mail Lost—Quick Dispatch—The Nethery House and Orangemen—The Royal Hotel—The Custom House—The Dead of the Conflagration... 114

CHAPTER XI.

The Old House on the Hill—A Wily Commissary—The Bags of Gold—What was Done at Midnight—The Dead of Night Deposit—The Old Vault—A Timid Money Lender—Mr. Peter Johnson—The Board of Commissioners—The Old Gentleman's Little Joke—The Inspection—How it was Discovered—The Fight with the Flames—" How much will I Get"—What he Got—The Oil Barrels—Dashing the Water on the Kerosene—A Lively Time on Reed's Point Wharf—The Bridge of Fire—On the Ferry-Boat—The Western Union Telegraph Office—The First Despatch............................ 129

CONTENTS.

CHAPTER XII.

A Thrilling Incident—The Burning House—The Tall Figure on the Hall—Escape Cut Off—The Only Way Out—The Street of Fire—Walking on Coals—The Open Boat—The Way to the Wharf—Terrible Suffering—The Awful Death on the Street—Worn Out—The Escape—Saved—The Firemen—How they Fought the Flames 144

CHAPTER XIII.

A Chapter of Incidents—Agony on Board—Coming Up the Harbour—The Story of the Moths—The Newly Married Lady's Story—No Flour—Moving Out—Saving the Drugs—The Man with the Corn Plasters—Incendiarism—Scenes—Thievery—The Newspapers—Enterprise—Blowing Down the Walls—An Act of Bravery—The Fatal Blast—Danger and Death in the Walls—Accidents—The Fire and the Church—The Ministers 155

CHAPTER XIV.

"I went againe to the ruines, for it was no longer a Citty"—The Drive by Moonlight—Through the Ruins—After the Fire—A City of Ashes—The Buried Silver—The Sentinel Chimneys—The Home of Luxuriance—A Recollection—The Moon and the Church—Back again 167

CHAPTER XV.

Aid for St. John—The First Days—How the Poor were Fed—Organization of the St. John Relief and Aid Society—Its System—How it operates—The Rink—The Car Shed—List of Moneys and Supplies received—The Noble Contributions............................. 175

CONTENTS.

CHAPTER XVI.

The Odd Fellows and the Fire—Relief Committee at Work—Searching out the Destitute Brethren—Helping the Sufferers—The Secret Distribution of Aid—List of Donations 203

CHAPTER XVII.

The Losses of the Masonic Fraternity—Great Destruction of Masonic Regalia and Paraphernalia—Organization of the General Masonic Board of Relief—Amount received in Aid of the Suffering Brethren 239

CHAPTER XVIII.

The Destruction—The Loss—Estimates—The Acreage and Streetage—Has the Land Decreased in Value?—Incomes swept away—What is Left—Hope!—The Insurance—The Corporation Loss—The Dominion Loss—Additional Deaths—The Wounded—The Orange Body 244

CHAPTER XIX.

The Books we have Lost—"The Lost Arts"—The Libraries of St. John which were Burned—The Pictures which were Lost—The few that were Saved—A Talk about Books and Pictures—The Future—What St. John Men must Do—Acknowledgments—Conclusion of the Story of the Fire 259

THE STORY

OF THE

GREAT FIRE IN ST. JOHN, N.B.

CHAPTER I.

The Great Fire—Its Extent—Its Terrible Rapidity—A Glance Backward—What the People Passed Through—The First Fire—Protective Movements—The People Who Lent the City Money—Minor Fires—Fire of 1813—The Great Fire of 1837—The Calamity of 1839—The Trials of 1841—The King Street Fire.

ONE of the most destructive fires of modern times occurred at St. John, N.B., on Wednesday, the 20th June, 1877. It was more calamitous in its character than the terrible conflagration which plunged portions of Chicago into ruin, and laid waste the great business houses of Boston a few years ago. In a relative sense, the St. John fire was a greater calamity, and its people for a time suffered sterner hardships. The fire in the large American cities was confined to a certain locality, but in St. John an immense area of territory was destroyed in the incredibly short space of nine hours, and fully two-fifths of the entire city were laid in ashes, and one thousand six **hundred and** twelve houses levelled to the earth. The fire raged with overwhelming violence, carrying in its wake everything that came before it. At one time three portions of the city were burning at once, and all hope of checking the conflagration died in the hearts of men as the terrific volume of flame thundered and crackled, and hissed in sheets over their heads. The blinding smoke rolled heavenwards in a thick heavy mass; the flying embers were carried along for miles, and the brisk north-western wind brought the destroying flame to a thousand households. Men and women stood paralyzed in the streets, fearing the worst and hoping against hope. Those who had worked all afternoon trying to save their property now sank to the earth and barely escaped with their lives, for the fire was upon them. Nothing appeared to stay the march of the fiend. Immense piles, that seemed to stand like an army of picked guardsmen, were swept away in an instant; granite, freestone, brick and marble were as ineffectual in staying the conflagration as the dryest tinder-box houses which fed the flames at every turn. Even old stone buildings that had stood for sixty years, in the outskirts of the city, and had withstood many a serious fire before, now crumbled and tumbled before the conquering scourge.* 200 acres were destroyed, all that part of the city south of King Street, regiments of houses, stores and public buildings were burned, and the fire was only stayed when the water-line prevented its going further. The boundary of the burnt district followed a line on the

---

* The exact acreage, from actual measurement is 200 acres; streetage, 9·6 miles.

eastern and northern sides of Union Street to Mill Street, Mill Street to Dock Street, northern and eastern sides of Market Square, centre of King Street to Pitt Street, Pitt Street to its junction with the water; thence around by the harbour-line to the starting point. In brief, this was the battle-ground through which the grand charge of the fire was made—unparalleled in its brilliancy by any similar exploit which the annals of military deeds unfold. Men, horses, rows of stoutest building material, steam, water, all succumbed and went down like chaff before the whirlwind. Nothing was too strong to resist, nothing too weak to receive clemency.

A glance at the earlier history of St. John will show that destructive fires have been of frequent occurrence, and its people have suffered much from this system of devastation. In 1784, on Friday, the 18th June, the first fire of which we have any knowledge took place. At that time it was considered a terrible blow, and the sparse population thought that many years would elapse before the little city could recover from the wreck which the fire had made. Eleven houses were burned, and a large number of discharged soldiers of the 42nd Regiment were the principal sufferers. About this time a woman and child were burned to death at the Falls, and seven houses in this quarter were destroyed.

In April, 1787, the people decided to take active measures for protection against fire, and accordingly the following document was drawn up:

We, the subscribers, taking into our serious consideration the alarming situation of the city for want of fire-engines and public wells, should a fire break out in any part of it, and, at the same time, being sensible of the present inability of the city corporation to advance money for the purpose, do severally promise to pay the mayor, aldermen and commonalty, of the City of St. John (or to such persons as they shall appoint), the several sums annexed to our names as a loan upon interest, for the purpose of importing from London two suitable fire-engines, and for sinking a sufficient number of public wells in this city.

" Which several sums the said corporation have engaged to repay to each separate subscriber with interest annually, as soon as their funds will enable them so to do, as appears by an abstract from the minutes of the common council, dated the 20th March last:

" City of St. John, N.B., 5th April, 1787.

	£	s.	d.
" Gabriel G. Ludlow (Mayor)	10	0	0
Ward Chipman (Recorder)	10	0	0
Jonathan Bliss (Atty.-General)	10	0	0
James Putnam (Judge)	10	0	0
Christopher Billop	5	0	0
Zeph Kingsley	10	0	0
Samuel Randall	10	0	0
Gilbert & Hanford	10	0	0
Isaac Bell	5	0	0
Robert Parker	10	0	0
BENEDICT ARNOLD	10	0	0
William Wyly	10	0	0
Mark Wright	3	0	0

THE GREAT FIRE IN ST. JOHN, N. B. 13

	£	s.	d.
C. C. Hall & Co.	5	0	0
William Pagan	10	0	0
John Colwell	5	0	0
Thomas Bean	10	0	0
Francis Gilbert	5	0	0
Samuel Hallet	3	0	0
William Hazen	10	0	0
James Ruon	5	0	0
John Califf	4	13	4
Isaac Lawton	5	0	0
Samuel Mills	5	0	0
Paul Bedell	5	0	0
William Wanton (Collector Custom)	10	0	0
Adino Paddock, M.D.	5	0	0
McCall & Codner	10	0	0
Thomas Horsfield	10	0	0
John McGeorge } Thos. Elliot } William Bainy }	10	0	0
Thompson & Reed	10	0	0
Christopher Lowe, (King's Printer)	5	0	0
W. S. Olive, (Sheriff)	5	0	0
Wm. Whittaker	5	0	0
Peter Quin	3	0	0
Charles Warner	5	0	0
Abiather Camp	5	0	0
James Peters	5	0	0
Daniel Michean	3	0	0
Fitch Rogers	5	0	0
Munson Jarvis	5	0	0
Nehemiah Rodgers	5	0	0
Edward Sands	3	0	0."

On the 2nd February, 1786, the corporation paid Peter Fleming £136 6s. 8d. for two fire engines. These must have proved ineffectual, for the reader will notice that the above loan was made up hardly a year afterward, and the present sum was raised for the special purpose of buying London engines, and sinking wells.

The movement was not inaugurated a moment too soon, for in 1788 the following year, a fire occurred in the store of General Benedict Arnold, of revolutionary fame, which threatened to become very serious before it was got under way. Arnold's store was situate in Lower Cove, where the sewing machine factory adjoining John E. Turnbull's sash factory stood, till the late besom of fire swept it away. A good deal of excitement was occasioned at the time of the fire in Arnold's premises. His former partner, Hoyt, charged him with setting fire to the store. Arnold sued him for slander, and recovered a verdict of twenty shillings!

The next fire broke out in 1816 in a large two-story house on the corner of Germain and Britain Streets, occupied by a military physician named Davis. The doctor and his wife were saved from burning by the heroic conduct of their next door neighbour. A party of soldiers were engaged the next day sifting the ashes and searching for the silver which had melted; not a trace of it was found however.

The fire of 1823 was a very serious one, and caused great destruction. It began on Disbrow's Wharf and took along with it nearly both sides of Prince William Street;

the old wooden building on **the latter street lately occupied** by *The Telegraph* newspaper, alone escaped. The lot on which it stood cost Dr. Adino Paddock five shillings in 1786. During this fire over forty houses were burned, and the loss of property and goods was estimated at £20,000, which in those days was felt **to be enormous.**

The fire of 1837 will linger long in the memory of many of the inhabitants of St. John. It was the most wholesale destruction of property which the people had ever known. Many to-day contrast the misfortunes of that day with those of the present hour. Even when the flames were carrying death and destruction on **all** sides on that warm day in June, 1877, men stopped **to compare** notes and whisper a word or two about the fire **of 1837.** Of course the loss was not as great then, or the number of lives lost so large, or so much valuable property destroyed as at the present time, but the people were less able to bear the trials which came upon them then, and many never recovered from the shock. The city was young and struggling to gain a foothold. The city was poor and the people were frugal. They were not able to bear the burdens which were in a night entailed upon them, the magnificent system of relief from outside sources was not in operation, and without help of any kind save that which they themselves brought into requisition, the citizens nobly worked long and hard to rebuild their little seaport town. There was a prejudice against insurance, and many lost every dollar they possessed. The hardships **of** those days are remembered by many who passed through them then, and who once more endure the horrors of a great calamity with almost Spartan **courage.** The time of the '37 fire was in the very heart of a rigorous winter, on the 13th of January, and we can only picture the destruction of Moscow to enable the reader to understand how terrible the sufferings of the people must have been, when snow and ice were on the ground, and not a shelter covered the heads of the afflicted women and tender babes. It was a day remembered long after by those who had passed through its trials. The fire originated on Peters's Wharf, and in a moment, like lightning, it darted along South Market Wharf and extended up to the ferry boat. Both sides of Water Street and Prince William Street between Cooper's Alley and Princess Street were destroyed. The old Nichols House was saved; it was occupied then by Solomon Nichols and stood on the corner of Cooper's Alley and Prince William Street, lately the site of Farrall & Smith's dry goods store. It was originally built of wood and it was a marvel that it was not carried away with the rest; but it stood like an oasis in Sahara, or the old sentinel who was left on guard and forgotten after the army had fled. One hundred and fifteen houses were consumed, and nearly the whole of the business portion of the city, and one million dollars' worth of property were destroyed.

Hardly had the people recovered from the disaster of 1837, when another scourge came upon them causing nearly as much destruction as before. This was in August,

THE NORTHERN AND EASTERN PANORAMIC VIEW OF ST. JOHN, 1828 OR '30.

1839, when a fire started in Nelson Street and burned the entire north wharf, both sides of Dock Street, Market Square, with the exception of the house standing on the site now occupied by the Bank of British North America, and a house on Union Street west, occupied by Mr. Hegan. It didn't cross Prince William Street. The old Government House, Union Street, escaped.

The spring of 1841, 17th March, was the scene of another fire, when four lives were lost and much excitement prevailed. Mr. Holdsworth, of Holdsworth & Daniel, (London House) perished while endeavouring to keep off the sparks from the roof of his store.

On the 26th August, a £30,000 fire in Portland carried off sixty houses; and on the 15th November, 1841, a fire broke out on the South Wharf and burned the whole of that wharf together with Peter's Wharf, south side of Water Street, and the large brick Market-house in Market Square, which was occupied by butchers in the ground flat, and used for the civic offices in the second story. This building could have been saved, and was lost through gross carelessness. Incendiarism was rampant and the greatest excitement filled the public mind.

In 1845, 29th July, forty buildings were burned from a fire which took its start in Water Street, and in 1849 the famous King Street fire broke out in a store in Lawrence's building. The Commercial Hotel, then kept by the late Israel Fellows, father of James I. Fellows, Chemist, was destroyed, together with the Tower of Trinity

Church, which had to be pulled down that the Church might be saved. Pilot Mills climbed to the cupola and secured the fastenings by which it was brought to the ground.

The fire in Prince William Street of March 8th of the present year, which broke out in the building owned by the Ennis and Gardner estate, and resulted in the loss of seven lives and nearly two millions of dollars' worth of property, is still fresh in the minds of our readers.

Thus the reader will see that St. John has had a goodly share of the great fires, which, in a moment lay prostrate a city, and plunge her inhabitants into almost hopeless ruin. We come now to that day of our last and greatest tribulation when the city was shook to its very foundation and was well nigh thrown out of existence.

CHAPTER II.

The Late Fire—Its Origin—Bravery of the Firemen—The High Wind—
The Fire's Career—Fighting the Flames—Almost Lost—The Escape
from the Burning Building—Destruction of Dock Street—Smyth Street
in Flames—The Wharves—Demolition of Market Square—Something
about the Business Houses there—The Banks—Fire checked at North
Street.

THE great fire, for we must distinguish it by that title, since in vastness it overpowers all other similar calamities which have befallen St. John, originated in the late Joseph Fairweather's building, York Point, Portland, at half past two on Wednesday afternoon, 20th June. The writer and Mr. Frederick R. Fairweather were walking down King Street at the time of the alarm, and, in company with hundreds of others, visited the scene of what promised at the time to be a very small affair indeed. When the place was reached, McLaughlin's boiler shop was in flames and all efforts of the firemen to put out the fire were checkmated at every turn by the fierce north-west wind which was blowing a perfect gale. In a few minutes the fire spread with alarming rapidity, and houses went down as if a mine of powder had exploded and razed them. The wind lifted from the roofs immense brands and sparks, and by three o'clock the city was in flames at a dozen points. Lower Cove was on fire, and the dryness of the houses rendered them as useless to withstand the blaze as bits of paper would have been. The huge blazing brands were carried along in the air for miles around, and wherever they dropped a house went down. The engines were powerless, and the firemen, though they worked like heroes, availed but little. The wild, mad flames, now in sheets, now with a million tongues of angry fork-like columns, dashed against the wharves, levelling them to the water's edge, ripping up the pavements of the streets, and crushing houses out of existence in a single swoop. Nothing could be done. The leaping demon swept all before him. Hare's Wharf with its buildings bowed before the destroyer, and with a roar which thrilled every heart, and unnerved every man who stood there, the whole force of the fire dashed into Smyth Street and shattered every building in it. J. W. Nicholson's wine vaults, Harrison's flour warehouse, Logan & Lindsay's storehouse, Robertson Place, which exceeded in value half a million of dollars, were snapped up in a second. The flames spread into Drury Lane and Mill Street, and soon both sides of Dock Street were in the common ruin. But while this was going on, the rear of the London House, in Market Square, was threatened and the old barracks in Lower Cove were on fire. A reinforcement from Carleton and Portland fire departments came to the assistance of the firemen at this juncture, and every man worked with a will. The hose was directed with admirable expertness but the high wind baffled the efforts of all who stood before it. It could rise higher than the water, and it could travel faster than man. A mass of flames at the end of Smyth Street and Drury Lane burned close to an engine, but the dauntless firemen, holding boards over their heads to protect their faces and eyes from the heat, gave battle to the relentless foe. It was a fight of water and human endurance against fire, and fire prevailed in the end. The unequal combat lasted some minutes, and it was only when death seemed imminent that the men drew away, and even then they only yielded the ground inch by inch, till they could no longer stand up before the charging enemy. The fire was now going with headlong speed down Dock Street. Frantic women wildly sobbing filled the roads with the few sticks of furniture and portions of bedding which they had managed to save. Children hastened along crying aloud, and making the scene more dreadful as they ran barefooted over the hot sidewalk. Men with picture frames and books rushed past, calling and threatening, and moaning. It was a scene terrible in its reality. People were driven from street to street, and hurled forward, till, with horror in their blanched faces, they turned and saw in their rear the wild flames hemming them in. With many a shriek they dashed into the side streets. Some ran along Water Street, only to meet the flames there, and a few sought refuge in rafts and boats, and sped to Carleton, losing in the excitement every dollar they owned in the world. The old McSweeney lime-stone building, which came to a point on the corner of Union and Dock Streets, early succumbed and was a mass of crumbling ruins. It was near this edifice that a woman rescued her child from instant death, and pulled her away just in time to escape being buried in a mass of stone, which came tumbling down in a thousand pieces. The Rankine bakery, another building known far and wide, suffered demolition, and was soon a heap of ruins. Some young men, three in number, entered a store on Mill Street, to avoid the dust and smoke. In a little while they saw with agony the flames burst in upon them from the rear door, ten or twelve feet from the entrance. They called for help, and attempted to gain an exit from the place which was now filled with heavy black smoke. Three times they sought the door, and every minute they began to realize the imminence of their danger. The flames and smoke drove them back, and now the water from the hose came tearing into their faces, knocking their breath away, and saturating them with the wet. Two jumped with the frenzy of madmen and the wildness of despair, and landed into the street safe, but paralysed with fear. The other man groped his way on his hands and knees along the floor and felt for the door. He succeeded after enduring much suffering, in crawling into the street. All that these three saved was on their backs. In the midst of the commotion in Dock Street, merchants were busily engaged in securing their books and private papers, and hurrying out with them. Some trusted to their safes and locked their doors. The sweep in this street was a clear one. The old "Hammond House" went shortly after the McSweeney building, and the Figaro Opera House followed shortly after. This building was built a few years ago, as an exhibition hall, by Otis Small,

Esq., and leased to Major George Bishop, as a concert room. He occupied it awhile, and Pete Lee succeeded him in the lesseeship and management of the concern. Some excellent performances of the variety kind have been given in this building. The hall was comfortably seated and tastefully arranged. Latterly it was converted, by Prof. Neilson, into a ball-room and dancing academy, when it received its new name, " Figaro Opera House."

Dock Street was soon in ashes, and it was while this street was burning that a grand rush was made by the merchants and private bankers, to the Bank of New Brunswick. Piles of bank notes, bills of exchange, mortgages, bonds, specie, books of account, ledgers, &c., &c., were placed in tin boxes, when practicable, and deposited, through the courtesy of George Schofield, Esq., of the bank, into the vaults. They were not a moment too soon, for now the splendid front of the Market Square was in a blaze, and Hall & Fairweather's store on South Wharf was burning. An immense amount of damage was being done. On this square a vast deal of business had been done for many years, and leading merchants had made and lost fortunes on its site. The London House, Messrs. Daniel & Boyd's wholesale establishment, represented a large value. It stood in the centre of the square, and the gradual sinking of this structure was a sad but grandly imposing sight. It was here where enterprise was to be found, and Daniel & Boyd's name was ever the synonym for honesty, integrity, and truth. It was in this spacious warehouse where the busy merchants were to be seen, eager to help the young men of the city, and anxious to develop the resources of the country. In every good work, in every deed of charity, Thomas W. Daniel and John Boyd headed the list, and to them many a young merchant to-day is indebted for that teaching, which, in after life, made him honourable in his dealings. This prominent house was started in 1831 by Holdsworth & Daniel. The fire of 1839 carried their store away, and for a while the firm occupied the store known as Jardine's, Prince William Street. In 1839, the land on the market square was purchased by Mr. Thos. Daniel for £4,000. (In 1811 this place was used as a blacksmith's shop.) In 1847, Mr. Thomas Daniel left the firm and went to England. His nephew, the present head of the house, Thos. W. Daniel, began business on his own account, and soon after 1852, he admitted John Boyd as a partner in the house, under the style of T. W. Daniel & Co. Shortly after the style of this firm was changed to Daniel & Boyd. On the corner to the right of Daniel & Boyd, No. 1 Market Square, was the staunch old drug establishment of the late W. O. Smith, Esq. Mr. Smith, the father of our present ex-Mayor, opened here after the fire of 1839, and the business has been conducted here till the late fire, by his son, A. Chipman Smith, since 1871, when his father died in March of that year. In the adjoining store, so many years occupied by Lawton & Vassie, Messrs. Manchester, Robertson & Allison, may be said to have begun business. They left here, W. W. Jordan taking the store, to occupy their commodious premises in King Street, which alone

VIEW OF KING ST., SHOWING ST. JOHN HOTEL, 1837.

kept off the fire from the north side of King Street. The saving of this building was one of the marvels of the present calamity. It really held the key to the whole of this side of the street. But for the laundry and the well managed protective means employed by the firm and their friends, the destruction of this house and the entire street would have been accomplished. Men stood idly in the courtway folding their arms and telling one another that the building could not possibly be saved, when Mr. Manchester, in his short impulsive way, told them if every one did as they were doing, it could not; but he intended to use every effort in his power before he gave it up. The firemen here worked with a will, and were rewarded with a splendid result. It was on this side of the street that the Western Union Telegraph Office was situated, and it and Mr. J. W. Hall's new building were the first to go. The Maritime Block—a splendid structure—in which the banks, Maritime, Montreal and Nova Scotia, were established, and which faced the Market Square, went down while it was yet daylight. In this building the offices of the school trustees, Dun, Wiman & Co., A. P. Rolph, Lumber Exchange, and Board of Trade were held. While Mr. Rolph was engaged in getting his things ready to move out, Mr. Richard Thompson's men were hastening in with silver-ware and jewelry, thinking in their excitement that this building was at all events safe. Mr. Thompson's loss is very heavy, and the damage to his elegant and costly stock is considerable. The lot on which the Sheffield House stood was offered some years ago, at private sale, to John Wilmot, Esq., father of Senator R. Duncan Wilmot, by James Brimner, for £2,000. Mr. Wilmot refused it, and attended the auction sale when it was knocked down to him for £2,950. The police office went next, Watts & Turner's, H. & H. McCullough's, and round again to the north wharf, carrying Lewin & Allingham, Chas. R. Ray, W. H. Thorne & Co. (retail), and Thomas M. Reed, along with it. The destruction on the north wharf totally demolished the establishment of Jas. Domville & Co., and the books of the firm which had been taken to the Maritime Bank for safe keeping, were subsequently burned there. The saving of the Bank of British North America, the only monetary institution in the city which resumed business the next day as usual, was one of those wonderful events which only occur at .are intervals. The fire roared lustily in the rear of the bank, but something seemed to command it to halt there, and advance no further. A large barn went down, and now it was deemed certain that the bank would go next, but no, the fire crossed the square, dashed along Water Street, cut into Ward Street, destroyed a slip full of schooners and wood boats, slipped into Tilton's Alley, and rushed along with frightful rapidity on both sides of every thoroughfare in its way. On the one side of the city the fire was stopped at North Street, having reached J. & T. Robinson's house and store.

CHAPTER III.

The Fire in King Street—Recollections—The Old Coffee House Corner—The Stores in King Street—The Old Masonic Hall—The St. John Hotel—Its Early Days—The Bell Tower—King Square—A Night of Horror—The Vultures at Work—Plundering the Destitute.

THE fire entered King Street in the western side from Germain and Canterbury Streets. It began by burning down Lawton & Vassie's brick store, erected on the site which contained the famous Bragg building. This stout building and Bowes & Evan's premises were soon buried in the common ruin. The fire went along King Street, destroying Mr. Sharp's dry goods store, Jas. Adams & Co's., James Manson's magnificent palace, including his safe and all his valuable papers, John K. Storey's and Magee Bros., Imperial Block. This last place is quite historic. This block was erected in 1852, by the late John Gillis. It was built on the site where the memorable coffee house stood. Here of an evening for years and years the old men of the place used to sit and gossip and smoke and sip their toddy. Here in 1815 they met to learn the news of the war between France and England, and read the story of Waterloo four or five months after it was fought and won. In this sort of Shakspeare tavern, the leading merchants of the day met and chatted over large sales, and compared notes. Here a verbal commercial agency was established, and here delightful old gossips, like busy Sam Pepys and garrulous old busybodies, like Johnson's Bozzy, met and told each other all about everybody else's affairs. What a time these old fellows had every night sitting there in that quaint old coffee house, chatting and smoking, smoking and chatting again. And there were Ben Jonsons in those days, who wrote dramatic pieces and showed them to their friends over a cup of hot spiced rum. And poets too, full of the tender passion, sighed out hexameters of love in that old coffee house so dear to some of the men we meet to-day who lost everything in the flames on that dark Wednesday in June. Ah, yes, the grand old coffee house was torn down in 1852 to make room for the handsome pile of stone and brick which perished only the other day. The corner is again bare, and the few who remember the coffee house are fast passing away.

The fire now gained great headway, and soon it was seen taking prodigious leaps, going ahead, and then seemingly to dart back again and finish what it had already begun. The people everywhere were in the wildest state of excitement. In the back streets the fire was progressing and destroying the residences of the men who were trying to save their business property in the marts of commerce. People sent car loads of their more valuable goods to places which appeared to be safe, but which turned out in the end to be of only temporary security. Men had their stores burned at four and five o'clock, and their goods burned at seven and eight o'clock. It was only putting off the evil for a few brief hours. Cartmen charged wildly and exorbitantly—some having to pay as high as fifty dollars to have carted away a cartload of stuff. On every roof in King Street clerks and employers stood with hose and buckets of water, but nothing that man could do or devise held the flames at bay, or kept them off for the brief space of a moment. The fire was determined on a clean sweep, and despite the most strenuous exertions it had its own way, and baffled the efforts of those who attempted to stay its fierce will. Beek's corner, lately in the occupancy of H. R. Smith, bookseller, and a perfect feeder of a fire like this, was an easy prey, and with a loud roar its rafters fell, and a well-known corner was no more. Mullin's shoe store, a building of similar construction, went down in another moment, and now the only brick building in the block from Canterbury Street to Germain Street was attacked by the fire. This was Pine's brick building, a fine structure which several years ago Mr. George Jury Pine built, and in which I. & F. Burpee commenced business, and George Stewart, of Stewart & White, began trade. Messrs. Della, Torre & Co. occupied No. 30, and Geo. Stewart, Jr., Druggist, held the other store, No. 32. The present owner of the building, Stephen Whittaker, of Fredericton, had lately begun the erection of a spacious rear addition, and improvements on a liberal scale had been commenced in the upper stories. The rest of the building was known as the Russell House. This building went to pieces about six o'clock. The photograph rooms were destroyed before Pine's building went, and the flames sped quickly, carrying be-

30   THE GREAT FIRE IN ST. JOHN, N. B.

fore them the stores of Bardsley Bros., Scott & Binning, W. K. Crawford, Geo. Salmon, and Hanington Bros.' drug store, formerly Fellows & Co.'s establishment on Foster's Corner, corner King and Germain Streets. The contents of this store were quickly snapped up by the fire, and pills and plasters, soaps and perfumes were spilled about in hopeless profusion and confusion. Mr. T. H. Hall's twin buildings were across the street, but a barrier like that was an easy jump for the infuriated flames. They leaped into the windows, attacked the wood-work, and with a strong pull the two splendid stone buildings were borne to the ground, and thousands of dollars' worth of property lay scattered about in all directions. Mr. Hall occupied the corner store as a book-store, and T. L. Coughlan had the other. Dr. J. M. C. Fiske, dentist held the room overhead.* The Gordon House, Fred. S. Skinner's grocery store, a row of wooden shanties, Landry's brick building, with a rich stock of organs in it, Logan, Lindsay & Co.'s large grocery, A. & J. Hay's, Geo. Nixon's, Wm. Warn's bath-rooms, W. H. Watson's, Geo. Suffren's, W. H. Patterson's, Taylor & Dockrill's, George Sparrow's, R. McAndrew's, and the United States Hotel, only lived a short time in the very heart of the fire.

The fire closed here for a moment, engaging a building dear from long and good service to the people of St. John, and eminently historical in its way. The United States Hotel, as Mr. Hinch, the photographer, called it, when he

---

* The Orangemen of St. John District met in this hall.

took possession of it a few years since, was known for many years as the old Masonic Hall. It stood on the corner of King Street and Charlotte Street, and was commenced by the Free and Accepted Masons in 1816. It was decided to erect this Temple of Masonry at a meeting of the craft held April 1, 1816. The lot of land was leased from the corporation of Trinity Church, and on the 28th September following the corner-stone was laid, on which was inscribed the following :—

"This stone of the Masonic Hall was laid on 28th Sept., 1816, of the era of Masonry 5816, and the reign of George the Third, King of the United Kingdom of Great Britain and Ireland, in the mayoralty of John Robinson, Esq., by Thomas Wetmore, Esq., H.M. Attorney-General of N.B., as Grand Master, substitute of John Pike, Esq,. Grand Master of the Society of Masons, Nova Scotia, and the jurisdiction thereof."

The movement was not successful in a pecuniary sense, for in 1819 the building was sold at sheriff's sale, at suit of James Hendricks. The purchaser was Israel Lawson. Mr. Lawson had the building completed, and leased the third or upper story to the Masons. The room was 60 feet by 30 feet, with two large ante-rooms. It was in this room that all the concerts, balls, public parties, and public meetings given in the city were held for many years. Up to 1836 the house was known as the Masonic Hall, but after this year its name was changed. The St. John Hotel Company was formed, and the building was purchased from Mr. Lawson and converted into a hotel. It was called the "St. John Hotel," and Mr. Cyrus Stockwell father of the Honourable Mr. Stockwell, editor of the *Boston Journal*, opened it on May 24th, 1837. He was its first proprietor. A copy of the company's original seal is given below. It was made of brass, and was two inches in diameter.

This was the first hotel in St. John. It was here that Governor-General Poulet Thompson and Lord Elgin stopped, and all the notables who from time to time visited the city. In 1840, Mr. Stockwell retired, and Messrs. W. & J. Scammell succeeded him in the management of the hotel. These enterprising gentlemen set to work at once to remodel the building, and they soon had it in splendid working order. The same energy which the present firm of Scammell Bros. throw into their business, was characteristic of the old firm of Scammell Bros. in 1840. In 1851, W. &. J. Scammell left the St. John Hotel, and took up their quarters in the Waverley House, nearly opposite. The picture which accompanies this sketch of the old

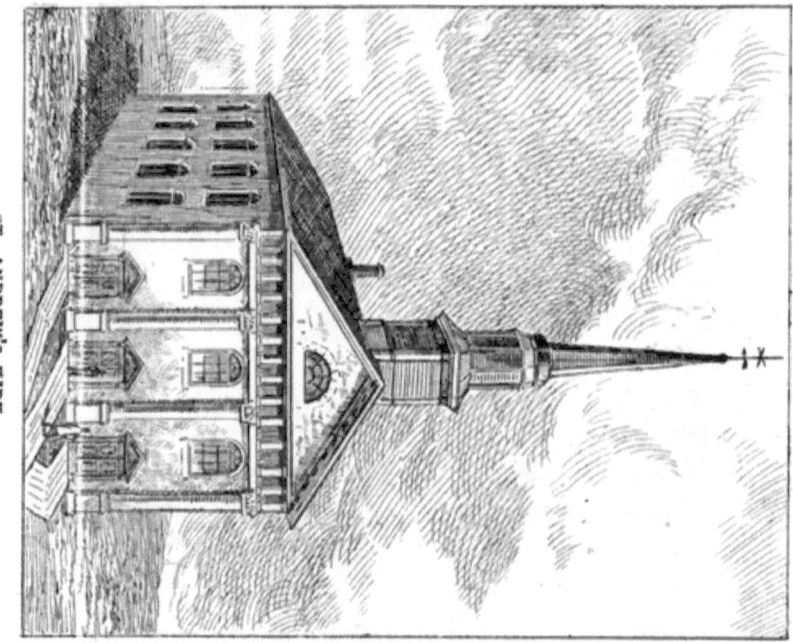

ST. ANDREW'S KIRK.

VICTORIA SCHOOL HOUSE, CORNER OF DUKE AND SYDNEY STREETS.

hotel represents the building as it appeared in 1837. It is taken from an old picture, and as but two or three copies were known to exist before the late fire, it is a question now if more then one copy was saved. The old St. John Hotel is full of associations, pleasurable in every case, to travellers who used to come to St. John thirty and forty years ago. Even in 1858, when Messrs. Whitney & Adams kept it, it was still a home for the stranger. There was a freedom about its old rooms, and a positive luxuriance which one looks for in vain in the hotels of our later days. About 1861-62, people used to sit in Ned Sharland's book-store, which was on the ground-flat, and sketch the Bell-tower, which was then certainly "a thing of beauty," even if Mr. Warner found it the reverse in 1874, when he climbed up to the triumphal arch and found it was made of wood, painted and sanded, instead of solid stone, as he thought it was. This bell-tower was erected in 1851, and the large bell which for years tolled out that fire was at hand, was made in 1852, and came from Meneely's, West Troy, New York. Before that day, men struck a gong from a scaffold whenever there was a fire. The tower was useful even in its latter days, if its beauty had departed three years ago. The cut which we supply will give the reader at a distance some idea of the old tower, as it appeared in its lusty young days. When the city comes to be built up again, the site of the late hotel must not be forgotten. It is eminently adapted for an hotel. It is centrally located, and has a frontage of 120 feet on King Street, by 100 feet on Charlotte Street.

King Square did much to stay the onward march of the fire. It was a haven of rest for those weary ones who were flying from the flames, with the few things they had saved from the burning. It was the camping ground of the soldiery, and the hospital bed of the sick and wounded, who were borne to the fresh grass, and laid there until help was brought to them. The Square, the first few days of the fire, was filled with furniture, and books, and household utensils. It was in this square that half-famished women, that night, hugged their little ones to their hearts, and rocked them, hungry and cold, on the sward till they went to sleep, only to awaken again and cry for something to eat. It was here that women gathered into slips the flying feathers that danced upon the grass and were the playthings of the wind, trying to save enough of what remained to make a rest for their heads. It was here they sat with wildly staring eyes, looking out into the night, while all around them the embers flew about, and the heavens were red with the sporting flames. It was before this that the Bell-tower fell with a deafening crash, and many a heart quailed in the Square, for this told that another historic fragment was swept away, and that the terrible fire was near at hand. Sobbing children ceased their wailing for a time, and feeble mothers prayed that God in His mercy might avert the calamity, and stay the warring flames. There was no more sleep for the tired ones. They must wander about, ringing their hands and crying aloud in their awful despair. Even men who had faced a thousand dangers, quailed before the advance of the fire. The streets were alive with hurrying pedestrians. Horses were driven at breakneck speed, and the clattering hoofs told that danger was at hand. Human vultures stood, with their "pickers and stealers," ready to pounce upon everything that could be seized, and the presence of an appalling danger did not deter them from plundering the unfortunate and the destitute. It was the old war again, of the strong against the weak and powerless. A female vampire helped a widow lady to gather her little things together in a bundle, while her children stole the silver and jewelry, and made off with their plunder. Rough half-grown men stopped children in the streets, and snatched from their arms the treasured fragments from a broken home, which they were trying to rescue from the elemental spoiler. Loafers and thieves held high carnival, and despite the agony which was felt on all sides, these miscreants never for an instant forgot that they were thieves, or neglected to ply their calling when chance threw anything in their way. All night they roamed the streets, and thrived on the misfortunes of others. Ask them for assistance, and they knocked you down. Give them something to hold a minute, and they made off with it. The vilest scum that ever filled a penitentiary stalked abroad that night, and their lawlessness but added to the horror of the hour.

CHAPTER IV.

The fire in Germain Street—The first brick house in St. John—Old Trinity—The Loyalists—Curious ideas about insurance—The rectors of Trinity—The Clock—The Royal Arms.

THE fire along Germain Street was of great volume, and dealt out destruction in a thoroughly wholesale manner. A good many buildings of more than ordinary note were situate in this pleasant street, and to these may be added a large number of churches, some of them being of especial importance in an historical point of view. The fire came along briskly, carrying Foster's Corner, Foster's shoe store, and the little buildings adjoining, till it reached Dr. Ring's residence, the old Disbrow property, the first brick **house** in **St. John**. The doctor had lately improved it by extensive building operations, but in an hour or two hardly a fragment remained to mark the spot, save parts of the well-built walls and the tall chimneys. Mrs. Chas. K. Cameron's millinery store and Hamilton & Lounsbury's place of business were in the two stores in this building, and they very soon were lost to sight. Lordly, Howe & Co.'s furniture warerooms, filled with new stock, were greedily devoured by the flames, and Geo. Hutchinson, jr., who kept the time ball **in** working order, lost all his jewelry **and** stock. The precious stones and gold and silver ornaments in his safe were totally ruined also. The Mansion Hotel, a small boarding house, was soon among the general mass of debris, and the fire whizzed across the street, and directed its entire force on Old Trinity. First the steeple went, and then the whole body of the old church was in a sheet of flame, and there was barely time left to save the historic Royal Arms which Captain Frank B. Hazen got out of the building, and a few prayer books in the vestry, and the minister's surplices, which Colonel Chas. R. Ray rescued from destruction. The communion plate was in a safe, and it too was saved; but this was all. During the burning of this sacred edifice the greatest consternation prevailed among the people who lined the streets. Now surely there was no resisting the fire. The hoarse roar of the tornado of flame seemed to sound like a mocking laugh, and when the rafters of the oldest church in the city fell with a dull thud, all felt as if a friend had been torn ruthlessly from their gaze. Many exhibited real emotion; and there were women who cried that afternoon, as they thought of this last relic of their loyalist forefathers being swept away in the cruel and all-devouring fire. Trinity Church has a very remarkable history of its own, and the picture which we supply of it will be perhaps the most attractive of our illustrations to the great mass of the residents of the city. It was ever a monument of the piety and religious tenets of our first settlers. A heritage which they left to their children. It never laid claims to architectural beauty, but it was commodious and homely; and men felt while inside its grand old walls that there was something more than the mere name in religion after all, and the word which they heard was true and good. The Loyalists who settled here in 1783, on that memorable 18th of May, were composed of that stuff which the poet tells us warriors sometimes feel, and they diligently set to work to build on this sterile, rocky soil a city that future ages would acknowledge. They had thrift, integrity, great zeal, enterprise and piety, and these **attributes** were their strongest points. The man who possesses all these characteristics can give battle to the world and he will **conquer**. They had true courage in them, these pioneers. They had stability, nerve and character, and were just the men to found a city and plant the seeds of civilization in a community. They erected simple houses at first, and then a church was built in which they could worship **that** God who had befriended them and journeyed with **them** to their new homes. The first church was erected in Germain Street, between Duke and Queen Streets, in the lot where Mr. James McMillan lived till he was burned out of it the other day. The faith adopted here was that of the Church of England—as the major portion of the Loyalists were of that persuasion. When the city lots were divided, the " Old Burial Ground " was laid aside for church and burial purposes, and at the south-west corner— where the court-house now stands—it was intended to build a church, and a frame for that object was obtained. The fire of 1784, however, passed over this section of the city, and the founders changed their ideas about the locality in which the projected edifice should stand. The Germain Street building had not been consecrated, and the people continued to worship there until 1791, when the **Trinity Church was erected.** The first church then continued to be occupied by various denominations, by the Methodists first, and then by the Baptists, until meeting-houses and chapels of their own could be built; latterly it was used as a private dwelling-house and school-house. The first sermon in Trinity was preached on Christmas Day, 1791, by Rev. Dr. Mather Byles, rector. The following year a bell was put up, and, in 1803 or 1804, stoves, for the first time, were placed in the church. The first Bishop of Nova Scotia, Right Reverend Dr. Charles Inglis, performed the consecration services of the church. This eminent divine was **grandfather** of Major-General Sir John Inglis, whose deeds of valour at Lucknow will never be forgotten while glorious exploits in military history **live in the memory of men.** Thomas Horsfield and Fitch Rogers were the first churchwardens of Trinity, and the vestrymen were Hon. Gabriel Ludlow, Ward Chipman, **Munson Jarvis,** Thomas Whitlock, Nathan Smith, Thomas **Elmes,** William Hazen, Colin Campbell, Nehemiah Rogers, Isaac Lawton, Thomas Bean, and Samuel Hallet; vestry clerk, Colin Campbell; sexton, James McPherson. General Coffin and **Thomas Whitlock gave the** ground for the building, and Messrs. Bean & Dowling were the builders. This Mr. Bean was the gentleman who, in June, 1811, when the church wanted to borrow £200, agreed to lend it that sum on the express condition that the insurance policy then on the building should be at once cancelled. **An** order was passed, cancelling the policy without delay. **Thus was**

Trinity for a while without insurance. Had Mr. Bean's ideas prevailed to-day the congregation would, in all likelihood, mourn the loss of $20,000, which is the amount that was on the building at the time of the fire. When the edifice was finished, it was found to be of a peculiar shape, and its breadth was out of all proportion to its length. This was not an accident, however, for the builders wisely thought the city would grow, and that as the requirements of the people needed it, the church might be made larger. Little change had taken place in the interior arrangements of the church at the time of its destruction. The same pews had stood over four score of years, and all the alteration that was made was a slight cutting down of the backs of some of the centre ones. The side pews remained the original height. For seventy-three years the old organ has been in constant use in Trinity. It was brought from London in 1804, and cost a good round sum. The freight on it alone was one hundred guineas, but the owner of the vessel which brought it over, Hon. Wm. Pagan, remitted the amount back to the corporation of the church. To its last days, this organ has been a good instrument. In 1792, Mr. William Thomson presented Trinity with a bell, for which he received a cordial vote of thanks. This bell was in active service till 1857, when the bell which tolled a few days ago its last sad peals, was mounted in the belfry. The town-clock, as every one was accustomed to call the clock which told of the passing hours, too, has a history. In 1810, Mr. John Venning erected the tower and cupola

KING STREET.

VICTORIA HOTEL.

He had nearly completed his work one May morning, when owing to a light fall of snow the staging became slippery, and when Mr. Venning stepped upon it he slipped from it to the roof, and from thence to the ground, where he was picked up dead. In 1812, the clock was placed in position, and has remained there, till the events of Wednesday ended its career. Barraud, of Cornhill, London, was the maker, and it cost £221 19s. sterling; the Common Council voted £50 towards it. Up to 1814, the church paid for having the time-piece wound, and in this year the winding cost £6 15s., when the church people decided that they would no longer attend to this service, and maintained that the commonalty should see to it. The Council, on December 24th, 1814, resolved to act on the suggestions of the Church corporation, and took upon themselves the duty of keeping the clock wound up and in repair. Edward Taylor assisted in putting up the clock and assumed control of it, till Mr. Wm. Hutchinson, father of Geo. Hutchinson, jr., took charge of it. Previous to 1857, it had three dials, but in this year a fourth was added, and a spire was placed upon the church.

In 1811-12 the church was lengthened, and in 1857 it was enlarged again.

The first rector was the Rev. George Bisset, A. M., an Englishman. Before the revolutionary war he was assistant to the rector of Trinity Church, at Newport, Rhode Island. He became, two years later, the rector of that church, and remained in that position until 1779, when the British forces evacuated the island, and Mr. Bisset went to New York. At the close of the war he came to St. John and was chosen rector of the new parish. In 1786, he went to England on private and public business, and while there raised quite a large sum to further the interests of his church, and to assist materially in the building of the edifice. But in 1788, without seeing his hopes realized, he died, and was buried in the Germain Street church-yard, and subsequently his remains were interred in the Putnam tomb, in the old burial ground, where they still lie.

A Harvard graduate of the class of 1751, was the next rector of Trinity, the Rev. Mather Byles, D.D. For fifteen years, he had laboured as a Congregational minister at New London, and then left that church to link his fortunes with the Episcopalians. He joined the Church and became rector of Christ's Church, Boston, Mass. He left his charge, when the British troops abandoned Boston, and went to Halifax, N. S., where he became Garrison chaplain. When Mr. Bisset died Dr. Byles removed to St. John, was made rector, and preached, as we have said, the first sermon that was ever preached in Trinity Church. In his latter days Dr. Byles was very infirm and required an assistant. He was rector of St. John for 26 years, and died at the age of 80 in March, 1814, loved, honoured and respected. He was a man of fine parts, an excellent talker, of quick and lively nature, and he possessed a rich fund of anecdote and humour. A bundle of his sayings and doings has been published.

Rev. George Pidgeon was **the third** rector. He was a

learned graduate of Trinity College, Dublin, and was born in Kilkenny, Ireland, in 1761. He was an ensign in the rifles, and had served in America during the war. He subsequently went to Halifax, took orders in the Church, became rector of Fredericton and Ecclesiastical Commissary for the Province in 1795, and in 1814, on the death of the incumbent, he was made rector of St. John. His health failed him, however, and for a time the church was closed, when finally he died, May 6th, 1818. He was buried in the old burial ground, and his monument may still be seen there.

The fourth rector was the Rev. Dr. Robert Willis—a Navy chaplain and a very eminent man. His ship was at Halifax coaling, when intelligence reached him that Mr. Pidgeon was seriously ill, and that the church in St. John was closed in consequence. He left at once for St. John where he officiated for several weeks, and on the death of Mr. Pidgeon was chosen rector. The Stone Church and St. George's, Carleton, were erected during his incumbency, and this caused a division in the Parish. Dr. Willis became rector of St. Paul's, Halifax, in 1825, and Archdeacon of Nova Scotia, which offices he held until the year 1865, when he died at the age of 80. He was the father of Rev. Cuthbert Willis, rector of Salisbury, who was formerly of the 15th regiment of foot.

In 1825 the Rev. Benjamin Gerrish Gray, D. D., succeeded Dr. Willis as rector of St. John. He was born in Boston 1768, and on the departure of the British troops from that city, while yet a child, he went with his father to

Halifax. He graduated at King's College, Windsor, completed his education in England, and was ordained minister in 1796 by Bishop Inglis at Halifax. Some years were spent by him as minister among the Maroons, a discontented body of savages which the British Government placed in Nova Scotia to the great annoyance and fear of the inhabitants. The Doctor spent several years in connection with various missions throughout Nova Scotia until 1819, when he became rector of St. George's, Halifax. He laboured as rector in St. John on the death of Dr. Willis, for fifteen years, when in 1840 he resigned his position. He lived till 1854, when at the advanced age of 86 he died full of honours and respect. He was a man of elevated tastes and liberal ideas. He loved science, art and literature, and was a well informed and polished writer and thinker. In 1833 one of the greatest calamities which ever befell man happened to Dr. Gray. His house in Wellington Row took fire, and before aid could come it was burned to the ground, together with the rector's wife and a female domestic. No sympathy could alleviate the suffering of the distracted husband, no words of man could take away the agony of his deep grief and sorrow. It pressed heavily upon his mind, and he was never again the same man. At this fire he lost his valuable library which contained many rare and costly books and manuscripts, together with the complete records of his parish.

He was succeeded by his son, Rev. John William D. Gray, D.D., a very able man. He was born in 1798, at

Halifax, and graduated at King's College, Windsor. He became rector of Amherst, N.S., and in 1825, when Dr. Willis resigned his office in St. John, a movement was made to get the rectorship for Dr. Gray. This was not done, however, for the father was appointed, and the son became his assistant. In 1840, on the retirement of Dr. Benjamin Gray, the sixth rector received the appointment, which he held until his death, in 1868. For twenty-eight years this eminent clergyman laboured for his church and his people, and all remember him as a kindly, thoughtful, generous man. He had abilities of the highest order, and, whether as a preacher or a writer, his reputation filled no second place. He wrote with a nerve and a boldness which carried all before it, and his extensive erudition and vast powers of concentration of thought made his works valued and esteemed. His notable writings were chiefly controversial pamphlets, and few entered the lists with him and gained a victory. His vigorous pamphlets on the Catholic question, and the Moses and Colenso controversy will be remembered by many who read these pages to day, and all will regret that the great rector never published a theological book or placed his ripe thoughts on some enduring record. He was an able exponent of the Scriptures, and he wrote in a superior and beautiful style. His sermons were models of elegant English and sound doctrinal ideas, and no rector of Trinity ever filled the position so grandly and so loyally as good old Dr. Gray. He died at the age of seventy years, and in the forty-seventh year of his ministry. He was accounted the best reader in the Province, and his delivery was forcible, and distinguished for a certain gracefulness of style. **The** Rev. James J. Hill, M. A. succeeded Dr. Gray. **He is a** native of Nova Scotia. His failing health caused him to resign the rectorship in a few years. At a meeting of the St. John Parish, held on the 21st of July, 1873, the Rev. F. H. J. Brigstocke, of Jesus College, Oxford, was unanimously nominated to the rectorship. He had been in orders twelve years, and for five years had been curate to **the Dean** of Canterbury. Mr. Brigstocke assumed his **duties in** October, **1873, and is** the present rector of the parish.

The stained-glass windows in the chancel of the old church were placed there in 1859, and were presented by John V. Thurgar, Esq., a respected retired merchant of **this city, whose** old stand was burned down on the North **Wharf** during the great fire.

The old arms of Trinity Church have an historic interest of very great importance. A glance at them will reveal the fact that they are military arms and not those of the church. They have escaped fire once or twice, and in the early years of their existence witnessed many a heated controversy, **and experienced** marvellous escapes from destruction. The first we hear of them was in Boston where they adorned the walls of the Council Chamber of the Old Town House. On March 17th, 1776, they sailed out of Boston Harbour and were carried to Halifax, where they had a temporary abiding place in the old **chapel there. They** were afterwards placed, in 1791, in

Trinity Church, where they have remained ever since, until Captain Hazen rescued them from the flames on Wednesday afternoon. A story is current that a hundred years ago, these arms were snatched from Trinity Church, New York, when that edifice was in flames, but this lacks confirmation, and the best authorities are unanimous in holding that their peculiar build unfitted them for church use, and that they were certainly intended to adorn the walls of council chambers. That they were with the British army, whether on its march or at its station, is settled beyond dispute. This ends the story of old Trinity, the most historic edifice in the city—the first church—the quaintest structure—the last link which bound the old and the new together. The school-house fronting on Charlotte Street was burned at the same time as the church.

CHAPTER V.

The Old Curiosity Shop in Germain Street—A Quaint Old Place—
"Rubbish Shot Here"—Notman's Studio—The Mother of Methodism—Destruction of the Germain Street Methodist Church—Burning of the Academy of Music—The Old Grammar School—Presbyterians among the Loyalists—The "Auld Kirk"—Saint Andrew's—The grants of Land—Legislation—The building of the Kirk—Ministers—The "Victoria" in Flames—Fascination of the Fire—The "Victoria" in Ruins—What might have saved it.

THE fire has destroyed Mrs. Lyons's "old curiosity shop," —an establishment known far and near as a place where everything, from a needle to an anchor, might be got. Mrs. Lyons is an old inhabitant, and for years was a constant attendant at every auction sale, and her judgment has more than once influenced and controlled the bidding. She bought everything, and, what is more curious still, she managed to sell it afterwards at a fair profit. Old books, old pictures, cheap prints, crockery, bedding, carpets, furniture; all had a home in that asylum for decayed rubbish. It was a pleasant place in which to while away an odd hour or two. The things were, at least, worth looking at; and one could sometimes turn over a good book or two, or dip into the pages of an old magazine and find a bit of poetry here and there, or a pleasant essay that was worth glancing over. Of course, nothing out of this stock could be saved, and the curious and out-of-the-way knick-nacks of the people were swept away

TRINITY CHURCH.

BELL TOWER AND KING SQUARE.

THE GREAT FIRE IN ST. JOHN, N. B. 49

in a very short time. Mrs. Lyons is a very heavy loser by the calamity, and narrowly escaped with her life. Indeed she was reported missing at one stage of the fire.

Mr. Notman's beautiful studio with its gems of neat things in art, and its hundreds of elegant picture frames, went next. The premises had only recently been opened, and the reception room was a perfect gallery of beautifully arranged pictures and chromos, and India ink copies. A number of oil paintings, some of them of considerable value, a good many choice bits in water colour, some decidedly clever engravings together with pieces of statuary, and a bronze or two perished in an instant. Not a **negative** was saved, and the fine picture of Mr. John Melick's handsome boy, which was so artistically finished in India ink **by** Mr. James Notman, shared a like fate. The studio was **full** of handsome work, and lovers of the æsthetic whenever they had a spare minute or **two** always wandered into Notman's and inspected the **new** things he had there. It was a place of resort for the cultivated mind, and the eye always rested on something pleasing and charming. This building went so rapidly that the occupants barely escaped with their clothes. The fire crossed the street on both sides, and after sweeping down Mr. Edward Sears's house on the corner, and carrying with it Mr. Tremaine Gard's jewelry establishment, it rushed along levelling all before it, till Horsfield Street was reached. On this corner the Mother of Methodism was situated—the old Germain Street Methodist Church—called in olden times "The Chapel." This structure was located a few feet off the street, **and when** the fire caught and hugged it **in its grasp the concourse** of people beheld a sight not easily **effaced from** their memory. **The** flames shot up, and **for awhile** nothing but an avalanche of fire was to be seen. The hot, thick volume roared out and crackled as timber after timber went down before the whirlwind, and rent asunder in an hour, an edifice which had withstood the blasts of the elements for seventy years. In 1808, on Christmas day, this chapel was opened, and dedicated to **the service** of God, by the Rev. Mr. Marsden. The leading layman at that time was the late John Ferguson, an influential citizen and a prosperous merchant. He did much for Methodism in his time, and it was through his exertions that the chapel was built. For many years this commodious building was the only place of worship that this body of Christians had in the city, and the various clergymen who from time to time preached from its old-fashioned, homely pulpit, developed sterling qualities and superior talents. Among its body of laymen were men distinguished alike for their zeal and religious principles. Such clergymen as Revs. Messrs. Priestly, Wood, Dr. Alder, John B. Strong, Bamford, Wm. Temple and H. Crosscomb, will be affectionately remembered by old members of this congregation, as ministers whose interests were ever closely identified with those of their hearers. The present **Chief of Police,** John R. Marshall, has been a member of this church all his life, and for thirty years he has led the singing. It was an unpretentious building with no attempts at architectural display. A few years ago, to meet the wants of the community, it was enlarged and extended back, and the gallery was placed nearer the pulpit. While this building was burning the hospitable residences of James Lawton, Esq., and Wm. Davidson, Esq., were being reduced to ashes, and Dr. McAvenny's fine dental rooms adjoining those houses, went down also.

The burning of the Academy of Music* took place almost at the same time. Not a vestige of this splendid hall remains to tell of the dramatic triumphs that have been witnessed on its stage, or the matchless oratory that fell from the lips of Phillips, Beecher and Carpenter. Here it was that a few years ago the great performance of Richelieu took place, when Couldock enacted the Cardinal Duke, and Louis Aldrich was the impetuous De Mauprat. Here on this stage Carlotta Le Clercq won some of her grandest triumphs. Here Warner and Lanergan gave their wonderful interpretations of the Moor and Iago. Here Chas. Koppitz led his great orchestra the day

---

* The outside dimensions of the Academy were 190x51 feet. The front 65 feet high, showing three stories in front. The finish was Italian in its general style, very rich and pleasing to the eye, with heavy and elaborate carved work. A large bust of Queen Victoria adorned the summit of the building, while over the main entrance an excellent bust of Shakespeare indicated the uses for which the building was intended. The front doors were massive in style, of solid walnut, and weighed sixteen hundred pounds. Inside.—The parquette was reached by a wide entrance; on either side of this entrance were broad and easy stairs leading to the balcony; while above this was the gallery for the gods, which was approached from a separate entrance. The parquette was furnished with 600 opera chairs, and the seating capacity of the whole building was 1,200. The scenery, ample in supply and excellent in character, was painted by Gaspard Maeder. The building when finished cost the Company over $60,000.

before he died, and here some of the sweetest voices have been heard emulating the notes of the nightingale. This building, which for several years enjoyed a splendid reputation, well stocked with scenery and properties, centrally and admirably located, seemed to melt into nothing on the day of the fire. The walls fell with a loud crash, and the grand temple of amusement, in which our people felt so much pride, was a thing of the past. It was owned by a joint stock company, and the late Dr. George E. Keator was the first president. On his death, Dr. Allan M. Ring was made president, and he has retained the office ever since. John R. Armstrong, Esq., has been the secretary from the beginning of the institution. It is only about a year ago that it was frescoed and painted and greatly improved inside. The Academy presented a noble appearance from the street, and the reader can form an intelligent idea of how it looked from the illustration which we give. The Knights of Pythias, New Brunswick and Union Lodges, occupied the upper story as a lodge room. It was neatly and attractively fitted up, and the knights took great interest in having it properly cared for. The loss with which this young organization has met, is quite large and is therefore severely felt.

The last theatrical performance at the Academy of Music was on Tuesday evening, 19th June, when Louise Pomeroy, an actress of charming genius, sustained the *role* of "Juliet" in Shakespeare's tragedy of the affections, "Romeo and Juliet." On Wednesday night she was to have performed "Rosalind" for the second time in St.

John, in the delightful comedy of "As You Like It." The company then playing were under the management of Mr. William Nannary, with Mr. P. Nannary as assistant manager, and Mr. W. E. Kelly, of Halifax, business agent. Mr. George B. Waldron was stage manager, and his wife, Isabella Waldron, the leading lady. The other members of the organization were R. Fulton Russell, F. G. Cotter, G. T. Ulmer, Harry Pierson, Belvil Ryan, Mr. Padget, Mr. Eberle, J. Reddy, Mr. Vanderen, Mr. Donaldson, W. F. Edwards, C. Mason, Lizzie May Ulmer, Pearl Etynge, Little Bell Waldron, Mrs. Edwards, Mrs. Vanderen, Miss Hill, Mabel Doane, and Florence Stratton. All of these artists suffered by the fire. Some saved their wardrobes, only to have them stolen afterwards.

After Dr. McAvenny's office was burned, the fire shot into Messrs. Miller and Woodman's double house, the late residence of Hon. A. McL. Seely, and it was soon shattered to its basement. The fire then spread as far as Duke Street, burning on its passage Dr. W. Bayard's house, and the old McGrath residence, which latterly contained Dr. James E. Griffith's office. On the other side, the Grammar School was the first victim after the Old Chapel.

This building was a plain wooden house of rather squat appearance. It was erected on two lots of land, 80 feet front by 200 deep, which in 1807 were sold by Thos. Horsfield for £100. The first teacher was James Brimner. In 1818 Dr. James Patterson took charge, and remained head master till nearly the close of his life.

Rev. Mr. Wainright, afterwards rector of New York, and who died Bishop there, was at one time a teacher in the Grammar School. The masters who have taught here have been judiciously selected, and the school has been very successful from the first. Messrs. Hutchison and Manning, and Rev. Mr. Schofield, and latterly Rev. Dr. Coster, are all gentlemen of fine scholastic attainments and excellent imparters of knowledge to the youth. For many years the Corporation gave a gold medal annually to the bright boys of this institution of learning, and many of our prominent lawyers, doctors, engineers and merchants have been educated here. H. W. Frith, Esq., was for many years secretary to the Board who controlled this school, and continued in that office till the new school-law came into force. The Grammar School in its last days was a free school of the highest grade.

It has been said of Scotchmen that next to love of country they revere their religion. Indeed, the love is as warm for the one as it is for the other. The Bible and Home. God and Scotland. Their religion has been compared to their native Grampians, and some have said that it was as hard, cold, determined and unyielding as those grand old hills themselves, the very name of which sends a thrill through every Scotchman's breast. Every Scottish poet has sung of home, every native bard has written hymns and psalms. Burns's "Cotter's Saturday Night" contains the germs of the Presbyterian faith, and Tannahill, Thomson, Campbell, Hogg and all the other tuneful minstrels have sung in the same key, and told of the old

faith which the Covenanters felt on their bleak hill-tops
years ago, when it was deemed by some to be a crime to
worship God in more ways than one. It is as rare to find
a Scotchman unacquainted with the leading events in the
Bible, the gist of the shorter catechism, and the whole of
the Psalms of David, including the cxix, word for word,
as it is difficult to enter a city all the world over, and
not find the sons of the old land filling the leading positions in the place. Our readers may be sure that among
the sturdy loyalists not a few Presbyterians were to be
found. When they reached St. John, they settled in
Lower Cove, and the first thing they did was to consider
the advisability of building a kirk. In 1784, the leading
men drew up a petition for a grant of land on which to
lay the foundation for a house of worship. It was sent
to Governor Parr, and on the 29th of June, of the same
year, the grant was issued under the Great Seal of Nova
Scotia. John Boggs and others, for the Church of Scotland, were the grantees. Their associates were Andrew
Cornwall, James Reid, John Menzie, Charles McPherson,
William Henderson, John Gemmill, and Robert Chillis,
their heirs and assigns in trust. The document runs as
follows, and sets forth that the grant was, "for the erection, building and accommodation of a meeting house or
public place of worship for the use of such of the inhabitants of the said town as now or shall hereafter be of the
Protestant profession of worship, approved of by the
General Assembly of the Church of Scotland * * *
and further for the erection and building and accommo-

dation of a dwelling house, outhouse, casements and conveniences for the habitation, use and occupation of a minister to officiate and perform divine service in the meeting house aforesaid, according to the form and professing aforesaid * * * and further for the building and erection of a public school house and public poor house, with proper accommodation and conveniences for the use of the inhabitants of the said Township of Parr,* forever, and upon this further trust and confidence to secure and defend the said piece and tract of land, and all such buildings, edifices, and improvements, commodities and appurtenances, to and for the several and respective public uses, intents and purposes aforesaid forever, but to or for no other or private use, intent and purpose whatsoever."

It further states that in case of the lands coming into possession of any other persons, they shall take the prescribed oath of allegiance within twelve months, and in case of their neglect to do so, the lands shall revert to the Crown. The grant was registered at Halifax, 29th June, 1784, and at Fredericton on December 23rd, same year. These lands were situate on the north side of Queen Street, extending east and west from Sydney to Carmarthen Streets, and north from Queen Street 100 feet. They contain 10 city lots and form a block of 100 by 400 feet.

Charles McPherson, once the owner of "Coffee House

---

* St. John was formerly called Parr Town.

PINE'S BRICK BUILDING KING ST., THE ONLY BRICK BUILDING.

PRINCE WILLIAM STREET.

Corner," survived the other trustees, who died before any of the buildings mentioned in the grant were set up. A change had come over the people's views since then, and the site was not approved of by those interested. It was not central enough, and in 1815 it was decided to ask for a site in the upper part of the town. Wm. Pagan, Hugh Johnston, senr., John Thompson, James Grigor, John Currie, Alexander Edmonds, and William Donaldson were the new Committee whose duty it was to provide "a meeting house for the use of such of the inhabitants as are of the General Assembly of the Church of Scotland." In this year the survivor of the trustees of 1784, Charles McPherson, relinquished his interest in favour of the new Committee. James Grigor selected the present site of the church in Germain Street, and in 1815 he purchased it for £250 from J. V. Thurgar's uncle, Mr. John L Venner. The lot is 100 feet in width and 200 feet in depth. Mr. Grigor and wife, by deed, on the 20th June, 1815, just sixty-two years ago, on the day of the fire, conveyed the property to Wm. Pagan and the rest of the Committee. On June 4th, 1816, another grant of land was given to the Committee by the Corporation of St. John. This lot was in Duke's Ward, and known on the plan as one of the public lots, letter B, bounded on the east by Carmarthen Street, on the west by Sydney Street, and on the south by lots 1086 to 1077 inclusive. The latter lots are on St. James' Street. This also was in special trust for the Kirk of Scotland in this city, and the grant was unconditional. This block was four hundred by

E

feet square, and a vacant field. The Committee built houses upon it some years after, and laid out the street from Sydney to Carmarthen, known as St. Andrew's Street. William Campbell was Mayor, and Charles J. Peters, Clerk.

The Act 56 George III., cap. 28, passed 16th March, 1816, recites to this effect:

" Whereas sundry inhabitants of the City of St. John and its vicinity, being of the Protestant profession of worship, approved by the General Assembly of the Church of Scotland, have, by voluntary subscription, aided by a grant* of money out of the Province (1814), erected a large and handsome building for a place of public worship, which shall be in connection with the said **Church** of Scotland: And whereas, the title of the lots on which the said church has been erected, situated in Queen's Ward in the said city, and fronting on Germain Street, is now in the possession of the inhabitants of the said city, who hold the same in trust: Be it enacted, that the minister and elders of the said church, commonly called by the name of Kirk, whenever such ministers shall be chosen and appointed, the said lots shall be vested in them, they being known by the name of the minister and elders of the Church of Scotland in the City of St. John."

In 1818, Act 58 was passed, and this statute authorized the Kirk's ministers and elders to have full power to purchase, receive, hold, and enjoy lands, and tenements, and to improve and use the same for the purpose of support-

---

*Legislature granted £250 towards erection of kirk.

ing and maintaining the building erected in St. John for a place of public worship, and of its minister for the time being; but such rents, with the rents of pews, shall not exceed annually the sum of £500.

An important discovery was made in 1832, when it was found that the legislation that had been had was entirely at variance with Presbyterian usage, which separated the spiritual from the temporal affairs of the church, leaving the spiritual department in the hands of the minister and his elders, and vesting the management of the temporalities in a body of trustees to be named. A new bill was prepared, and accordingly the following was speedily enacted by 2 William IV. cap. 18, " that according to the form and usage of the Church of Scotland the spiritual and temporal affairs of the said church are kept separate, and that the present acts of incorporation vesting the temporal affairs of the St. Andrew's Church, in the City of St. John, in the minister and elders is at variance with the form and usage of the said Church of Scotland."

All previous acts were repealed, and the following gentlemen, who were the committee of management then: Thos. Walker, Robert Rankin, John Wishart, John Robertson, James Kirk, Robert Keltie, James Burns, Henry Flood, William Parks, William Walker, James Robertson and Daniel Leavitt, with the elders, John Paul, Robert Robertson, Thomas Nisbet, William Hutchinson, Angus McKenzie and John Gillis, were appointed interim trustees until the election of twelve other trustees as provided by the Act, could be had. This Act is still in operation, and it fixes the annual rents at not more than £500, and prescribes the proceedings as to the election and choice of trustees, ministers, and elders, the sales and leases of pews, lands, &c.

In 1815 the kirk was finished, and the trustees were Messrs. Pagan, Johnston, Thomson, Grigor, and Edmond, Rev. Mr. Waddell, father of Dr. Waddell, many years resident physician at the Lunatic Asylum, preached the first sermon. The Rev. Geo. Burns was the first regularly appointed minister, he had been an assistant minister in Aberdeen, Scotland, Mr. Hugh Johnston who had been commissioned to go to Scotland for a clergyman, chose Mr. Burns who was a young man of 26 years of age, and a doctor of divinity. The degree was conferred on him by the University of St. Andrew on his departure for America, and the new Kirk was called "St. Andrew" in compliment to Dr. Burns's *Alma mater*. The young doctor arrived in St. John on Sunday, the 25th of May, 1817, and on that day preached his first sermon from Psalm cxxii, 1, "I was glad when they said unto me, let us go into the House of the Lord." Dr. Burns continued minister until 1829. He left St. John May, 1831, and on the 5th February, 1876, he died in Edinburgh at the ripe age of 86. The Rev. Robert Wilson was the second minister of the Kirk, and he officiated from 1830 to 1842. The Rev. Andrew Halket succeeded him from 1842 to 1848. He died in the fall of 1875, at Brecken, Scotland. The Rev. Wm. Donald, D.D., was the fourth minister of this now influential church, he was ordained at Aberdeen, in May, 1849, and on the 18th of June he reached St. John, and took immediate possession of his charge. His ministry was a long and able one, and no minister was ever loved more and respected higher than this teacher of the sacred word. He was ever kindly disposed towards his people and his congregation were ever devoted to him, their interests were his interests, and his interests were theirs. When he died 20th Feby., 1871, the whole city mourned, and old St. Andrew's refused to be comforted. The Rev. R. J. Cameron, who was Dr. Donald's assistant for some time, succeeded him in the ministry of the church. The Rev. Mr. Mitchell, who began his labours on the 30th January, 1877, was the last incumbent. During the long career of the old kirk—the oldest Presbyterian church in the Province —it has changed but little since it was erected. Some trifling alterations have been made in the interior, but externally it has remained for over three score years the same. Three memorial tablets had been placed upon the walls, the first was in memory of William Pagan, the second William Campbell, and the third Dr. Donald. The first Presbyterian minister who died in St. John was the Rev. Thomas Wishart.*

There are some interesting items in connection with Old St. Andrew's personal history which are worth recording.

---

* Three members of the congregation of this Church were lost at the time of the fire—Mrs. Thos. Reed, Mr. Joseph Bell, Capt. Wm. M. B. Firth.

The solid silver communion service which was used was the gift, in the year 1818, of the Earl and **Countess of** Dalhousie, and Miss Campbell gave the two peculiarly **shaped** silver plates which contained the bread when the the Sacrament was administered. These articles were saved, and are now in the possession of William Girvan, Esq. Mrs. James Lawton, about the year 1839, presented the Church with the Pulpit Bible. This was unfortunately burned, as well as the two oil paintings which hung **in the** vestry, and **were** portraits of Revs. Drs. Burns and Donald. It was to see these pictures that Dr. Burns's nephew came to St. John on the very day of the fire, but before he arrived they were no more.

Very little time was lost between the destruction of Trinity, the Germain Street Methodist, and "Old St. Andrew's." They took fire nearly at the same time, and within an hour of each other the three were consumed. **The** fire was extraordinarily rapid in its work, and the **frame** buildings seemed to add zest to its voracious appetite. An engine might have saved the Victoria Hotel, but it was far away, and helplessly the people looked on and saw one after the other of their cherished churches, hotels, houses of entertainment and dwellings, sink down before the red glare of the serpent, which wound its coils round-about and encompassed all with its fangs and fork-like tongue. It was a sight that the eye sickened **at, and the** heart grew faint, and despair fell upon **the** people, and many moved away. But there were others who gazed on the tottering ruins with a fixed and glassy stare, and as the huge boulders came thundering down from the heights above, and the half famished flames shot out in long, thin lines from the windows, and darted back again like a wiry thing of life, and shouts rent the air from the lips of the wounded, these men never moved from the spot on which they stood. The church was in ashes, and the great walls of the Victoria were red with the demon flames. They scaled the heights, they flew back again. They hid in the chimneys, they ran along the roof, they melted the sashes and tore down the door-ways. The marble steps were in fragments, and all through the long corridors of the house the shrieks of startled women rang, and hastening refugees from the flames leapt with the courage and skill of acrobats into the crowded street. It was a time in which men held their breath. The fascination of that sight was terrible. All were dismayed. All were paralyzed. The "Victoria," that Grand Hotel which was St. John to every traveller who came here—that massive pile of brick and stone—was no longer the standing monument of the city's enterprise. An engine might have saved it, but the engine was not there.

This spacious hotel was commenced by a Joint Stock Company in 1870, and was built on the corner of Germain and Duke Streets. It was opened for business July, 1871, with Mr. B. T. Creagen as Manager, and the following Board of Directors :—Otis Small, Esq., President; John Magee, A. Chipman Smith, John McMillan and William F. Harrison, Esqrs. The hotel building cost one hundred and sixty-five thousand dollars, and furnishing seventy-five thousand dollars. In the Fall of 1873, the Victoria Hotel Club assumed control, and Mr. John Edwards was appointed manager. At the time of the fire the hotel was under the management of Mr. George W. Swett, a very popular and courteous gentleman. Many of the guests sought refuge in the squares, and some escaped from the building with scarcely more clothes than they had on.

CHAPTER VI.

The Odd Fellows' Hall—The fire in Horsfield Street—The Sweep along Germain Street—The old Baptist Church—Some early Ministers—Two fiery ordeals—The Brick Church—The Ruins—The Bay View Hotel—An old Landmark gone—The blazing Barracks—St. James's—The Hazen House—St. Malachi's Chapel—The first Roman Catholic Church.

THE Independent Order of Odd Fellows is a very numerous and widely respected body in St. John. Its roll of membership embraces many of the best names in the city, and the order has grown from a very humble beginning to quite an influential position in the community. It is only a few years ago that some zealous members of the order banded themselves together and formed Pioneer Lodge, No. 9. In a little time the lodge grew so rapidly that it became too cumbersome to work, and new lodges had to be made—first it was Beacon, then Peerless, and latterly Siloam, in this city alone; besides, the order is strong in Moncton and also in Fredericton. An encampment, too, flourishes, and is largely adding to its membership. The Odd Fellows' Hall was pleasantly situate in what used to be No. 5 Engine House. The hall was commodious and neatly furnished, and the ante-rooms were convenient and well adapted for carrying on the exercises of the order. The ground flat and second story were occupied by Mr. Richard Welch, and the Odd Fellows met in the room immediately overhead. The loss by fire to the order was quite extensive, though a good deal of the regalia and paraphernalia were saved through the forethought of some of the members who managed to get into the building in time. The fire swept both sides of Horsfield Street, and carried along with it the dwelling of P. Besnard, Esq., and the house where James Hannay, the historian, lived. Mr. Hannay, who was at Oakpoint during the conflagration preparing his history of Acadia, lost a number of valuable books, including some high-priced and scarce volumes.* Some two or three hundred pages of his history were printed, but these were destroyed in the printing houses where they were kept. Fortunately Mr. Hannay had with him one copy of the sheets as far as printed, so the loss is not irretrievable. A portion of the unprinted manuscript, however, shared the common fate of everything that came in contact with fire on that fatal day, and this the historian had to re-write. In this street the old Theatre† once stood, in which professionals and amateurs read Shakspeare and Massinger to admiring audiences. Among the amateurs, some of our readers may remember, were the late Richard Seely, who was accounted a good actor in his day, and the late Col. Otty, whose Othello was a really creditable performance. While the fire was rendering desolate this street, the other wing of it was ruthlessly invading Germain Street, to the very water's

---

* Smith's History of Virginia, Ed. of 1627, on large paper : Smith's History of New York, large paper edition, 1758, presentation copy to Governor Ellis, of Georgia : and a very valuable historical library on New England and Acadian History.

† This was the old Friary

THE GREAT FIRE IN ST. JOHN, N. B.

edge. Otis Small's corner house, the Thomson House, some of the inmates of which had to flee in small boats, the residences of the Messrs. McMillan, father and son, the old Bayard House, the Seed's property, the former residence of W. O. Smith, Esq., No. 119, and then in the occupancy of the inmates of the Home for the Aged, some of whom got away in hardly enough time to save their lives.

Mr. Carey's Parsonage was on fire very soon after this, and all efforts to save it or the old Baptist Church next door, proved unavailing. In a short time only a blackened wall of smouldering ruins stood there to tell in more eloquent language than words could relate, of the sad havoc which the fire-king had made. For many years this church was to the Baptists, what Trinity, St. Andrew's, and Germain Street Chapel were to their denominations. It, too, had a history of its own, as dear to the people who Sunday after Sunday sat within its walls and heard the word of God spoken, as the historic data which filled every niche and corner of the first English Church in the city. It was first built of wood three score years ago, on the old site where the brick church stood, a period ago since, and such men as John M. Wilmot, Thomas Pettingill, and Jeremiah Drake, were the leading pillars and supporters of a body of Christians distinguished alike for their charity, faithfulness, and liberality. The church was organized in 1810, ground was broken in 1818, and the large frame building was opened for service July 12th of the same year. Wm. Stenning and Thomas

Harding purchased the site, and the former gentleman superintended the building of the edifice. For many years this was the only meeting-house which the Baptists had, and there are men living to-day who remember the struggles and trials which the denomination experienced in trying to plant a foothold in the sparsely populated district which St. John then was. The pastors of this church were known far and wide as earnest and faithful men, and such names as Samuel Robinson, Casewell, Bill, Henry Vaughan, and G. M. W. Carey, live in the hearts of all people and add lustre to any faith. When the question of tearing down the old structure which had withstood the storms of nearly half a century, and the replacing of it with a new one to be built of brick was proposed, there were many in the congregation who had grown up with the church through the long decades of time, and who had watched the building step by step, advance to its completion, and proudly take its place among the sacred edifices of the street of churches. These men opposed the measure, but the march of new ideas prevailed, and in 1863, the last of the old church was borne away and a handsome brick building was begun. The former vestry was converted into a parsonage, and the Rev. Henry Vaughan, son of the late Simon Vaughan, of St. Martin's, was the minister in charge. The church cost forty thousand dollars. Mr. Vaughan died in 1864. When Mr. Carey, the present pastor, arrived in St. John in 1865, the church was being built and he preached for a while in the basement, and in December, 1866, the first sermon in the church proper was preached by the same eloquent minister. A tablet was erected to the memory of his predecessor in the church. In 1873 this church was partially destroyed by fire, but the enterprising congregation soon had it up again. Thus has this edifice passed through two ordeals of like character. The church had just begun to recover from its first disaster. The liberality of its people had placed it out of debt, and while in the enjoyment of a splendid prosperity it was stricken down before the very eyes of the powerless people who loved it most. No one could do anything but watch the rapid demolition, and behold the rafters swing and the building rock and shake, and observe the long sinewy flames grapple with the walls and hurl them to the earth. There were strong men that day who wept when they witnessed the destruction. And when the sad work was done, some gathered near the ruins and looked down upon the site that had held a church while they were yet babes, and old gray-haired veterans who had worshipped here all their lives, felt that death would not be so bitter now since church and home were gone forever. The insurance on this church was very light and the loss is very heavy. The pastor saved literally nothing of his own effects, and his fine library and the intellectual labour of twenty years, passed from his gaze with the rapidity of the whirlwind.

The fire next crossed the street, and attacked Mr. Harding's houses, destroying his residence, and that of Mr. Joseph Allison. Queen Street shared the common fate; and on the side of Germain Street opposite the church, **in the building where** Mrs. Crane had her seminary for young ladies, the inmates were forced to escape in the International steamer, and get away from the fire by water. The street was impassable, and all hope of getting through to a locality which had not yet been reached by the flames had to be abandoned. Terror seized the ladies for the moment, but the courage which sometimes comes with despair, made them cool enough to think of the water. The strength of iron came to them, and in a moment they **were saved. It was before this house that** a woman fell on her knees and offered up prayer; **and here it** was that another woman, fearing the judgment day at hand, **gave** utterance **to** loud wails and cries, that sent a pang **to** every heart. In the melee, an old lady belonging to **the** Home for the Aged was lost, and her feeble sisters in adversity moaned and mourned for her all through the night. The next day she was found, and joy came to some hearts that had known no like emotion for several years. Those kindly old **ladies living so long together were** as one family, and a vacant **chair at the table** cruelly reminded them **of the** broken homes they had too often seen. The houses across Queen Street, on this same side of Germain Street, were not long in following. Pagan Place, the old residence of the late Edward Allison, Stephen Blizard's house on the **other** side, John **W.** Cudlip's residence, in Germain Street, seemed to burn at the **same** time. The Bay View Hotel—a valuable structure that reminded the spectator of the old feudal time, when castles were residences of the great, was erected in the year 1819, by Henry Wright, Collector, and used as a private residence up to about twelve years ago. It was built by day's work, and in those days the workmen received every Saturday night their pay in Spanish doubloons. Change was very scarce, and there was no paper money. Mr. Henry Wright died in 1829, and the house then fell into the occupancy of the late Wm. Wright, Advocate General, and John Boyd, M.D. Mr. Wilson was its lessee latterly, and it became an hotel under his management. It held a commanding position, and looked far out to sea. Strangers always paused to look up to the splendid front and defiant head, which reminded them of the old strongholds which render **historic** every inch of the old land across the blue water. **And** to-day, the ruins look even more picturesque and grand than the building did in its proudest days. Another landmark has been taken away, and it did not long survive those who dwelt in its spacious halls in the days of the long ago.

But while the fire was busy with this portion **of the** City, it was also extremely active and equally destructive in the lower part of St. John. The barracks **were** even burned down long before it was deemed likely **that** the Victoria Hotel would go. The sparks travelling **in** this direction with great rapidity, soon communicated with the long, low building which was built for the troops in 18 9.* The fire, when it reached here had full scope.

---
* Before this the troops lived on Fort Howe Hill, and the artillery at Hare's Wharf.

Nothing **stood** in its way, **and it** really spent its greatest strength here. The majority **of the** houses in this quarter were composed of wood, and so many of them were close together, that four or five houses were burned to the ground in about the same space that in ordinary times would be spent in consuming one. The burning of the barracks was witnessed by several thousand persons, and, for a while there **were** some who fancied that the blaze would cease **with** the destruction of this property. But, alas, for the fallacy of human hopes. The great headway of the flame was made, and nothing could stop it, till from sheer exhaustion, it spent itself. But the eager wind kept fanning it into fury whenever it shewed signs of abatement and not until it reached the barren banks along the water's edge did it relinquish its grasp on men's household goods and homes. Even then it did not stop at once, for small scrubs or trees, bits of shrubbery and grass fed it for a while. Indeed the fire may be said to have taken a new lease of life in those back places, and the rookeries of whole streets were swept into ruin and their inmates hurried into greater misery than they had ever known before. In Main Street, St. James (Episcopalian) Church was burned; it caught very soon from a flying spark. This church was erected in the summer of 1850 by Trinity Church. The parish was set off from Trinity in 1852, but the church was built two years before; the dividing line of the parish was south of Queen Street; the first rector was the Rev. John Armstrong who was succeeded by his son, Rev. Wm. Armstrong who held the rectorship nearly twenty years.

ACADEMY OF MUSIC.

NEW POST OFFICE.

The building was of the Gothic cruciform style of architecture and Mr. M. Stead was the architect. It had no tower. The first wardens were the late John M. Robinson, Esq., father of the agent in this city of the Bank of Nova Scotia, and the late Wm. Wright. The church was situate on the south side of Main Street, between Sydney and Carmarthen Streets and the lots ran through to Sheffield Street. The Sunday-school building was built in the rear.

The Sheffield Street Mission House and the Carmarthen Street Mission House (Methodist) were structures of late origin, and for a while did much good in the locality where they were placed. The fire visited them very soon and they were burned in a short time. All along Carmarthen Street the flames sped quickly, completely encircling every house with which it came in contact, and whenever they met a crossing street the fire drove through it with seeming greater fury and impetuosity. The lately erected Adam's terrace—a row of comfortable dwellings just finished within the year—burned with a tremendous roar that was heard above the din, for blocks away. In these houses were the families of Robt. Turner, Fred. R. Fairweather and W. C. Watson, Esqs., and so quickly did the flames spread that hardly a stick of furniture was saved, and hundreds of valuable books were burned. Judge Watters's residence, the home of Attorney-General King, Henry A. Austin's, Madame Caritte's, and the Henderson houses, hardly lived thirty minutes in the winding sheets of flame. The fire came up Carmarthen Street, up Prin-

cess Street, up Leinster Street, up Duke Street, up **Orange
Street, to the rear of** those streets and down King **Street
east and also in its** rear on a portion of the south side.
Many believed **and** there seemed good grounds for that
belief, that but **for the** torch of the incendiary, Leinster
Street would have been preserved. **No one** doubts but
that it was set on fire by some miscreant either through
madness or through the hope of gain. This is **beyond** dispute. The fire was going in the opposite direction,
nothing could bring it up towards King Square and
the head of Leinster Street. **It was** out of all reason to
suppose **that the** sparks could be carried to these points
for the wind was opposite, and the open square had, till
late in the evening, kept the flames away and broke **the
connection.** The old* Hazen House built by Dr. Thomas
Paddock, which is still standing to-day, and passed safely
through the fire, stood invincible at the head of a column
of buildings. The fire was confined to its own seething
territory, and this block between Leinster and East King
Street, and the whole of King Square were safe. But as
the night advanced,† a house far away from the reach of

---

* The lot where the Hazen House now stands (King Square) was bought in 1790, by Mr. Thomas Horsfield for £6 5s., and sold by him five years later for £5, to a number of gentlemen who erected a grist mill there. In 1800, they abandoned the enterprise, and in 1818, the spot was used as a barracks at the time when one-third of the militia were called out for a few months, when war with the United States was threatened. A day or two after the fire in June, 1877, the Bank of New Brunswick opened a temporary office there for a few days, and a soldier of the 97th regiment kept guard over the building at night. Some of the 62nd also did duty here.

† The fire broke out in rear of Dr. Boyle Travers' residence.

flying cinders, was observed on a sudden to be throwing out flames, and from that moment all knew the eastern portion of the city was doomed to destruction. Christian Robertson's mammoth stable, with its splendid livery appointments, and large stock of feed and hay, representing large value, was only a plaything of the moment. Old St. Malachi's Chapel, the first Roman Catholic Church in the city, caught from the sparks which were borne on the breeze from the stable. Its destruction was complete. The first service held by a clergyman of the Faith in St. John, was in the City Hall, Market Square, 1813, by Rev. Charles French. St. Malachi's Chapel was opened by that gentleman, October 1st, 1815. Among the priests who succeeded him in that place were Father McQuade, who in 1819, had thirty women and thirty-five men for a congregation, and Fathers Macmahon, Carrol, and Dumphy. Mr. Carrol came from Halifax, and was the nephew of the first Roman Catholic Bishop of the Maritime Provinces—Bishop Burk. Of late years St. Malachi's was used for school, lecture, bazaar, and other purposes. Some of the most eloquent efforts of J. C. Ferguson and R. J. Ritchie, have been delivered from the platform of this Hall, on temperance and other topics. St. Malachi's was used as a church until the cathedral was opened under Bishop Connolly's charge. The St. Vincent De Paul Society met in this hall for several years, as well as those other excellent institutions, the C. T. A. and St. Joseph's Societies.

CHAPTER VII.

A hard-working Manager—The Dramatic Lyceum—The Temperance Hall—The Water-Works Building—A Hard Fight—Another Rush of the Homeless—The Weary March of the Unfortunates—History of the Water Supply—Early Struggles—Changes—The Old Way—The St. John Water Company—Placed in Commission—The Company To-day.

THE cosy Dramatic Lyceum, endeared to old theatre-goers on account of many pleasant memories, was reduced to ashes after the fire had destroyed the marble establishments of Jas. and Robt. Milligan and S. P. Osgood. Like Robertson's stable it was not long in the throes of dissolution, for it parted company with the earth in a few brief moments. It had been built a score of years and more, and for a long time it was the chief place of amusement in the city. Its builder was the father of theatricals in St. John, and no man ever did more for his chosen profession than he. He worked with the vigour which only an enthusiast feels, and now at the close of his long managerial career, extending over a quarter of a century, he can look back with pride and satisfaction on the work he has done. He has taught the people all they know of dramatic affairs to-day. He has educated and elevated their tastes, and by the production of the great masterpieces of Shakespeare, Jonson, Massenger, Bulwer, Goldsmith and Sheridan, he has instilled into the minds of the citizens a love of all that is admirable and beautiful in our common literature. He it was, who at great pecuniary sacrifice brought such an artist as Charles Mathews

here, and it was under his management that Charles
Dillon, E. L. Davenport, Frederic Robinson, Wyzeman
Marshall and the famous comedian, Wm. J. Le Moyne,*
played short engagements in our city. When the plain, but
comfortable Lyceum was built, it was the first step towards
a regular theatre that had been made, and in his early days
Mr. Lanergan had much to contend against and many old
prejudices to break down. A hundred arguments were
brought to bear against his enterprise. Many good people,
unskilled in the knowledge of the world, and who had never
in their lives attended a theatre, were the most open in their
denunciation of it and its teachings. Fathers were exhort-
ed to keep their boys at home, and men and women were
enjoined not to attend the performances in this "devil's
house." But Mr. Lanergan showed his patrons that he
could furnish a species of amusement harmless in its character and respectable in its quality. He selected from
the wide range of plays only those which taught good
lessons, and the ladies and gentlemen he secured to give
utterance to the thoughts of the masters in literature,
were persons of irreproachable character and conduct.
He saw his efforts rewarded at length, and during the last
ten years of his career his audiences comprised the *elite* of
the city. The old Lyceum was ever a pleasant place. It
was cosy and easy and roomy, and one could always see
an acceptable performance on its little stage. The build-

* Mr. Le Moyne's second appearance in St. John was at the Academy of
Music, in October, 1876, when he appeared in a round of favourite characters
from dramatizations of Dickens' novels, under the management of Mr.
Charles H. Thayer, of Boston.

ing was sold to the Irish Friendly Society a few months ago and it was used by them for concerts, entertainments, &c. On the night of the fire it was under engagement to a minstrel party.*

---

* As many readers take interest in the programmes used on first nights of theatres we give a copy of Mr. Lanergan's opening bill, at the Lyceum. It runs as follows:

ST. JOHN DRAMATIC LYCEUM.
SOUTH SIDE KING'S SQUARE, ST. JOHN, N. B.

Manager and Proprietor.......................... MR. J. W. LANERGAN.
Stage Director................................... FRANK REA.
Scenic Artist .... D. A. STRONG.
Machinist and Property Maker.................. D. J. MORIARTY.
Ticket Master................................... T. A. ALLISON.

"Those who live to please,
Must please to live!"

GRAND OPENING NIGHT!

The above new and elegant place of amusement will open for the first regular Dramatic Season, on Monday evening, June 15, 1857, with a full, Efficient and Talented Dramatic Company,—comprising the following well known Ladies and Gentlemen:

Mr. W. A. DONALDSON, }
 " N. DAVENPORT,   } .... From the Boston Theatre.
 " N. C. FORRESTER, }

 " FRANK REA.............. From Wallack's Theatre, New York.
 " F. S. BUXTON............ From The Canadian Theatres.
G. F. TYRRELL; J. C. WALLACE; E. B. HOLMES; D. J. MORIARTY; P. MORIARTY and J. W. LANERGAN,

Mrs. J. W. LANERGAN, }
 "   FRANK REA,   } .... From Wallack's Theatre, New York.

Miss E. HOMAN .... From the Boston Theatres.
Mrs. F. S. BUXTON ....   "   Canadian   "
 "   J. C. WALLACE..........
 "   N. C. FORRESTER........   "   Boston   "
and " J. C. MORIARTY ....   "   "   "

The entertainment will commence as above with the National Anthem!
GOD SAVE THE QUEEN,

By the Orchestra.—After which an Original opening Address written, and to be delivered by
G. F. TYRRELL.

THE GREAT FIRE IN ST. JOHN, N. B.   79

After this temple of art was overthrown the fire burned along the square till it struck the Hazen building, now owned by C. M. Bostwick, who had but recently renovated

---

To be followed by Sir E. L. BULWER's Chaste and Elegant Comedy in
5 acts, entitled
MONEY!

" 'Tis a very good world that we live in,
To lend, or to spend, or to give in,—
But to beg, or to borrow, or to get a man's own,
'Tis the very worst world that ever was known."

Alfred Evelyn .... Mr. J. W. LANERGAN.
Benjamin Stout, Esq..........(first appearance) FRANK REA.
Sir John Vesey ....   "   "   N. C. FORRESTER.
Lord Glossmore .... G. F. TYRRELL.
Mr. Graves ....(first appearance) Mr. F. S. BUXTON.
Sir Fredk. Blunt ....   "   "   N. DAVENPORT.
Capt. Dudley Smooth ....   "   "   W. A. DONALDSON.
Sharp .... J. C. WALLACE.
Toke ....(first appearance) D. J. MORIARTY.
Clara Douglas .... Mrs. J. W. LANERGAN.
Lady Franklyn ....(first appearance) Mrs. FRANK REA.
Georgina....................................... Mrs. J. C. WALLACE.

The entertainments of the evening will conclude with the Amusing farce,
with NEW READING, *of*
MR. & MRS. PETER WHITE.

Mr. Peter White............................... Mr. F. S. BUXTON.
Major Pepper ....   " N. C. FORRESTER.
Frank Brown ....   " E. B. HOLMES.
Widow White .... Mrs. J. W. LANERGAN.
Mrs. Peter White ....   " FRANK REA.
Kitty Clover................................... " J. C. WALLACE.

PRICES OF ADMISSION.
Parquette 1s. 3d.—Dress Circle 2s. 6d.—Private and Family
Boxes $4, 5 & 6 each.
☞ Private and Family boxes can be secured in advance by application at the Box Office.
DOORS OPEN AT HALF PAST 7—COMMENCE AT 8.
Ladies unaccompanied by gentlemen not admitted.
Good order is expected and will be rigidly enforced.
PRINTED AT DAY'S JOB OFFICE, 4 MARKET STREET.

it from top to bottom. But this corner house was too much for the fire, the fiend was baffled in its object, and though late through the night it made several inefficient attempts to raise its head, when the morning dawned, the Hazen Building was still safe and defiant, for the flames were at its feet helpless and weak. The fire crept along the square and passed the burned district when it divided itself into two wings. The right body went up Leinster Street, and the left wing proceeded around by the square, attacked the Court House, was repulsed, when it burned the buildings adjoining No. 2 Engine House, and made a sortie in rear of the jail. It was well nigh successful in its object, and indeed a portion of this edifice was burned. The prisoners were made secure, and a grand exit took place under the immediate supervision of Deputy Sheriff Rankine. Two or three of the culprits managed to escape, but they returned next day, after wandering about the city, and gave themselves up, fearing lest they would starve in the desolate and destitute town. The jail successfully resisted the flames, but not so the old Temperance Hall which stood beside it. This antiquated and wholly unattractive meeting-house was put up about thirty years ago, and was originally intended for a school in connection with the poor-house, which stood on the corner of Carmarthen and East King Streets. The Temperance Order was organized in St. John, May 12th, 1847, and the leading men were Hon. S. L. Tilley, C.B., Lieut.-Governor of the Province, Chas. A. Everett, the Smilers, John Rankine, W. H. A.

Kerns, S. B. Paterson, O. D. Wetmore, and of late years, Samuel Tufts, Edw. Willis, A. G. Blakslee, J. A. S. Mott, and Sheriff Harding. The organization met in King Street till they were burned out, after which they settled in the Temperance Hall near the jail, where they have remained ever since. The interior of this block was burned, and only the Court House, which was opened for the first time for Supreme Court uses by Judge Botsford at the January Circuit of 1830, the Registry Office, and the City Prison were left. It was only by dint of the most strenuous exertions that these buildings were kept proof against the levelling qualities of the left wing, which again and again reared its front till it was firmly laid low at eleven in the evening of that terrible day. The old poor-house in Carmarthen Street was hemmed in by the united forces of left and right, and it easily succumbed without even a show of resistance. The defence of the office of the Superintendent of Water Supply* was one of the memorable events in connection with the history of the fire. In the yard people from all quarters of the city had stored their goods in the vain hope that the fire could never reach them. The situation of the office seemed to promise safety. It was far away from the business portion of the town, and no one dreamed of

---

* On these premises was situated the St. John Meteorological Observatory. This was destroyed, but all the instruments belonging to the Dominion were saved. Night and day observations have been made here under the superintendence of Gilbert Murdoch Esq., C. E., during the last 25 years.

its being attacked from the contingent which moved along Carmarthen Street. Here at least many persons thought, was a place of safety. From four o'clock in the afternoon, while the rich row of buildings in the Market Square were struggling against overwhelming odds, load after load of furniture, merchandise and general chattels poured into the spacious yard, and even the office itself was for a time a vast warehouse. It was only when the work of the incendiary showed itself in Leinster Street and old Malachi's toppled over, that the destruction of the well-equipped office was considered imminent. Then it was that heart-sick and weary men and women, who had worked all day, and who had lost nearly all they possessed, and had hoped what little they had taken to the water-office yard would be saved, began to realize the situation. Where could they go now? Where could they take the only remnants which reminded them of the bright home they had had that morning. Twice had they gathered up the fragments, and in each removal the little heap grew smaller than before. But it was worse now. In the afternoon teams could be had for five dollars a load, and now as high as thirty, and even fifty dollars were refused by inhuman drivers. Calamities sometimes make barbarians of men, and the nearer the flames got, and the hotter the breath of the fire became, the more exorbitant was the price asked by owners of vehicles; and the more inhumanity mankind exhibited. Women cried and groaned as they fell on all that was left, and some begged piteously for help. But when they got a dray or a sloven, where could they go? The wild behemoth could overtake them where'er they went. But on came the fire, both sides of the street, back again by Carmarthen Street, up by Carmarthen Street. Here the force united, and crushing out all before it, drove with tremendous energy and iron-like rigour into the very heart of the building. In an instant it was on fire in ten places, and the huge pipes alongside that looked so like an array of mounted cannon, were all that remained in the yard the next day. The blacksmith shop, oil-house, stable, and everything near showed scarcely a trace of what they had been. The great bulk of the valuable records, papers and plans and specifications of the office were saved through the untiring vigilance of the superintendent, his valuable aids and the workmen in the employ of the Company. Nothing, indeed, that could not be replaced in a little time was lost.

In this connection, a brief sketch of the water supply of St. John will not be without interest. It is only half a century ago that the inhabitants of this city were dependent on wells for the water which they drank and used. Even at later date than that it used to be sold about the streets from tall casks, at a penny a bucketful. The chief wells were in King's Square, Blockhouse Hill— the vantage ground of many a well-contested fisticuff battle between the rising generation; Princess Street, near Charlotte; Queen Square, the foot of Poor House Hill, which in winter made such a splendid coasting road; and in Portland close by the first public hydrant, now in

Main Street. In 1820, agitation was made for a better system of water supply ; but it was not until 1825 that the question took definite shape, and an Act for the incorporation of a water company, with a capital of £10,000 passed the Legislature. Surveys were at once made, and estimates were laid before the stockholders, but the capital subscribed was deemed insufficient to enable them to go on with the work in hand. The money was accordingly lent out on interest until the next year, when each stockholder received back the sum he had paid in, with three per cent. added. A number of new wells were sunk at once, and every effort made to secure for the people a fuller supply. In 1832, Hon. William Black, Nehemiah Merritt, James White, John Ward, George D. Robinson, Thomas Barlow, Hugh Johnston, John M. Wilmot, James Hendricks, Thomas Millidge, Robert W. Crookshank, Zalmon Wheeler, Robert Parker, William B. Kinnear, Richard Sands, Lauchlan Donaldson, Charles Simonds, James T. Hanford, William Leavitt, and Noah Disbrow had an Act passed for the Incorporation of the St. John Water Company. It started with a subscribed capital of £20,000, five per cent. of which was to be paid in a year from the date of the passing of the Act. The shares were placed at £5 each. Directors were to be elected every year, and consist of thirteen in number, and seven of the old directors were to remain in office each year. In 1834, a new Act was passed, amending the one which was sanctioned two years previously, but the Company was not regularly organized until 1837. Colonel

Baldwin, C.E., during this year, made surveys, and on his advice the first practical attempt at bringing the water into the city from Lily Lake was made. An engineer was appointed, and, under his management, the first City Water Works were built. The water was not brought, as in the opinion of eminent engineers it should have been, directly from Lily Lake to the city by its own gravitation, but was taken from the tail of Gilbert's Mill, and conducted thence by a sluice to a reservoir or a cistern, which was placed a few yards to the south-west of the Marsh-bridge. An engine and pumping-house was erected over the cistern, a steam-engine and gear were procured, and the water was sent through a ten-inch main to the reservoir, which was on Block House Hill. The water was first brought through the pipes to the city in October, 1838. The supply passed through a very limited number of pipes, and the inhabitants, up to 1850, could only get water two hours each morning. The Company, from its first organization, suffered the pangs of financial troubles. The stock had met with many takers, who subscribed readily, but when called on for their payments failed to respond. A loan of £5,000 was received from the Legislature, which relieved the company somewhat for the nonce. In 1850, an appeal was made to the citizens on public grounds, and they were earnestly solicited to take up the new shares which were offered. The money from this source was to be applied to the extending of the works to, and bringing the water from, Little River at Scott's Mill, five miles away from the city. This course had been recommended by Chas. W. Fairbanks, Esq., C.E., of Halifax, under whose supervision the water had been introduced into that city. The city took up 900 shares, and private individuals bought the balance. The site at Scott's Mill was purchased, a small dam was built, and a twelve-inch main, four and a half miles in length, was laid. This main the company connected with the ten-inch main that was laid in 1837-8. The same main is still perfect, and to-day works as well as ever. In 1852 an Act was passed, authorizing a further increase in the capital to the amount of £10,000, to be made preference stock. This was necessary to meet the growing demand of consumers, and to enable the company to extend their pipes through the streets. In April, 1855, an Act was passed to allow the company to transfer their property and works to the City Corporation and Sessions. This step was deemed prudential for many reasons, the chief of which was the great difficulty the company experienced in running the water and sewerage systems separately. The conveyance was made. The Act authorized the Commissioners to issue debentures, bearing six per cent. interest, payable half-yearly, and redeemable at periods not exceeding forty years from their date. Two of the commissioners, one of whom should be chairman, were to be appointed by the Common Council, and another by the County Sessions. John Sears, Esq.—who lost in the great fire all his private papers, historical recollections which he had been collecting for forty years, and a number of rare oil paintings and portraits, an irreparable loss—was the first chairman, with the late John M. Walker, and John Owens, Esquires, as Commissioners. In 1864, Edward E. Lockhart, Esq. the present chairman, was appointed to the office, and the late Thomas King, and J. D. Woodworth, Esquires, Commissioners. On Mr. King's death, Mr. Stephen K. Brundage was appointed, and Mr. William Seely took Mr. Woodworth's place.

The first step taken by the commission was the improvement of the works. The dam at Little River reservoir was built higher and stronger, and during the progress of operations on it, it burst twice, and Gilbert Murdoch, Esq., the chief engineer, narrowly escaped drowning on one of these occasions. A twenty-four inch main was laid from the reservoir, and almost at the same time, and for most of its length, beside the ten inch main put down in 1850. This came across the Marsh bridge, and was connected, along with the twelve inch main, with an iron chamber, from which the water flowed into the original ten inch main, running up Brussels Street to the reservoir; a twelve inch main up Waterloo Street; a twelve inch main which went by the city road to Portland, and mains which have been put down later. The reservoir in Leinster Street was also thoroughly improved.

A new twelve inch main was laid up Erin Street, through St. Patrick and Wentworth Streets, to Princess, in 1868. The twelve inch main that is laid up Waterloo street, also goes along Sydney to Princess streets, and the Portland twelve inch main is extended nearly to the spot where the defunct street railway stables were, on Main Street, where an eight inch pipe joins it, and carries the water as far as Rankin's mill, by way of the steamboat wharves.

This brings the history of the water supply down to about nine years ago. Since that time, the progress which has been made upon it has been great and rapid. A vast amount of money and skill have been expended to bring the works down to the splendid state of perfection in which they are now. The water supply is excellent, and the system of sewerage is unsurpassed anywhere. Under great natural difficulties the work has been prosecuted, but the engineers and their workmen, by dint of perseverance, have surmounted the many obstacles which beset them on every side. Before leaving this subject, a remark or two may be made about the source from which our people receive their supply of water. The Victoria spring is situate on a hill-side, about a mile this side of Loch Lomond. Its waters form the head of Little River. Lake Donaldson is near the spring, and the Victoria is supposed to drain it. The stream from the spring flows into Douglas Lake, a sheet of water on the south side of the Loch Lomond road, eight miles from the Marsh Bridge. It is three miles from Lake Douglas to the reservoir. Lake Latimer, one of the feeders of Little River on the south side, is nearly as high as Loch Lomond. Its waters are as clear as crystal. Lake Buck, which also flows into Little River, lies about a quarter of a mile away from it. Long's Lake which is on the right side of Little River as it flows towards Court-

NORTH SIDE KING ST. AND BELL TOWER.

KING SQUARE AFTER THE FIRE, ENCAMPMENT OF THE 97TH REGIMENT.

eney Bay, is about a mile to the north of Loch Lomond Road, and empties itself into the reservoir. That a still further head may be had when wanted, the Commissioners purchased land through which they can bring a strong supply of water from Loch Lomond. There is an abundance of water in Little River for the immediate requirements of the city, but the supply can be doubled easily by tapping Loch Lomond.

The water in the Little River Reservoir is one hundred and sixty feet above high tide level; and in the Leinster Street Reservoir it is one hundred and thirty-two feet. A good deal of nonsense, during the excitement of the present fire, was talked about an inadequate supply of water to meet the wants of the exigency, but this was found to be fallacious. There was plenty of water all the time, and while there was much reckless and needless waste, there was sufficient of the element to meet the demands of the firemen and hose-men. It is a popular cry to raise at a fire which cannot be got under way, that there is no water. On the best authority the writer is happy to be able to place it on record that the supply of water was in every way adequate to the requirements of the hour.

CHAPTER VIII.

Burning of the Leinster Street Baptist Church—The Varley School—Centenary Chapel—The Gas Works—$17,000 worth of Coal burn in Ten Days—The Tall Sentinel—St. David's Church—The Reformed Presbyterian Church—The Victoria School—Gigantic Ruins—An Accident—Sketch of the School-house.

AFTER destroying the fence which enclosed the premises of the Water Company, the fire crossed the street, burned Mr. Wm. Murdoch, jr.'s, house, and turned its attention to the Leinster Street Baptist Church, which was soon brought to the level of the earth. This building was cleanly and squarely burned, and nothing approaching to the semblance of an edifice could be seen on the spot half-an-hour after the fire ceased. The building was completely swept away. The corporate body of the church was organized in 1858, under the pastorate of the Rev. E. B. Demill, son of Nathan S. Demill, with a membership of sixteen. The church was begun 1861, and in two months and a half the basement was finished and ready for service. In three years afterwards the church proper was completed, and the parsonage was erected in 1874. The former cost $13,000, and the latter $6,500. The second minister who presided over this congregation, was the Rev. W. V. Garner, who officiated for the first time in 1864. He was succeeded, in 1867, by Rev. W. S. Mackenzie, a trenchant writer and an excellent reasoner. The Rev. J. D. Pope followed him in 1874, and was the pastor of the church at the time of the conflagration. The early deacons and prominent men of the church, were the late Nathan S. Demill and **Saml. Kinsman.** Hon. A. McL. Seely, **A. W.** Masters, J. F. Marsters, and Stephen E. Gerow are the present deacons. The building was fully insured, and after the church debt of $3,000 is paid, the people will have about $15,000 with which to commence re-building.

The old Varley Wesleyan day-school, a brick building which a prominent Methodist—the late Mark Varley—designed for the purpose of educating, free, the poor belonging to his faith, made a resolute stand against the forces of the leveller. But in vain was water dashed upon the building. The intense heat drove the people back and no efforts of man could prevent the school-house from being in the end subdued. This property was erected a little more than twenty years ago and served its purpose long and well. A first-class education could be gained here. The teachers were usually men of brains, and the system employed for imparting instruction was simple and efficacious. After the school law came into force this school was no longer necessary under its old management, and the school trustees leased the building from the Varley Trustees, and it was used as an advanced school, at the time of the fire. The building occupied two stories. The upper room was used for girls and the lower apartment for boys.

The rear of Centenary Chapel adjoined the Varley school, and being built of wood and very large, it went up in a sea of flame without warning. The church was opened on its present site, corner of Princess and Wentworth streets, in 1839, the first Sunday after the fire in Dock street, and was designed by Mr. Burpee, an American architect. Mr. W. B. Frost put up the frame. The Rev. Dr. Wood, of Toronto, in 1838 preached the sermon on the laying of the corner-stone, and after the church was built he officiated for some years till 1846 when he left St. John. He was succeeded by the Rev. Henry Daniel and Rev. Mr. Sutcliffe, whose ministry lasted some three years. Rev. Dr. Knight and Rev. Mr. Cooney followed for four years. Then Rev. Messrs. James Hennigar and Cardy were the ministers for three years. Rev. Mr. Albrighton and Rev. Dr. Stewart, and Rev. Mr. Botterel held service for three years more. The Rev. Messrs. John McMurray and Wm. Wilson, were the clergymen for three years, and Rev. J. R. Narraway followed with Rev. Dr. Richey for the same period. After them came for two years Rev. Mr. England, who in his turn was followed by Rev. Mr. Lathern for three years and Rev. Donald Currie for two years. Rev. Dr. Henry Pope, who published a year ago, an acceptable series of sermons in two volumes, entitled, "Draughts from the Living Fountain," succeeded him for three years, and Rev. Howard Sprague, one of the most eloquent and popular divines in the conference was the last clergyman of this church. He was elected to proceed to England shortly after the burning, to get subscriptions and assistance for the rebuilding of the chapel. This church occupied the north-west corner of Princess and Wentworth Streets. The other three corners contained three splendid residences, those of J. V. Troop and Chas. McLauchlan, jr., Esqs., Simeon Jones and Alexander Lockhart, Esqs. These houses being solidly built and very strong were a good while in burning, but they went at last and a large portion of the furniture and other household goods that were got into the street were stolen afterwards by the ghouls which infested the place. One lady lost in this way a valuable box of furs, another her jewelry and a third a work-box of ornate design and curious pattern, which contained many little nick-nacks of value and interest. In this street depredations of a wholesale nature went on unchecked all through the night. The houses of Mr. W. C. Godsoe and Mr. T. Amos Godsoe were both burned, and a house near by was pillaged by the mob even while the walls were swaying to and fro. Mr. J. W. Scammell's house on Princess Street and Mrs. Chas. Patton's residence caught fire from blazing brands which consumed them speedily, and the heavens were soon alive with burning bits of wood, which being borne on the breeze sailed lightsomely away. The fire burned several houses in Pitt Street, and though the occupants of Orange Terrace moved out quickly, their residences were saved, the paint only on the doors and front being singed.

The Gas house which is located on Carmarthen Street was long in catching, but when the fire did reach it, its destruction was one of the most beautiful sights which were witnessed that night. An immense heap of coal took fire and the flames mounted to the sky. The great blaze lasted nine or ten days afterwards and the value of the coal was over $17,000. Nothing was left on the spot but the tall sentinel-like chimney, blackened in the fire, and standing like a monument over the wreck of an institution, which the morning before represented a value exceeding two hundred and sixty thousand dollars. The company under the excellent direction of Robert Blair, Esq., the President, had just received a new lease of life and impetus. Since his assumption of the duties of the office, the stock rapidly rose in value, the price of gas was reduced, and improvements on a large scale had been inaugurated. In a single night these works were swept away and only blackened heaps of ruin remain. But the energy of Robert Blair has not departed, and in less than six months gas will again burn as brightly as ever in the less luxuriant halls of the stricken population who can afford it. The works were built in 1845, and in the evening of the 18th of September of the same year, gas was first turned on in St. John. Philip Peebles, Esq., C. E., now of Quebec, was the engineer who furnished the plans, and Geo. Peebles, Esq., C. E., was the Superintending Engineer. The latter remained for a time and took charge. The first Secretary Treasurer was Mr. Robert Reed. Mr. Gilbert Murdoch C. E. was Superintendent of the works, and had charge of the pipe-laying and distributing arrangements. Mr. Robert Britain, the present Secretary, succeeded Mr. Reed in the office, and was subsequently appointed Manager. Robert Blair, Esq., was made President but a short time since. The price of gas up to 19th June 1877, was $3.00 per thousand feet.

One hundred thousand feet of gas were in the holder's close, and the flames not a block away. The direst danger was imminent, and an explosion terrible in its character might occur at any minute. No one can say how many lives might have been lost, or how much valuable property destroyed. No provision had been made to prevent this blow-up, when Mr. Robert Britain with a prudence and forethought wonderful in a time like the present, sought the President and pointed out to him the vast extent of the danger which was so near. Mr. Blair immediately gave Mr. Britain full charge, who notwithstanding that his own private residence was being burned before his eyes, and his furniture and books, wholly uninsured, were being swept away, stuck to his post like a hero and averted a calamity, which might have resulted in the instant death of hundreds of people. Such grand conduct as this deserves more than a mere mention. Words are weak rewards for such conduct.

Leinster Street was burned wholly, both sides down to Pitt Street where the fire ceased, excepting one house, on either side which were spared. The whole of East King Street, south side, from the jail to Pitt Street, Princess Street both sides to Pitt Street were all destroyed. Mr. J. S. Turner's walls in Princess Street remain in fair condition, but the house is totally gutted. Orange Street fared the same fate. The handsome residences of A. C. Smith, H. D. Troop, J. A. Venning and J. W. Hall, Esqs., were devoured early by the flames. On Sydney Street two churches suffered severely. Both of these were of the Presbyterian faith, St. David's (Free) and the Reformed Presbyterian Kirk. The former situate in Sydney Street, was built in 1850, and Rev. Dr. Thompson, afterwards an eminent divine of New York, was its first pastor, and preached the opening sermon in the new kirk. Before the kirk was erected, this body worshipped in the old St. Stephen building, King Square, and Dr. Thompson preached there when the congregation gathered. The Rev. Wm. Ferrie, at one time editor of a little journal called *The Protestant*, was the second minister, and on his retirement from his charge, he was succeeded by the Rev. Neil McKay, and Mr. Ferrie went to New York. Mr. McKay was followed by the present pastor, the Rev. Dr. David Waters, whose loss in the fire was very large, the greater part of his library having been burned. The Doctor was away at the time in Halifax, and only reached the city when all was lost.

The Rev. A. McL. Stavely is the senior Presbyterian clergyman of St. John. He came to the city in the ship *Eagle*, August 3rd, 1841, having been ordained minister at Kilbrought, Ireland, June 12th, of the same year. On the 7th of August, 1841, he preached his first sermon in the first Reformed Presbyterian Church which was then in the building in Lower Cove, opposite the Public Schools, known as the Wheeler property. He was the first minister of that denomination who came to the city, and has continued ever since in charge of this body. In 1850, the Lower Cove Church was sold, and has been since used for manufacturing purposes. The church on the corner of Princess and Sydney Streets, and which was burned, was erected in **1850**. The house adjoining and which was originally intended as a parsonage, was purchased by Mr. Stavely, as his private house, and he has been living in it for twenty-seven years. In 1870, at a cost of $2,000, the basement of the church was excavated, and a fine new hall for general purposes was made. By the fire Mr. Stavely loses heavily, and his library, the accumulation of many years, was destroyed.

Probably, the greatest wreck of the day was the destruction of the costly and splendid new Victoria School— a building which presented a massive front, and occupied a commanding position on the corner of Duke and Sydney Streets. This was the edifice which many who lived up the street as far as Carmarthen Street firmly believed would act as a barrier to the flames, and keep off the fire from their houses. Some so implicitly believed this that until the high walls fairly bent over, not an effort was made to remove even a picture from the rooms. O, said the householders on Upper Duke street, that immense pile will never burn; we are safe enough. But the proud edifice where a thousand children received **daily a free** education, did burn, and the sight though terrible, was one of the most impressive of the day. Now there was hurrying and packing in three score houses at once, and loud cries to teamsters and shrieks to servants and porters rent the **air**. Those, who talked the loudest before the school was in **ashes**, exhibited the **greatest** despair when they saw what they believed up to this moment to be their surest safeguard, encircled in the fury of the flames, going down before their eyes. First the wood-work around the sashes gave way, and lights shot from half a hundred windows, and the crash of glass as it was hurled to the pavement showed that the great fire had abated not a jot. The hot slates on the roof came down the giddy height in scores, and one man pinned to the earth by a falling slate was carried away insensible of pain but with a two-inch wound upon his scalp. The flames crackled for a while and then the dull, heavy sound of weighty bodies falling inside sent a shudder through the waiting, watching crowd below. The woodwork snapped and sang in the blaze, and the great stones on the windows and cornices crumbled into fragments. And still the watchful and waiting crowd stood in the street, straining their eyes trying to look through the smoke, and seemingly unable to comprehend it all. It was only a building that was burning after all. Only another splendid edifice to add to the total of this day's fell work. Yes, this was the last, surely it might be spared. But the despoiler would not leave one. All, all must be swept away in the general scourge.

As the last vestige of the school-house went down all hope for the city passed away from men's minds. If that strong building could go so easily, where would the fire end. Men who had lost their stores and houses wandered about aimlessly, surveying the work of sorrow that was

THE GREAT FIRE IN ST. JOHN, N. B.

going on so unceasingly and relentlessly. It was a hopeless thing now to try to save anything.

The Victoria School-house, of which an illustration is given, was begun in the spring of 1875, and was occupied in the following May. Messrs. McKean & Fairweather made the design, and it was erected under their supervision, by Messrs. Flood & Prince. It cost $46,000; heating, $4,000. The workmanship and materials employed in its construction were of the most substantial character. The foundation was on piles, capped with Georgia pine; and the basement above ground was faced with granite. The fronts were of pressed brick, relieved with Preston bands, window heads and cornices. The slope of the roof was slated and the deck was gravel roofed. The building was 82 feet on Duke Street and 68 feet on Sydney Street, three stories with high French roof, and a basement 12 feet high. The basement contained two play-rooms, janitor's apartments and furnaces and fuel. The 1st, 2nd and 3rd floors contained four rooms each, 28 x 32, with clothes-rooms and teachers' closets. The top floor had two rooms, 26 x 30, and a large Exhibition Hall, 16 feet high, 26 x 75. These rooms were separated by folding doors and could be thrown into one room on occasion. The building was heated by hot water, and ample provision was secured for ventilation by means of tubes carried between the floors and entered through a main central shaft through the centre of which the wrought iron smoke pipe was carried. A central projection on Duke Street of 4 x 24 feet was brought up as a tower, above the main roof and finished with a steep high roof. This roof and the main roof were finished with a cast iron cresting. The lot was enclosed with a neat iron railing set in a free stone wall. The school-house was well equipped with furniture.

In Duke Street the meeting-house of the Disciples of Christ (Christians) was situate. This church was built of wood and of course burned very rapidly. The members had their first place of worship in Charlotte Street where Mr. Jack's buildings were. About twenty years ago they removed to this building in Duke Street. Brother Tuttle was the first pastor and Mr. Eaton was the second, Bro. Patterson the next, and Elder Geo. W. Garrity was the fourth and last. A few years ago a division took place in the church, and a new edifice was built at the head of Jeffrey's Hill, and about half of the members of the old congregation linked their fortunes with the new order of things.

The old Madras School on the south side of Duke Street, and the Roman Catholic School-house on Sydney Street, adjoining the Victoria School and which was formerly taught by the Christian brothers were burned also.

CHAPTER IX.

Queen Square—Incidents in the Burning—The Old Pitcher—" God is burning up the World, and He won't make another "—Saved from the flames—Overtaken by Fire three times—The Night of **Terror on Queen** Square—Alone amidst Perils—The Lone House on the Square—Three People under a Table—The sailor—" If I Die to-night sir, hunt them up"—The escape—The Deserted Streets—An Anomaly—The Marine Hospital—What a few Buckets of Water Did—The Wiggins Orphan Asylum—The block in Canterbury street—The *News* office—Savings Bank.

SOME of the most terrible incidents of the fire took place during the burning of Queen Square. The flames carrying away Mr. Manson's residence on the corner of Sydney Street and the square, had entered Mr. A. L. Palmer's house soon afterwards, and then the whole block was hurried to destruction. The square was filled with the savings of the people, not alone of those who lived hard by, but many things were here that had been carried to the vacant space from a long distance early that day. There was bedding in abundance, and all round about little heaps of general household stuff lay guarded by women and boys. This for a time was the haven of safety, and the broad field looked like a vast warehouse. Chairs and bedsteads and even stoves and old pipes were piled in hopeless confusion one upon the other. In the hurry people had taken that which they had seen first, and the common things of the kitchen were saved while the rich furniture of the drawing-room was left to perish. A man congratulated himself upon saving an old tub and a dipper, while the books in the library lay untouched save by the fire, and private papers that he could easily have slipped into his pocket, burned before his eyes, A lady told her husband to be careful and take a bag which contained the massive silver plate of her family for a century, and in the moving it was found that he had saved the rag-bag instead. A man who had been a prosperous merchant lost his all, and the little savings he had scraped together in a decade of years seemed to melt before him, but he that night knelt and thanked his God that his wife and child were by his side. These treasures were near him and all else might go. He had his strong and willing hands still left, and a firm spirit, and though for a while he would miss the little comforts he had been accustomed to, yet would he battle with the world again, and in the coming years try to win back some of the fruits he had lost. Men in the excitement knew not what to take first, and pianos were thrown out of three-story windows, while carpets that had worn worthily and well till they had become heir-looms in the family, were carefully borne down stairs on the broad shoulders of stout porters. A thousand human beings stood in the square watching the flames lashing the buildings before them. John Boyd, Esq's residence, one of the handsomest buildings in the city, richly furnished and equipped with costly books, was attacked on both sides, and soon forced to yield and go down like the less substantial buildings at its side. The house of G. B. Cushing, Esq., was of wood, and it was not

long before the site on which it stood was level with the
ground. Before the house of Mr. E. L. Jewett, once the
home of the late Dr. Gray, had taken fire, a gentleman
tried to save it by standing on the roof and dashing a
pitcher of water on the sparks as they caught vulnerable
spots. For an hour or more he stood there with his
pitcher, when it became evident to him that no effort that
he could make would save the building, and he got down,
leaving the pitcher standing on a ledge of the chimney.
The fire shortly afterwards burned the building, and left
the long chimney standing against the sky; and the next
day when the spot was visited, and people walked over
the heap of ashes that had once been a household, all that
was saved was the old pitcher, that still stood on the
ledge of the chimney solitary and alone. It told the story
of the desolation more eloquently than tongue of orator
could speak, or pen of a Macaulay could describe. The
house of ex-Mayor Woodward, with its hundreds of curi-
osities and old relics, including Major André's gun and a
score of Continental dollars, caught in the rear, and lived
but a few minutes in the flames. But so it was all round
the square. When Mrs. Stevenson's strong house was
going to pieces, a flock of pigeons hovering near it were
drawn in by the heat; they whirled about for an instant,
turned and rushed into the vortex, and perished in a
second. A cat, maddened and wild, cut off from all
escape dashed along, when the fire pursued her, and she
stood still. On Thursday morning she was still standing
in the same place. Her frame only could be seen, with

head up and tail, erect; it was a ghastly sight. It was during the conflagration on the square, that a little child, five years old, sat by the window of his grandfather's house, then in fancied security, and looked out at the flames. The little fellow for awhile could not speak. He became pale with terror, and with a loud cry he burst out with this thought: "O, pa, pa, come and see! God is burning up the world, and He won't make another, and He won't make another!" It was in vain they tried to pacify him, he still continued his cry, and it was only when far away from the dreadful scene which roused so strangely his youthful imagination, that he became calm.

But there were other incidents in this quarter of the city which deserve more than a passing notice. There were deeds of heroism done and hours of agony endured that should be recorded and remembered. There were exploits exhibiting a broad humanity and great self-sacrifice performed, that should not be forgotten or go down unrecognised. We had heroes in our midst that night, and the man who climbed three stories of a house enveloped in the flames, and snatched the sleeping infant from its crib, and brought her safe to her agonized mother in the square below, is as surely as brave as "he who taketh a city," or marches against the invader of his country. If there are decorations of honour to be given, let them be bestowed on those noble ones who saved lives that day. A case has come under the writer's notice which deserves the fullest publicity. Mr. D. R. Munro, after working at John McDougall's place in York Point for some time, and

MARITIME BLOCK (1873) SHOWING VIEW OF PRINCE WILLIAM ST
Climo, Photo.

THE BUILDING WHICH PREVENTED THE FIRE FROM
EXTENDING UP KING ST.

then going to the assistance of an old lady who was striving to save her bedding, started for Lower Cove in the direction of Mr. Tucker's house. On his way he noticed with alarm the extraordinary headway which the fire was making. Trinity and St. Andrew's were on fire, and the Victoria Hotel just catching. Some of the streets were so blocked up with people, and thick with flame and smoke, that he could not pass them. He had to go through Chipman's field, but he could not get further along Prince William Street. Germain Street was the only way open to him, and by this thoroughfare he journeyed till he reached Queen Square. Here Mrs. Freeman, the rigger's wife, was gathering together her scattered effects, when her little children raised the cry, " Quick, quick, mother's on fire! Save my mother!" Mr. Munro and a companion rushed in, seized Mrs. Freeman, wound a carpet about her, and tried to smother the flames with their hands. As soon as the carpet was removed from her person, the fire again seized her, when her clothes had to be torn from her and she was rolled on the grass with a table-cloth wrapped tightly around her. This saved her life, and she escaped the awful death which seemed so imminent. Mrs. Tucker's house was by this time in great danger, the leaping flames were expected momentarily to snatch it from its base, and people were beginning to get the furniture away before the shock came. For a moment Mr. Munro lay on the grass, unable to resume his exertions. He had worked from three in the afternoon till it was nearly eight o'clock, and with hands and face burned he

H

rested on the grass. But his rest was of short duration, for on looking up a sight met his eyes which filled his soul with horror. Mrs. Tucker's house was on fire and she herself seemed in the very heart of the flames. He almost flew to her, the courage of the lion and the quickness of Mercury seemed to come to him all at once, and he was by her side in an instant. Three times her bonnet caught, and as often was the blaze extinguished. Mrs. Tucker seemed deaf to all requests of her friends, who in vain entreated her to go away and leave her house and furniture to their fate. She still remained by the few things she had borne away, and it was after eight o'clock before she sought a place of safety. A sailor was working in the cellar of her house, passing the things he managed to lay hands on through the window. He was not aware of his danger, for when he had got in, the flames were a good distance off, and when he was discovered the house was on fire. In a few moments, it would come crushing down and bury him in the ruins. Mr. Munro hastened to his relief. Through his labours the man was rescued, for he had not been out a hundred seconds, when, in a mass of ruins, the house came tumbling down. The sailor, who gave his name as Robert Angus, 2nd officer of the ship "Asiana," sought with Mr. Munro a refuge in the square, for all hope of getting away by any of the streets was cut off. Both sides of Charlotte Street and Sydney Street were on fire, and from St. Andrew's Street all means of exit were away. The two men stood on the square and looked around them. Strange emotions filled their breasts. They were alone, standing in the centre of one of the greatest conflagrations they had ever seen. All round them the giant flames gathered, and closer and closer, and narrower and narrower the circle became. The Pagoda in their rear was blazing. The posts here and there burned at the tops, like so many huge candles. Not a soul was to be seen on the square but themselves. The streets were deserted. Every one had fled. The little nests of scattered effects burned on every side of them, and the stench from smouldering feathers and domestic animals who died by the score, was intolerable. Neither man for some minutes spoke. Both looked out into the night. One can guess what thoughts entered their heads. The advancing fire interrupted their reveries, and as they could not escape from the plain in which they were imprisoned, they looked about them for means of preservation from the intense heat, which became greater at every moment. An old pine table was brought up to the camping ground they had selected. A headstone of marble that was lying at their feet, was placed at the head of it, and a carpet was wrapped around them. In this primitive wigwam the men resolved to pass the night. The prospect before them was gloomy enough. Just before getting into this cabin, an old woman came hobbling up towards them, crying aloud for help. They invited her to share their kennel. She accepted the invitation and the three refugees watched the flames on every side of them for two hours. There was silence for a while when the sailor, who all through had exhibited such nerve and cool ness, now showed signs of trepidation and fear. He began to talk of his home in England, of his wife and children, and the strong man who could do so much for others, fairly broke down and wept bitter tears. " Who will take care of them now, sir," he broke out with a wail. " If I die to-night, hunt them up and tell them how I died. It is not for myself I feel, but for them, poor bodies. You know my name and ship, sir, any of my mess-mates will know what to do if you tell them what became of poor Bob Angus." It would indeed move a sterner heart than Mr. Munro's, to hear a man like this talk in a way like that. The sailor who had breasted the billows of the ocean so long that he had begun to look upon them as his playthings, crouched that night in his little box in Queen Square, weeping for the loved ones at home, far, far away. Mrs. Donovan who sat beside the sailor tried to cheer him up, but it was useless, and her words of comfort only made him feel worse and writhe in greater agony.

At last, for there is an end to all things, a bold sortie was proposed, and each of the prisoners sought to force a way out of their natural prison. Each took a direction, and in the dead of that awful night they made their way. The hydra-head of the monster ruin withered them at every turn. Giant walls fell crumbling at their feet, and the fire flashed and the flames flickered on the heaps of debris which they encountered on the sideways of their journey. Not a soul could be seen in the streets. They met no living thing. The silence was as terrible to them as it is to the lonely pilgrim of the forest, or the traveller in the distant arctic, who shrieks ever and anon lest he go mad from the effect of that awful solitude. When the parties met at the corner, they separated and each groped his way homeward through the desert of desolation. Mr. Munro's loss is very heavy. In working for others he neglected his own interests, and many of his personal effects have passed away.

On St. James Street, two buildings stood. One was a very massive and very beautiful structure, of no precise form of architecture, but very chaste and elegant for all that. The other was an old wooden barn-like house that had been decaying for years, and was only waiting to be torn down by some passing high wind. These two buildings were situate within a stone's throw of each other, and the one could have been saved just as well as the other. A little nerve, a little will, and a few pails of water would have done the work. The Marine Hospital was built in a garden. It was a useful sort of affair in its day, but it had long ago done all the good that was expected of it. Its day was past, and it must soon have given way to a **fine** brick structure, to be located on its site. When the **fire** came tearing along, decimating the buildings in every block, Mr. Barnes, the keeper, and a few of the inmates stationed themselves in good positions, and began a vigorous defence of the old place. A number of well directed buckets of water, plied rapidly when the fire showed itself, was all that these men did, and the old building was saved. The fire was stubborn, for it tried a hundred times to gain a foothold, but the men who defended the hospital were just as indomitable, and the defence was a great success. The hospital now stands in all its grim shabbiness and ugliness, though a barn near by, filled with goods of all kinds, including a piano, of course, perished. People from a distance, who came days afterwards to witness the desolation, ask with amazement why this great house was saved, and the noble charity almost opposite, was allowed to burn. But it is hard to always fathom the short-sightedness of man. All praise is due to Mr. Barnes and his assistants, for saving even one public building, and it is a pity his example could not have been followed opposite, when the Wiggins Orphanage caught. Only one man was left in charge, and it is not expected that he could do everything in a time when all were at their wits' end and full of excitement. This splendid charity was instituted in 1867, and was founded by the late Stephen Wiggins. It was opened July 1, 1876, and erected at a cost of $80,-000. Mr. Wiggins left this magnificent sum for a male Orphan Asylum, under certain provisions. These were, that each child to be admitted must be born in the City and County of St. John, preference always to be shown to fatherless children of mariners; the children must be not under the age of four nor over ten years at the time of admission, and not to be continued in the institution after reaching the age of fifteen years. No teacher could be employed who was a Unitarian, Universalist or Roman Catholic, and no Governor could act in that capacity if he were of that belief. The Governors consisted of nine gentlemen. Those at the time of the incorporation were, the Rev. William Scovil, Charles Merritt, Frederick A Wiggins, Hon. John W. Weldon, Beverley Robinson, J. D. Lewin, Geo. C. Wiggins, Henry W. Frith, and the Rector of St. James' Church. When the building burned, there were twelve orphans in the Asylum, but they were safely rescued and sent to Long Island. The present Board consists of the following gentlemen: Chas. Merritt, Hon. J. D. Lewin, Rev. Wm. Armstrong, Rev. W. Scovil, Hon. J. W. Weldon, Geo. Sidney Smith, B. L. Peters, H. W. Frith Rev. F. Brigstocke, with James U. Thomas, as Secretary. At a meeting of the Governors, held on Monday, the 2nd July, it was decided to rebuild the Institute very soon. The reader will notice from the cut which is given of the Orphanage, that it presented a very pretty front, and was exceedingly well built.

In Mecklenburg Street, all that fine block of buildings on the north side, beginning with the residence of Mr. John E. Armstrong, and followed by Mr. John W. Nicholson's castle, the houses of the Messrs. Magee and others; on the south side Mr. Vaughan's well-built house, and on the corner the Stevenson property, mentioned just now, burned very readily. Mr. John Magee's family escaped with their lives only.

The fire in Canterbury Street levelled a block of buildings that were the boast of the city. They were built with great care and especially designed for the great wholesale trade which was done there. The street is a narrow one and runs from King Street to Princess Street, and is crossed by a small alley called Church. Of late years the street has grown from a comparative by-way or **short cut**, to an extensive wholesale stand, where merchants **of** large means and good business capacity have met their clients and customers. The stocks kept in these spacious warehouses have ever been large, and the appliances with which the stores were supplied actually made business a luxury. The centre building was erected and occupied by the **Hon.** Thomas R. Jones, wholesale dry goods merchant. His shirt factory was situate opposite, next door to the Printing House of McKillop & Johnston, who used to print *The Weekly Watchman.* The second pile was built by the same merchant for Messrs. W. H. Thorne & Co., wholesale hardware merchants, and the building on the south of the present edifice, was erected by The North British and Mercantile Insurance Company, Henry Jack, Esq., agent, and leased to Messrs. Everitt & Butler, wholesale dry goods merchants. Mr. Jack's office was in this building also. **The** *Daily News'* office was between the latter and the Savings Bank. It was erected some twenty years ago by the present Queen's printer and former proprietor of the *Daily News*—the first penny paper — George E. Fenety, Esq. The present proprietors, Messrs. Willis & Mott, purchased it last September. This year they made several improvements on it, enlarged it in the rear **and** improved the inside. **They** had begun work on the ground flat when the fire changed the **aspect of affairs.** All that was saved were three pages of **type, and the** late fyles of the paper. These were carried **as far as** Reed's Point, and were only considered safe **when they reached** water mark.

The building was of brick. **The offices were down stairs and consisted** of accountant's room, **editor's office and reporters' room.*** The Savings' **Bank on the corner of Princess and Canterbury Streets was a building of** singularly handsome proportions. It was built in the year 1859, by the St. John County Provident Society, which up to this time had an office in the old Commercial Bank building. In 1872, the Dominion Government took it off their hands, had it renovated thoroughly and changed, and commenced operations in it in 1873, as a Dominion Savings' Bank. The Assistant Receiver-General and Dominion Auditor had offices in the bank. Matthew Stead was the architect. The old Post **Office in** this street was leased a few months ago to The Paper Company, who had it repaired and well **furnished.** In the upper story *The Watchman* office was located. Messrs. Bowes & Evans' large stove establishment, and John Vassie & Co's wholesale dry goods house, entrance on Canterbury Street, were greedily devoured. The little street suffered severely, for it represented a very large sum of money. Two well-known institutions were also burned here, Conroy's hair-dressing establishment and McGinley's barber-shop.

---

* The first steam press in the Maritime Provinces was started in the *Morning News* building, then situated directly on the south end of what is now called Canterbury Street, but which was not then opened.

CHAPTER X.

Incidents—An Old Corner Burned Down—The Lenders and Borrowers—
"Twenty per Cent."—The Shylocks of the Curbstone—The Human
Barometer — The Vultures of Commerce—Chubbs' Corner—The Old
Commercial Bank—The *Telegraph* Office—The Bank of New Brunswick—A Hard Worked Cashier—The Post Office—Not a Mail Lost—
Quick Despatch—The Nethery House and the Orangemen—The Royal
Hotel—The Custom House—The Dead of the Conflagration.

BEYOND all question the successful resistance to the flames at the residence of James H. Moran, Esq., at Chipman's Hill, prevented the spread of the fire to the northern portion of the city. That house was attacked with great fury from front and rear, but the extraordinary and well applied labours of Mr. Joseph Dunlop, and his crew of workmen from the shipyard, aided by the city firemen, kept the flames at bay. The window sashes caught several times, and the men finding neither timber nor axes, boldly grasped the sashes with their naked hands, and despite some severe burning to themselves, they succeeded in tearing them away. This saved the building and stopped the spread of the flames along Union Street and beyond it. Mr. Moran was at his summer residence in St. Martin's during the conflagration, but on hearing of the calamity he hastened home, and made the journey of 32 miles, it is said, in two hours and forty-five minutes. While the fire was in Mill Street, a bright little fellow of thirteen, named Johnny Law, performed an act of considerable heroism and thoughtfulness. His employer, Mr. W. H. Gibbon, had gone to Grand Lake about wo days before the fire, and left his establishment in charge of this boy, who had the forethought when he saw the flames coming near the store to save the books and papers. The flooring above his head fell while he was getting out, but by crawling on his hands and knees, he managed to effect his release from a captivity that would soon have resulted in certain death. Besides this he saved a number of articles from the house, and saw to the successful removal of Mrs. Gibbon and her young children.

There was great ruin in Prince William Street after the fire. A good deal of the wealth of the city, and some of the chief buildings of the place were situate here. The destruction of the Imperial Building belonging to the Messrs. Magee, and which was occupied by them and Messrs. MacLellan & Co., the bankers, was but the work of a few moments. A large quantity of valuable merchandise likewise perished, and the newly commenced block of buildings adjoining exhibited even a vaster extent of ruin than it did on the night of the last great fire which raged in this locality, and which cost the city seven lives.* Mr. Robert Marshall's insurance office, on the corner of the Market Square, and indeed the whole of Prince William Street, both sides clear to Reed's Point, were reduced to ashes and debris. Jardine's grocery store, Messrs. Wis-

---

*March 8th, 1877.

dom & Fish's belting and heavy goods establishment, Benson's millinery store, Steeves, Bros., J. & J. **Hegan & Co's.**, Beard & Venning, The Devebers, James R. Cameron & Co., W. H. Hayward & Co., **George** Philp's banking house, and Chubb's book store on the **one** side, were as completely wrecked as the row of stores on the eastern part of the street which contained Barnes & Co's. bookstore, Peiler's piano warehouse, and Professor Devine's music store, the splendid book and publishing establishment of Messrs. J. & A. McMillan, which was first built in 1831, and was afterwards burned in one of the great fires which succeeded **that year, and, about** 1842, was rebuilt in the shape in which the fire found it the other day, the insurances offices of H. R. Ranney, Lawton's drug store, Stevenson's shoe-shop, Valpey's, Sheraton & Skinner's carpet warehouse, Simeon Jones & Co's., Eastern Express, Francis', and Z. G. Gabel's **corner** store.

Chubb's Corner—the home of the curb stone broker, **and** the place where more gossip has been talked during the last forty years than would furnish the stock-in-trade of forty well-organized sewing circles—was an early victim, for it went down with Furlong's palace about the hour of six. The mention of Chubb's Corner awakens a thousand memories. For many years **it** enjoyed the distinction of being the great centre of commercial speculation. Men came here to meet men who had money to lend, and those who had none came to borrow it. Stocks and merchandise changed hands on this spot a dozen **times a** day, and the cautious bill-broker who never had any **funds** of his own to lend, came here to scent the financial air. In this cheerful spot money **was** subject to **the fluctuations of** the market with **a vengeance.** The rate—aye, there's the rub—"if we **can only agree about** *that*," said the note-shaver, " I think I may take the paper. 'The man is a good man,'" he continued, unconsciously quoting Shakespeare, " and I think I may take his bond," and though nothing was said about the pound of flesh in the event of the notes not being paid at maturity, the modern Shylock meant it all the same, and was as equally determined to get it, too, as the old gentleman we see on the stage rubbing his hands together, and making horrible faces at the audience and the Christian merchant Antonio. The rate in this grim **corner was not** measured by the consciences of the money-lenders, **but by** the necessities of the applicant. One could tell in a much less expensive way than by borrowing money of these gentry, whether they were getting a good price for their coin or not, by simply watching their faces during the operation. The face of the note-shaver is a barometer. It requires no regulating and it is always correct. There, quick, watch it now. See how long the face is. No, he has no money himself, but— Ah, that's it, now watch. See, observe the countenance, listen to that chuckle? Yes, what is he chuckling about? Oh, that's nothing, only habit; now the face is hanging up again, and it is ready for observation. The lender is telling the borrower how difficult it is to get money, and how much Smith had to pay for a thirty days' loan yesterday. This is of no interest to Jones, who is hanging on the words of Mr. **Shylock** as a lover drinks in the soft nothings of his mistress, **but** it gives the lender opportunities to find out how " hard **up** " his victim is. Now watch the face again. Still long and bilious-looking. Twenty per cent. is not so high. It's only five dollars off of a hundred, and look at the time three months—and it falls due on Sunday, too. You'll get a day's interest out of me for nothing, you rogue. The face is positively joyous. The eyes snap and sparkle. The countenance has become quite round and full, and there are bright **spots** on the cheeks. The extra day without interest did it, and the two go off arm in arm. But after all they are not happy; one has paid too much, and the other stands ready to kick himself for not having asked more. O, Chubb's Corner, you have much to answer for, and perhaps the fire did some good in staying **this** kind of business for a time at least on **your** site. But the old corner was not given over entirely to the vultures of commerce. It was the place for many years where property, stocks, debentures, bonds, and all such securities were sold at Public Auction as well as by private sale. The old Corner was a meeting place too, where men met and talked over the times and their affairs. Men stopped here on their way to the Post Office, the old Bank and the Custom House, if it was not too late, to have a friendly chat with an acquaintance. Office boys **hurrying** along in the leisurely hurry that office boys always employ, stopped at Chubb's Corner and looked into the windows of the Exchange office, and wondered to themselves if the huge pile of money they saw lying about was good or not, and whether it would pass. And so the days came and the days passed away, and year in and year out, the old Corner still stood the centre of a busy hive. If those old walls could speak now, as daily, men tramp over their fallen forms, what tales could they tell, what stories of joy and sorrow might they not relate! Walls have ears and they heard much, but they could not speak and what they knew has perished with them.

The building on the Corner was put up by Mr. Chubb, shortly after he was burned out in 1839. The head of the old firm was Henry Chubb, Esq., whose father landed with the Loyalists. He succeeded in 1811 the business which had formerly been carried on by Mrs. Mott, wife of the King's Printer, for whom Mr. Chubb conducted the work of the establishment on the death of her husband. In 1842, Samuel Seeds was admitted partner in the firm together with the eldest son of Mr. Chubb, Henry J. Chubb. In 1846 the latter died and the surviving partners continued the business until the spring of 1855, when Mr. Chubb died leaving his share to Mr. Seeds and his two sons, Thos. Chubb and George James Chubb. In 1863, Mr. Seeds retired and the brothers remained in business until 1865, when G. J. Chubb bought out his brother's interest, and the firm has continued under the old style of H. Chubb & Co., ever since. An exchange office was added to the stationery and printing business during the American War.

The old Commercial Bank building which was lately

completely altered and renovated internally, was situate on the south-east corner of Prince William and Princess Streets. The corner stone was laid in 1839, and a grand Masonic demonstration took place, Rev. Dr. B. G. Gray officiating. Henry Gilbert Esq., was the President of the Commercial Bank at the time. It was used latterly for the civic offices, and the Water Commissioners had an office on the ground flat. *The Daily Telegraph* newspaper occupied the old wooden building adjoining, and about which notice is given in the first chapter of this history. Mr. Elder, the enterprising editor and proprietor of the paper, is a heavy loser by the fire. Not only did he lose his well-equipped printing office and appliances, his splendid reference library and collection of historic data, the gatherings of many years, but his bound fyles also, and in fact everything he possessed vanished forever.

The Bank of New Brunswick was for a long time deemed safe. It is true that the merchants hurried in with their books when the fire was still raging a quarter of a mile away, but the old building which was burned inside, exhibited after the fire, walls and pillars as strong and vigorous as they were half a century ago. The vaults preserved their contents, and millions of money were thus plucked from the burning. The old bank was an edifice in which the people took pride. It was a hale old veteran that had passed through many a disaster. When financial troubles darkened the days of the people, when the dread cholera spread disease and death in house-

BURNT DISTRICT, SHOWING GAS HOUSE CHIMNEY AND SMOKING RUINS, TAKEN FROM LOWER COVE.

Photo by C. F. Simonds

holds, when fires laid waste the best acres of our
territory, the old bank still stood erect, and withstood
the shock which threatened her on every side. It
succumbed this time, but only in a partial way, for its
pillars and a portion of its walls are as stalwart as of
yore. In May, 1821, a general meeting was held of the
stockholders of the banking company that had been organized the year before. At this meeting some honoured
names were read, and the following gentlemen were present: Henry Gilbert, Hon. John Robinson, Nehemiah
Merritt, Wm. Black, Ezekiel Barlow, Thos. Millidge,
Ward Chipman, jr., Zalmon Wheeler, Hugh Johnston, jr.,
Robert W. Crookshank, Robert Parker, jr., Stephen Wiggins, and Hugh Johnston, senr. On the seventh day of
May the directors were chosen, and the bank was ready
for business. The first President was the Hon. John
Robinson; and the other Directors for the year were
Wm. Black, Ezekiel Barlow, Lewis Bliss, Ward Chipman,
jr., Robert W. Crookshank, senr., Henry Gilbert, Hugh
Johnston, Nehemiah Merritt, Thos. Millidge, Robert Parker, jr., Zalmon Wheeler, and Stephen Wiggins. Of these
but one lives to-day, Lewis Bliss, Esq., who, at last
accounts was in London, England. The Hon. J. D. Lewin
was made President in 1857, and Wm. Girvan, Esq., whose
great industry is proverbial, was chosen cashier, March
1st, 1862. Mr. Girvan, on taking charge of his office, at
once went methodically over the old books, and in two
years, by dint of untiring application, he had the full set
from 1820 in shape. The books are in such excellent

I

condition, and so **well arranged,** that it is a pleasure to **refer to** them.

The Bayard Building, containing Mr. G. Em. Allen's office, the Attorney-General's office and others, with **two** stores underneath, and the new Bank of Nova Scotia building, which formerly belonged to Messrs. Andre D. Cushing & Co., were soon destroyed, together with Barnes' Hotel, which, only a few years ago, had an extension added, and was fitted up with every modern improvement. Stewart & White's large furniture warehouse and auction rooms opposite, in Smith's building, with their heavy stocks, were burned.

The destruction **of** the new **Post Office,** one of the **most** beautiful buildings in the city **at the** time of the fire, **was** one of the saddest spectacles of the day. It had only **been** opened a year, and its handsome design and rich finish had often been admired. The ornamental freestone work **on the** front, and the rich red granite pillars, gave the edifice a very fine appearance. The flames were twice extinguished by Mr. Parker in the tower where they made the attack first at six o'clock, at the place where the clock was to have been put. At three in the afternoon the mail matter was carefully put away in bags, and every preparation made for a speedy departu**re.** The first load of mail bags was hauled to a place of safety, to Reed's Point, and seventeen of them were carried by **hand** to the fish-market wharf, where a boat was seized and **sixteen** of the bags put in it. The doors of the Post Office were closed to the public at five o'clock, and by half-past six the fire had made such an onslaught that nothing could keep it away. Through the foresight of Mr. J. V. Ellis, the Postmaster, not a mail was lost, or a letter mislaid. The outgoing mails that night to the north and east, were despatched as usual, and with excellent executive skill, the Post Master was ready in a temporary office in the Market building, to deliver letters to applicants in less than twenty-four hours after the fire. In twelve hours after that the delivery system was in full working order, and in a few days merchants had the pleasure of receiving their mails in boxes of their own at the Post Office. The Registry Letter Office was ready for work, under Mr. M. J. Potter's management in a little while, and the opening of the Money Order Department's Office was not long in following. The clerks and other employes of the Post Office deserve the greatest credit for their promptness under a most trying situation, and their uniform kindness and courtesy were preserved to the last. Mr. Flaglor delivered the first and last letters at the Post Office, Prince William Street.

The old Nethery house in Church Street, where Mr. Geo. A. Knodell had his printing office, and Mr. H. L. Spencer his medical warehouse, was once the great headquarters of the Orangemen, and was built about the year 1823. It was in this building that in old times balls and parties, and dinners in connection with the order were given, and it was from here that on the famous twelfth of July, when Duncan Wilmot was Mayor, the Orangemen marched at the time of the memorable riot. Mr. Knodell has begun rebuilding on this site.

The Royal Hotel in Prince William Street, formerly Stubbs' Hotel, and for many years a leading house in the city, caught fire early in the afternoon from the sparks. The inhabitants apprehended no danger and the sparks were put out, but Mr. Waldron, Stage Manager of the Theatre, came to the conclusion that as it had taken fire once, it might soon again be stricken. He accordingly warned the others and proceeded to get his things together for a final exit. The Hotel did catch about an hour and a half after this, and all on the ground save the old tree to the left, were in ashes before night. Mr. Thomas F. Raymond succeeded Mr. McIntosh in the management of Stubbs' Hotel, and it was by him changed to the name of " The Royal." A great many public dinners and balls have been given in this house, and its spacious dining room for many years was considered one of the finest ball-rooms in the city. The last great ball given here was in 1871, in March, by St. Andrew's Society, on the occasion of the marriage of the Marquis of Lorne to the Princess Louise.

A large amount of property that had been stored away for safe keeping in the Custom House, was burned when that fine building went down. Hundreds of people believing strongly in stone and brick, sought refuge for their chattels here, and almost all available space was occupied with goods of every description. The merest trifles were saved after the building took fire, and an immense amount of material was consumed. Even Robert Shives' collection of diaries that dated back many years was lost, as well as a considerable number of his papers in connection with the emigration office of which he was the agent. Mr. Shives was suffering from illness during the fire and was too weak to be about much. Several merchants who had sent their account books to the Custom House for safety lost them in the great destruction which followed. The building was a good strong substantial structure built about the year 1841, by the late John Walker, Esq., and designed by him as a government warehouse.* He did not succeed however, in having it accepted as such by the government, and it was purchased by Mr. McLeod, of St. John, and Alexander Keith, Esq., of Halifax, and used as the Custom House. The Government of Canada bought it from George McLeod, Esq., M. P. some months ago. It was roomy and well adapted for customs purposes. When the Dominion Government took it off Mr. McLeod's hands they refitted it up completely. The storm drum and time ball and signal station were situate on the Custom House.

The International Hotel was formerly a double residence with the entrance on the second story. About twenty years ago it was enlarged and converted into an hotel under the management of Mr. A. B. Barnes, who called the house after its owner—The Lawrence Hotel. Mr. Barnes left

---

* It had a three story granite front on Prince William Street 250 feet long, by 92 feet deep towards Water Street, which face was built of brick four stories high. It cost Mr. Walker $120,000.

it some years ago and removed to his own premises nearer King Street, and Mr. R. S. Hyke, after it was modernized a little, assumed the management.

The fire in Water Street proved to be very destructive. Tisdale's corner, at the head of South wharf, and the home of the hardware business in St. John for many years; the grocery establishments of C. M. Bostwick and Geo. Robertson; John Melick's office, the ferry floats and waiting-room, as well as Adam Young's large stove warehouse and the Messrs. McCarty's place of business, were soon carried away. The good old house of Robt. Robertson & Son, that for half a century wielded great influence in the community, and whose ships to-day ride many oceans, with its stock of sails and rigging, lasted scarcely longer in the terrible heat than an hour's space. Walker's wharf and the premises in Ward street suffered greatly, and it was while trying to save his property here, that Captain William M. B. Firth lost his life. He was last seen in Prince William Street, blinded by the smoke and scorched by the flames, trying to make his way out. It is thought that finding all hope of gaining an egress from the suffocating street, he sank down in the roadside exhausted and weary, and death came to him there. His body was found the next day, but it was not until Saturday that he was fully recognised and claimed. He leaves a sorrowing wife and five grief-stricken children, who spent the terrible days of his absence in the greatest agony. There were many rumours about Capt Firth while he was missing. Some said that he was all right in Carleton, others averred that he had gone away in a ship, while others again stoutly maintained that they had seen him put out to sea in a boat and that he would turn up all right But when these tidings reached his poor wife, she always turned with a sad smile of gratefulness to those who brought her such news, in the hope that it might cheer her up, and said that her heart told her better. Her husband's place was by her side, and he knew it as well as she. What would he be doing out in a boat so long, when he did not even know whether his wife and family were alive or not; no, she never believed the rumours which came to her, thick and fast, as the hours of those anxious days went by; and when the dread news came at length, the widowed mother and her fatherless children had known it in their hearts long before.

Another terrible death was that of Mr. Samuel Corbitt, a gentleman esteemed and respected for his many good qualities, by all who knew him. He was a furniture dealer, and his store was in Prince William Street. A gentleman exchanged a few words with him while the fire was in full career. Mr. Corbitt went into his own building, to get some things and he never came back. The greatest sympathy is felt in the community for Mrs. Corbitt and family.

An old resident of the city, Mr. Joseph Bell—a painter, lived in Duke Street, where he kept his shop. On the night of the fire he went in to remove a painting it is said, but when he turned to come out he could not pass the flames, and he too perished, and was buried in the ruins of his old home. A man named Johnson is still missing, and it is probable he lost his life in the fire. Mrs. Coughlan, Timothy O'Leary, Michael Donohoe, and Mrs. **Fitzgerald**, are also supposed to **have** lost their lives in the same sad way, **and as** many are still missing, the loss of life, it is expected, will be quite large. The heavy buildings came down with such rapidity after they became hot, that it is feared that a good many people were buried in the ruins, and the intense heat which followed **would** render them never again recognisable, even if a portion **of the remains were found.**

An incident has come to hand which deserves more than a passing notice. Young Johnny Murphy, a mere child, who lived with his mother in Charlotte Street, bravely jumped from **the** second-storey window of his residence with his younger brother in **his** arms. The act was **that** of a hero, and worthy the admiration and applause of thousands. Such bravery and heroism should indeed be rewarded. The little fellow wears his honors **meekly.** '

CHAPTER XI.

The Old House on the Hill—A Wily Commissary—The Bags of Gold—What was done at Midnight—The Dead of Night Deposit—The Old Vault—A Timid Money-Lender—Mr. Peter Johnson—The Board of Commissioners—The Old Gentleman's Little Joke—The Inspection—How it was Discovered—The Fight with the Flames—"How much will I Get?"—What he Got—The Oil Barrels—Dashing the Water on the Kerosene—A Lively time on Reed's Point Wharf—The Bridge of Fire—On the Ferry-Boat—The Western Union Telegraph Office—The First Dispatch.

THE fire in that portion of Princess Street, from Prince William street to Charlotte Street, was a great leveller, and destroyed a number of useful buildings as well as a few very excellent ones. The Wiggin's building on Rocky Hill, north side, which was erected about twenty years ago found a fate which was common enough that day. The destruction of Ritchie's building, though not expected by some, followed soon after. It was admirably built, and the large number of division walls which it had, rendered it almost invincible against any element however strong. Look at it to-day after the fire has done its worst, and there is much of it standing that can be utilized again. Its splendid supports are ready for duty, and though the structure was on fire for seven hours and subjected to great heat, the walls show that they could stand a good deal of such endurance yet, and not crumble. The site on which this edifice was erected, has in common with some others which have been mentioned in the course of our story, a history of its own. A frame building many years ago, before Rocky Hill was cut down, was built here by Dr. Thomas Paddock, who afterwards disposed of it to Price, the Commissary, who subsequently sold it to the Government. The house was used as the Commissariat for a number of years. About 1823 or 1824 a good deal of excitement was created by the arrest of Mr. Price who was charged with defalcation in his accounts. He was closely guarded, and after a court of enquiry was held, he was confined for a time and finally allowed to depart. The story goes, and there are many who remember it perfectly, that a wealthy gentleman knowing that Price lived too fast, and had become involved, had offered to lend him the bags of money which would make good his position when the commissioners came to examine his accounts. It was proposed that they be sent over and deposited in the house, and after the examiners were satisfied and had left the city, the bags of coin would be conveyed back again to the owner. This was satisfactory, and Price thanked his good friend. In those days commissioners did not move as rapidly as they do now, and the board did not arrive for a few days. In the meantime, the money was in Price's possession, and he slept at night the peaceful sleep of the innocent and just. But delays are ever dangerous, and Mr. Price's friend was the timidest of the most timid men. He had no sooner sent his bags of gold out, when he began to ruminate. What if the commissioners decided to take the money with them and deposit it somewhere else? What if the thing leaked out and his friend Price got dismissed, and he lost his money? It worried him, and though Price slept, the money-lender did not. He began to grow more and more anxious. Every day he grew worse, until at last just as the commissioners had arrived and Mr. Price was getting ready to show them around in the morning, and give them his papers to examine, and show them the money, the friend acted on the thought which was burning his heart out, and he sent for Peter Johnson. Now Mr. Johnson, who figures in our narrative, for the first time was a negro, and he it was, who, in the dead of night when all was still, wheeled the mysterious bags of bullion to and from the old vaults in the Commissariat. The money-lender sent for Peter Johnson and told him that he had altered his mind, and that the bags and their contents must be home again that very night. Peter proceeded at once, and stealthily approaching the vaults, opened the heavy doors with his key, got out the money, and wheeled it home again, and Mr. Commissary Price slept on in babe-like innocence. And so did his friend. And so did Mr. Peter Johnson. And so did the Board of Commissioners. In the morning, Mr. Price rubbed his hands and dressed himself with scrupulous propriety, that he might meet his masters in a becoming manner. And the Board of Commissioners got ready too, and they drove round to Mr. Price's in a body, and before entering on their duties there was much merriment among them, and one facetious old gentleman who was always joking and saying good things, you know, remarked to the others in his delicious way, that almost every man had a price, but none had a Price like their's, and then he chuckled and slapped Price on the back, and Price chuckled, and the Board chuckled, and I have no doubt whatever but that Mr. Peter Johnson and his master would have chuckled too had they heard it. And then the party went down to the office and began to overhaul things, and everything was all right, and the books were found correct. And then a stupid old member of the Board asked to have the money brought in to be counted, just to comply with the regulation, not that they doubted friend Price. O, no, but an absurd form demanded it," &c., &c. And Mr. Price was affable and kindly, and said, " O yes, gentlemen, I shall be quite happy to show you the funds which are all safe in the vault, I assure you. Saw them myself no later than the other day," &c. &c. And everyone said that was all right, and the iron doors were unlocked and swung back! But where was the money? Mr. Price was as pale as death, and turned to the astonished commission, when he said, " Come, gentlemen, now a joke is a joke, what have you done with the money?" But Mr. Price discovered before long that the world was not quite a smile, and he was marched off to prison, and the facetious old gentleman said to the gentleman who only wanted the money produced to gratify an absurd whim of the Government, " Who would have believed it?" And so the Inspectors walked out, behind Mr. Price, who was placed in durance vile and suffered as we have seen.

In 1843 Mr. Oliver Goldsmith, a descendant of the family of the poet, and a gentleman who wrote poetry too, occasionally, and whose "Rising Village," a companion piece to "The Deserted Village," was not without some slight merit, called on Judge Ritchie and told him that he had received orders from the Government asking for tenders for the old building on Rocky Hill, and he suggested that he had better tender for it. The judge did so, and to his great astonishment, his was the only tender sent, and he got the whole of the property, including the house and a stone barn which were on it, for £500 sterling, three months after his tender was accepted. He immediately rented it to Dr. Simon Fitch, who was beginning practice and who occupied it for a number of years. It was idle for a while after Dr. Fitch left it, and then Judge Ritchie had it altered and modernized, and he and Mr. L. J. Almon lived in it. It was still located high up on the rock. The judge, whose taste for architecture is well known, often planned the style of building he would like to put up. In the evenings after reading a while it was no uncommon thing for him to draw near to a table, and with pencil and paper plan buildings of infinite variety. It was good employment for the mind, and less expensive than actual building, and the paper houses could be altered and improved and altered again at very little cost. One day the judge planned in earnest, and his ideas took practical shape. He pulled down the high house, excavated the rock and proceeded to build. In 1853 he began work and by the month of February, 1854, his building was pretty well up. He had expended some five thousand pounds on it, and was about leaving for Fredericton when

Mr. L. J. Almon came in and remarked to him that after he was in Fredericton a week or so he would feel rather foolish to get word that his building was burned down, and that there was no insurance on it. This troubled the judge, and he began to feel quite uncomfortable. He told Mr Almon to lose no time but go at once and effect insurance. Mr. Almon put £5,000 on the unfinished edifice. The judge went to the capital, sat in the Assembly, and in a few days received intelligence that his building had been burned to the ground. He returned to St. John at once and began to rebuild. This time he proceeded with great care, and the chaste and handsome building destroyed the other day was the result. The first occupants of the offices were W. H. Tuck, Duff & Almon, Chas. Watters, Geo. Blatch, Wetmore & Peters, E. B. Peters, St. John Insurance Co., the Electric Telegraph Co., D. S. Kerr, Chamber of Commerce, Thos. T. Hanford, the Masonic body and some others. The stores below were not rented for some time after the building was ready.

The Society of Free and Accepted Masons, after leaving the Old St. John Hotel, met for some years in the upper story of the residence of the late Mr. Marshall, father of Mr. John R. Marshall, Chief of Police. This house was on the corner of Princess and Sydney Streets. When Judge Ritchie's building was finished, the Masons rented about half of the top story, and had it finished and furnished for masonic purposes. They have occupied these apartments ever since. Up to January, 1868, the various lodges in the city held their warrants from either of the

Grand Lodges of England, Scotland, or Ireland. In the Province there were twenty-six lodges, viz: twenty English, three Irish, and three Scotch. When Confederation came to pass, it was deemed imperative by the leading masons of the Province to separate from their respective parent Grand Lodges in the mother country, and form a new Grand Lodge of their own for New Brunswick. This conclusion was reached only after mature reflection, and when it was found that the great political changes which had taken place in the country rendered it necessary. Three Grand Lodges were already represented in the Province. The Grand Lodge of Nova Scotia was working, and the Grand Lodge of Canada would be formed soon. Unless the craft established a Grand Lodge in and for the Province of New Brunswick, the exercise of masonic jurisdiction by so many governing authorities would only tend to hopeless confusion and detriment to the Order. It was a thing which could not be helped. Either an Independent Grand Lodge of New Brunswick must be formed, or a general Grand Lodge of Canada would be created, which would have entire jurisdiction all over Canada. At a preliminary convention of masters, past-masters and wardens, the subject was fully ventilated, and the motion to form a Grand Lodge of New Brunswick was carried by a large majority. The office of Grand Master of the new Grand Lodge, was first offered to R. T. Clinch, Esq., who was then District Grand Master, under the Grand Master of the Grand Lodge of England, but he declined the honour on account of the position which he

136 THE GREAT FIRE IN ST. JOHN, N. B.

held. Benjamin Lester Peters, Esq., was **then elected Grand Master** by acclamation; William Wedderburn, **Esq., Deputy Grand Master**; Hon. **W. P. Flewelling, Senior Grand Warden; David Brown, Junior** Grand Warden; Rev. **W. Donald,** D.D., Grand Chaplain, and Wm. H. A. Keans, Esq., **Grand Treasurer**; Mr. W. F. Bunting was **made Grand Secretary** at the meeting **in January,** 1868, **and the** following officers were appointed: John Richards, **Senior Grand** Deacon; Benjamin R. Stevenson, Junior **Grand Deacon;** John V. Ellis, Grand Director of Ceremonies; Robert Marshall, Assistant ditto; Jas. McDougall, Grand Sword Bearer; John Mullin, Grand Standard Bearer; Henry Card, Grand Organist; James Mullin, Grand Pursuivant; Edward Willis, S. S. Littlehale, Robt. R. Call, Hugh A. Mackenzie, Thos. F. Gillespie, John Wallace, Grand Stewards, and John Boyer, Grand Tyler. Grand Lodge was instituted in January, in the year of masonry, 5868. The craft has made great progress, and preparations before the fire were on foot for the erection of a fine new hall in Germain Street. The greater portion of the stock was subscribed, and operations were to be begun at an early day. The brethren lost heavily by the recent fire. All the warrants were destroyed, but these can be replaced. The private lodges met in several instances with irreparable losses, and the full set of jewels, which Bro. Oliver Goldsmith several years **ago** presented to Albion Lodge, No. 1, was not the least of these.

In the summer of 1863, the St. John Gymnasium (joint stock) Company began building the Gymnasium, which

INSIDE THE SAVINGS BANK
Photo. by G. F. Simonson.

was located opposite St. John's Presbyterian Church, King Street East. Its dimensions were 40 x 100, three stories front, and the Gymnasium proper was 40 x 80. The cost was a little over $5,000. The building was heated by steam, well lighted with gas, and neatly and tastily arranged, containing bath-rooms, parlours, drawing-rooms, &c. The first president was John W. Cudlip, Esq. Mr. J. S. Knowles was secretary, and Fred. A. Jones, the lessee and manager. Mr. M. W. Maher was the builder. A few years ago, the building was sold to Carson Flood, Esq., dealer in piano-fortes, and was by him converted into a commodious hall, suitable for dancing parties, tea-meetings, &c. The Gymnasium caught from the rear of the water-works, and was soon a heap of ashes. The *Globe* office in the Globe Building, Prince William Street, was burning about the same time as the Bank of New Brunswick, and the proprietors did not save even their tyles.

The fight with the flames on Reed's Point Wharf, which lasted from three o'clock in the afternoon until late the next morning, was one of the most dreadful encounters of the day. A prominent medical man of the city, who lost the house which he had considered fireproof, was hurrying away, when he found his services no longer needful, to a place of safety. All means of exit from the fire were cut off, except one—the route towards Reed's Point. He hastened in that direction, for he saw in a moment that soon that avenue would be closed against him. He fled down Germain Street to St. James's Street,

was located opposite St. John's Presbyterian Church, King Street East. Its dimensions were 40 x 100, three stories front, and the Gymnasium proper was 40 x 80. The cost was a little over $5,000. The building was heated by steam, well lighted with gas, and neatly and tastily arranged, containing bath-rooms, parlours, drawing-rooms, &c. The first president was John W. Cudlip, Esq. Mr. J. S. Knowles was secretary, and Fred. A. Jones, the lessee and manager. Mr. M. W. Maher was the builder. A few years ago, the building was sold to Carson Flood, Esq., dealer in piano-fortes, and was by him converted into a commodious hall, suitable for dancing parties, tea-meetings, &c. The Gymnasium caught from the rear of the water-works, and was soon a heap of ashes. The *Globe* office in the Globe Building, Prince William Street, was burning about the same time as the Bank of New Brunswick, and the proprietors did not save even their tyles.

The fight with the flames on Reed's Point Wharf, which lasted from three o'clock in the afternoon until late the next morning, was one of the most dreadful encounters of the day. A prominent medical man of the city, who lost the house which he had considered fireproof, was hurrying away, when he found his services no longer needful, to a place of safety. All means of exit from the fire were cut off, except one—the route towards Reed's Point. He hastened in that direction, for he saw in a moment that soon that avenue would be closed against him. He fled down Germain Street to St. James's Street, thence along the latter till he reached the wharf. There he saw an immense crowd of refugees from the district round about, numbering fully fifteen hundred persons. The men were very disorderly, and the liquor they had taken was showing its effect. There was fighting, and quarrelling and swearing. The roughest element of the city was here. A long row of barrels containing kerosene oil or petroleum lay upon the wharf, and the sparks from burning buildings near by came whirling along in dangerous proximity to the barrels. The danger was growing more and more near. Should these barrels ignite and explode, a hundred lives at least must perish. No time must be lost. Water must be carried up to the barrels and the fire kept off. An attempt was made to roll some of them over the wharf into the harbour, but they were too heavy, and the fire was leaping in great strides towards them. The doctor shouted himself hoarse trying to induce the crowd to help him, but he was answered with either a be-sotted stare or a vulgar oath. He kept on running to the water, filling his pail, and dashing it on the barrels till his arms ached. Once he got a response from some rough men on the wharf, and a bargain was made with three of them. He offered them all the money he had—three dollars,—if they would come and help keep the fire away from the deadly oil. But the assistance was of short duration, and after working for about twenty minutes the fellows gave up, and would work no more. Still, nothing daunted, the doctor toiled on. He had all the women put on board the International Line steamer, through the kindness of Captain Chisholm, who was busily employed on the other end of the wharf in beating back the flames which were massing there, and then with a will he continued his self-imposed labour. None but he seemed to realize their danger. Maddened by drink and worry, and perhaps driven to desperation by the havoc the fire was making, they did not appear to take in the deadly peril in which every one on that wharf stood. The crowd stood about idling away, smoking, drinking, talking, jeering, and quarrelling. A lithe young fellow of twenty sat dangling his legs over the wharf and smoking a cigar, when the doctor called on him to come down and give him a hand. He returned a careless reply, and in a sneering tone asked how much he would get if he gave his help. The doctor grew maddened at this, and turning on him in a moment, cried out, " I am an old man; I have lost all that I was worth, and have nothing left. I have been watching you for an hour, doing nothing while I was working; and as you won't come for asking, I'll make you come down here and carry water if I have to drag you to the very water's edge." So, saying he pulled the young man down, grasped him by the neck, ran him to the water, and giving him a pail set him to work filling it while he carried it to the barrels himself. The lesson was a salutary one, and the unwilling assistant will probably never forget it. He had some manhood left in him after all though, for he worked well and hard, and after a time he apologized to the doctor and said he was sorry for having spoken as he did. It was some hours after this episode, that the doctor hailed a passing tug-boat, and the captain learning what was wanted, ran his little steamer alongside the **wharf and got** ready his hose. In a few minutes the wharf was deluged with water and the great danger **was** averted. It was this hose and the well directed efforts of the doctor which saved the wharf and the lives of many people. It is a matter of regret that the name of the captain of the tug could not be got as he deserves well of the country, and should make himself known that he may receive something more tangible than thanks. Hemmed in by the streets of flame to the right and left of them and directly in their front, from fifteen hundred to two thousand persons were imprisoned on the wharf from three o'clock in the afternoon till four the next morning, when the fire had gone down, and one of loveliest mornings of the year dawned on the stricken city.

One of the prettiest sights was to be seen from the head of King Street, looking down in the direction of the market slip. When the schooners therein had caught, the flames mounted the masts and communicating with one another formed a complete bridge of fire from the north wharf to the south. It was like a gala-day celebration of fire-works on a large scale.

LIST OF VESSELS TOTALLY BURNED.

SCHOONERS.

1. Schooner "Angie Russell"; 25 tons; Boylan; Canning, N.S., was discharging cargo of fish; owned by Captain.

THE GREAT FIRE IN ST. JOHN, N. B.

2. Schooner "Brill"; 74 tons; St John, N.B., had discharged part of cargo and was going to Fredericton with balance; owned by McSherry's Insolvent Estate.
3. Schooner "Brilliant"; 18 tons; Patch; Campobello; light cargo.
4. Schooner "Bear River"; 37 tons; Winchester; Bear River, N.S., outward bound with cargo; owned by Captain.
5. Schooner "Ella P."; 23 tons; Thurber; Barrington, N.S., fish.
6. Schooner "Eliza Jane"; 27 tons; Bent; Bayshore, N.S.; salt.
7. Schooner "L. L. Wadsworth"; 12 tons; Brown; Westport, N.S.; owned by Captain; fish.
8. Schooner "Lily"; 8 tons; Israel; Weymouth, N.S.; outward bound; owned by Captain.
9. Schooner "Martha Rowan"; 25 tons; Peters; Westport, N.S.; fish.
10. Schooner "Parrot"; 27 tons; Hutton; St. George, N.B.; owned by Captain.
11. Schooner "Star"; 13 tons; Benson; Westport; fish.

WOOD-BOATS.

"Burnett," 46 tons, Captain Reed; "Linda," 26 tons; "President," 46 tons, Captain Orchard; and "Messenger," 33 tons.

Four lime scows laden with lime, two owned by Mr. Raynes, of Fairville; two owned by Mr. Joseph Armstrong, of Greenhead.

CASUALTIES.

Schooner "Justice," Westport, hauled out of slip badly burned.
Schooner "George Calhoun," lying in Walker's slip, mainmast burned, hauled out without further damage.

On board the ferry-boat between three and four o'clock in the afternoon, the appearance of the city burning in four places at once, was a grand as well as an awful sight. The passengers gathered together and wore very anxious looks, when it seemed for a time to be the intention of the captain not to land. The houses and stores of many who were on board were in danger, and all wanted to be at the fire. From the water it appeared to be levelling houses to the ground at the rate of one a minute, and the frightful ratio seemed never to slacken its speed. The ships lying near the wharves moved out into the harbour, and some sailed far down the bay. The path of the ferryboat was crossed more than once by vessels which had succeeded in getting away in safety, and collisions now and then were threatened; but fortunately none occurred. At length, to the relief of all on board, the boat succeeded in getting safely to her landing-place, and a grand rush was made up the floats for the head of Princess Street.

Perhaps one of the best and first specimens of enterprise which occurred on the night of the fire was that which was displayed by the chief officers of the Western Union Telegraph Company. The office was burned down, and only the books and some of the instruments were saved. The Fairville wire would not work, and no means of sending abroad intelligence of the ruin of the doomed city remained. It was fully eleven o'clock when R. T. Clinch, Esq., the superintendent of the company, Mr. Thos. Robinson, the manager, Mr. Dawson, Mr. Black and other gentlemen connected with the company, met the writer of these pages on Germain Street. The fire was still raging, though not at all fiercely in the lower part of the city. The party went down to the railway station, and we give an illustration of the building so that the reader may see the temporary Western Union Telegraph Office during the first few days of the fire, and after a little while a wire was put in working order. The first and only dispatch which left the city that night, and which on Thursday morning was read all over Canada, and in the United States, was sent forward, and each page was telegraphed as rapidly as it was written. In the morning the office was ready to receive and deliver messages, and those who stood by the counter, and every day watched the enormous crowd of people all anxious to be served first, can realize how hard the operators had to work in order to meet the requirements of the citizens. At one time there were between five and six hundred messages on the operator's table, and the sender might consider himself fortunate if his telegram got off three hours after it was written. Some miscreants in some instances cut the wires a few days after the fire, and the company had to send out twenty-five or thirty patrol men to look after them. Mr. Clinch lost no time in getting suitable quarters for the patrons of the company, and in a week he had a comfortable office, working finely, in the Market House. He began work at once on the new building which the company intend putting up, and in six months the new telegraph office will be ready for occupancy on its old site at the foot of King Street

CHAPTER XII.

A Thrilling Incident—The Burning House—The Tall Figure in the Hall —Escape cut off—The only Way Out—The Street of Fire—Walking on Coals—The Open Boat—The way to the Wharf—Terrible Suffering—The Awful Death in the Street—Worn Out—The Escape—Saved—The Firemen—How they Fought the Flames.

IN olden times men who had performed deeds of bravery on the battle-field were canonized as saints, and those who had shown daring in other ways were revered as gods. There is a fascination about the stories which come down to us through the long centuries of time, and from the middle ages, and we are accustomed, almost from the cradle, to revere the names of the great ones who have filled the world with the splendour of their exploits in the defence of cities and the protection of fair ladies. In the nursery we learn to lisp the names of stalwart knights and doughty warriors, and the great deeds which they performed, ages and ages ago, live again in the memory of all mankind. And it is well that it should be so. It is well that the splendid actions of the world's great men should be remembered for all time. Who is there who does not feel the blood mantling his cheek when he thinks of a Clive and of a Marlborough? Who can think of a Napier and a Wellington, and not experience for a time a thousand emotions coursing and careering madly through his breast? And Robert Bruce on his little palfrey giving battle to the last of one of England's proudest and sternest knights, in full view of Stirling Castle, the day before the great battle was fought, is a story which every Scottish lad is taught before he is old enough to read. And the lives of such men as Bonaparte, Turenne, Wolfe, the Great Frederic, Von Moltke, and a hundred others, are undying records in the histories of nations, the memory of whose deeds shall last when time shall be no more.

In a young country like ours, whose territory has not often felt the hostile tread of invading armies, and whose broad acres are almost wholly unstained with the blood of battles, the heroes we have developed have earned their reputation in another and nobler way. Halifax has had her England, whose name will be remembered as long as ships sail the seas; and in St. John, we have long learned to bless the name of a hero in humble life, honest Tom Sloven. And now from the ashes of the fire two names arise, which in after years, when their owners shall have passed away, will live in the hearts of the people, and leave there an imperishable record. We applaud success, and oftentimes let honest effort and endeavour go unrewarded. We worship the rising sun, and when a man works hard to achieve a certain success and fails, we are apt to pass him by. And though the object, in the instance which we are about to relate, was not successful in the end, let us never forget the deed which was attempted at the imminent risk of the lives of the chief actors. When the story of the fire is told at firesides in the years to come, generations now unborn will listen with blanched cheeks and curdling blood, to the great incident in the conflagration, when a woman perished by the roadside, and two men escaped a dreadful death.

Mr. John E. Turnbull's sash factory, in Main Street, despite all exertions, caught so quickly that the workmen narrowly escaped from the ruins with their lives. Mr. Turnbull crossed the street to his residence, which, like many others on that eventful day, he considered impregnable. He had worked long at the factory, and had stored in his house a large quantity of belting and tools of his workshop. He had carefully gathered up everything of an inflammable character, and had swept the yard clean, so that nothing could ignite and spread around the fire, that but too readily devoured everything in its way. A vigorous defence was inaugurated to save the house. Mr. Turnbull had good assistants. His sons were there, working like beavers, and Mr. Walker Frink in his department, stayed the flames for a long time. The neighbours, believing like Mr. Turnbull, that nothing could harm this house, had piled large quantities of furniture against its front, these were lying before the windows of the cellar, and after a while took fire. Mrs. Turnbull fearing that the house might after all be burned, and at the request of her husband, made her escape by the back window, and had to be lifted over the fence. It was well that she did go, for in a few moments the house was threatened from a dozen quarters. The fence in the rear was crackling, and Mr. Turnbull went down into the cellar and began to shove off the blazing furniture from the windows. He worked away at this for some time, never dreaming that the fire was so near him, or that escape would soon be cut off. He had lost his hearing some years before, and did not hear the roar of the fire nor feel its approach. His son James was up-stairs battling with the fire, and Mr. Frink was on the roof. James Turnbull, realizing in an instant the condition of his father and his infirmity, and knowing well the determined character of his nature, was about to rush into the cellar and tell him how near the fire was, when he turned and beheld a dark shadow in the doorway. It was coming towards him, and for a moment struck terror into his soul. The tall figure of a woman, deeply robed in black, holding up a long train in her hand, and with head-dress all aflame, stood before him in the hall. He advanced towards her, as soon as he could recover himself, and at once tore off the burning head-dress and stamped it with his foot. He then brushed the kindling sparks from her dress. She seemed demented and unable to understand the nature of these proceedings. Indeed she remonstrated with him, and begged him not to destroy her bonnet. *The fire had crazed her brain*, and after escaping from her house she had wandered into Mr. Turnbull's blazing residence, unheedful of the terrible burns she had received, and notwithstanding that she was on fire herself in several places. James, realizing the state of affairs at once, coaxed her to go with him to the cellar to see his father, but she hung back and implored him to leave her there. He was forced to drag her unwillingly along, and together they both arrived at the place where the father was still labouring to extinguish the fire that was coming from all sides. He knew nothing of the great headway that had been made upstairs, and had not even begun to realize the danger of his situation below. As soon as he saw the lady he told his son to go and fetch a mat and throw it over her, and he would be with them in a few minutes. This was done, but as often as this mat was wrapped around her, it was thrown off again. Some moments passed, and Mr. Turnbull finding that he could do no more, resolved to leave the house. He and his son and the lady went upstairs where a sight that would have appalled a heart of stone met his eyes. All hope of escape through the alley in the rear was cut off. The house was on fire in the back. The flames were melting the roof in a dozen places. On either side the blaze was at its height, and not a moment was to be lost. Escape lay in one direction only, and that was hazardous in the extreme. *They must face the fire and escape by the front door,* or perish where they stood. The position they were in was trying, but fortunately for them their nerves were strong, and they were cool and collected. And now they began preparing for the struggle. The warrior formerly buckled on his armour of steel before venturing on the fray, but the armour of the firefighters consisted of old coats and wet clothes. A coat was fastened around the lady, who was still unknown to Mr. Turnbull, and her head was covered. His son James enveloped in the same way, stood by her side. Mr. Turnbull tied a wet handkerchief across his mouth, and after putting a coat over his head, they began the memorable race for life. James seized the lady, lifted her on his shoulders and followed his father out of the door. She was heavy, very tall, and had passed in age the allotted three score and ten. In addition to this, she was unwilling to leave the house, and twice she had to be dragged away by main force from the sofa. In no instance did she seem to comprehend what was being done or how great her peril was. She was more concerned about her parasol and head-dress than she appeared to be about her own personal safety. James seemed endowed with superior strength, and he seized his burden with a sort of death grip from which despite her struggles, she could not escape. She afterwards became calmer, and while she made no attempt to get off his back, he had her full dead weight to carry. The three stepped into the street and walked into the furnace. The heat was intense, and holding down their heads they hurried along. They ran over blazing coals, and hands and feet burned to the very bone. They had not proceeded twenty-five yards from the house, which was situate near the corner of Main and Sydney Streets when they came upon a boat, thirty feet long, which was lying directly across their path on its side. They could not pass by the inside and had to go around by the bow. They were hastening along to Charlotte Street, and intended going down that street to the Ballast Wharf, and when the worst came the intention was to leap into the sea. But the lady grew very violent just as the boat was passed a few feet, and refused to go any further. She straightened herself up, and slipping from James's shoulders, fell prone upon the ground. In vain she was reasoned with, in vain she was asked to make an effort, in vain she was appealed to, she would not move, but lay on her back helplessly, saying, " O leave me alone, leave me here, I'm very, very comfortable." The great fire, like a whirlwind, brushed against the exposed flesh of the three human beings, and wore it to the bone. It was like some invisible fiend. Before them they saw no flames, but a dead white heat that was all the more terrible because it could not be seen. Every time the covering was removed from their heads as they sought to look out and see where they were going, this intense, imperceptible heat burned their very eyeballs. The trees alongside were grasped by this unseen power, and their trunks were twisted and turned in its cobra-like embrace. Every thing in the road seemed charged with an element that appeared to draw the flames on. Though Main Street is one hundred and five feet wide, and the fire was for the most part confined to the houses on the side of the road, a cat could not run the gauntlet that night, and live. No one can realize the awful power of the heat, which the Messrs. Turnbull and the lady they were striving to save experienced on that thrilling march through the melting valley, without having passed through a similar experience. It was a trial that can never be blotted from their memories.

So much time was lost in trying to induce their charge to continue on with them, that their chance of escape by Charlotte Street was cut off, and the only hope that re mained now, was to return by the **terrible route** they had come. The **battle** had to be fought **over again.** The race back had to be run once more. The boat must be crossed again, they **must go** nearly two blocks forward, **or** die in their tracks. The street **was** full of smoke now, and flying embers alighted **on their** shoulders and **burned** their clothes, and the wild heat and the scorching flames were madly tearing through to their faces. Their charge remained as helpless as before, **and there** was something pitiable in **her** beseeching cries, that almost tempted them to accede to her request and leave her there in the street. But not a **moment** must now be lost, the fire-king was trampling down all before him. The two men seized her. She struggled and would not move. **They dragged her** to the boat, and she fell from their **now powerless arms.** Weakened by the fire, and sick at heart **at their** ill success, they could do no more, and could scarcely resist themselves the desire to stay there by the upturned boat, and yield their lives back to Him who gave them. The old lady fell back, and died with a smile upon her lips. The men, too weak to carry her further, placed her close by the boat, and shouted loudly for help. But the streets were bare of people, and no sound could be heard but their own voices rising above the crackling of the flames. They ran over the lava-like street, stopping **every now** and then to catch breath. On, on, they sped, the **youthful** spirit of the one being roused **when** it lagged, **by the** inspiring words of the wiry **and vigorous elder. It was a** terrible journey, fraught by **direful dangers on every side**

Each foot of the way was gained by a struggle, every yard was won by a battle. It was not until Carmarthen Street was reached, that father and son could realize that they were saved. They removed the covering from their heads, and looked back at the road they had passed. A moment more in that fire would have been their last. A figure was coming towards them, as they, arm in arm, almost reeled up Carmarthen Street, and it proved to be the brother of the woman Mr. Turnbull and his boy had tried to rescue. He was told that his sister was left by the boat dead, and that no earthly power could have saved her. One can imagine his agony when he learned these tidings. The old lady proved to be Mrs. Reed, mother of Mr. T. M. Reed, a former mayor of the city. At three o'clock the next morning, Mr. Turnbull went back to Main Street, and on coming up to the unburned portion of the boat, found close by it, the remains of Mrs. Reed. Mrs. Reed lost in the fire two sisters—the Misses Clark, one of whom, it is thought, was burned in her house, on the corner of Sydney and Main Streets. These three ladies were highly respected and loved by all who knew them, and their afflicted relatives meet with the sympathy of all.

Mr. Turnbull's loss is very heavy and foots up fully twenty-five thousand dollars. He lost absolutely everything he possessed, and the deeds and bank-notes which he had in his safe were all burned. He does not despair now of being able to retrieve himself in some way. He

CANTERBURY ST., SHOWING RITCHIE'S BUILDING IN THE DISTANCE.
Photo. by G. F. Simonson.

PRINCE WILLIAM STREET.
Photo. by G. F. Simonson.

was the first man to erect a wooden shanty and send a flag flying from its summit.

A large number of persons escaped from the resistless and giant-striding flames by means of rafts and small boats. Others got a friendly sail to Partridge Island in the tugs and steamers which approached the wharves whenever it was safe to do so. Many of those who were on Reed's Point Wharf and the Ballast Wharf got away in this manner.

The contingent of firemen from Portland worked with a will, and did much to check the flames—as much, indeed, as mortal man could do in a fire like this, with a high wind blowing a perfect gale all the time. The city firemen performed, with their brethren of the adjacent town, signal service. They drew lines round the burning buildings and tried again and again to confine the fire to one place, and prevent its spread. But the effort was futile. The flames broke down the lines, rose up in a hundred new places, and drove the firemen and their engines away from the spot. Some splendid work was performed in the vicinity of King Street East, and down towards Pitt. Here they were partly successful, and did all that could be done under the circumstances. Many of them are heavy losers, having lost everything they had in their own houses, while they were engaged in trying to save those of others. In a fire which never ceased to rage at its height until it came to the water's brink, and which poured an unceasing stream of flame for nine steady hours, and which burned in fifteen sections of the city at

K

once, it was a difficult matter for them with only four engines, to do anything like stopping the conflagration until it had spent itself, no matter how efficient and perfect the organization might be. No one expected the firemen to accomplish anything. There was something in the air which seemed to breed a sort of contagion, and the fire paralyzed buildings in a moment, and no one could tell how they caught. The fire struck men down where they were standing, and an invisible heat bore to the earth the trees on the sideways.

CHAPTER XIII.

A Chapter of Incidents—Agony on Board—Coming Up the Harbour—The Story of the Moths—The Newly Married Lady's Story—No Flour—Moving Out—Saving the Drugs—The Man with the Corn-Plasters—Incendiarism—Scenes—Thievery—The Newspapers—Enterprise—Blowing Down the Walls—An Act of Bravery—The Fatal Blast—Danger and Death in the Walls—Accidents—The Fire and the Churches—The Ministers.

As the "Empress" was steaming up the harbour, from Digby, on the night of the fire, the passengers on board, many of whom belonged to St. John, beheld the city in flames. Some of them even saw from the water their own residences on fire, and witnessed the alarming rapidity of the flames and the almost powerless efforts of the people to stay their ravages. One can imagine the feelings of those passengers who had left children at home, and who now began to experience the greatest anguish and suffering. What made the matter worse was, that some time had to elapse before the captain could venture to approach his wharf, and this added largely to the bitterness of the fathers and mothers on board. A mother who had left a little one in the city, while absent on a journey to Nova Scotia, told the writer that the agony she endured while making the approach to the city completely deadened and prostrated her. She grew perfectly helpless, and for a time nothing could rouse her from the seeming state of insensibility under which she sank.

Those were terrible moments of suffering—awful moments of uncertainty.

Among the curious incidents of the fire which are constantly coming to the surface, is the rather good story which is told of one of our neatest housekeepers. Her house is noted for its spotlessness, and some who profess to know, say that such a thing as a spider's web could not be seen about the premises, even in the cellar or woodshed. The lady has a natural abhorrence of those pests, the moths which *will* get into our furs sometimes and defy all the camphor and snuff in existence to keep them out. One day, about six months ago, some handsome newly upholstered chairs were purchased, and duly placed in the parlour. In a week a moth was found in one of the new chairs, and there was much consternation thereat. The rest of the furniture was examined carefully, and the offending chair was sent to the upholsterer for his examination. The result proved to the lady's satisfaction that she was right, and that the flock which had been put into the chair with the hair had caused all the mischief. The whole set was sent back to the furniture-man, and he was ordered to take the flock out. He returned them after a time, but in less than a week the persevering house-keeper succeeded in finding moths in every one of the chairs. She sent them to another upholsterer this time, and was awaiting their return when the fire occurred, and they were burned up, moths and all, while her own house was untouched.

A newly-married lady fearing the fire would reach her

dwelling, succeeded in hiring a team, and putting into it her best furniture, bedding, husband's clothes, and all her silver, sent them up to her mother's house at about four o'clock in the afternoon. At six o'clock her mother's residence was burned down, and with it all that was in it, while her own house was about half a mile from the vicinity of the fire. The lady was quite annoyed when the folks came in for a night's lodging that night, shortly after tea was over.

Considerable consternation prevailed among the people when it was known that nearly all the flour in town had been burned. The estimated loss was considered to be about fifty or sixty thousand barrels. One man is said to have hurried out and paid $18 for a barrel, while there were several persons who paid twenty cents a loaf for bread.

A good many people who feared the fire was coming their way moved out, and put their furniture, etc., in the street, and watched it till after midnight, when the expected flames not arriving, they marched the effects back again. The goods were almost as much damaged as if they had remained in the fire. Large quantities of material were lost in this way, and a lady saved an old pewter-box which once contained her husband's sleeve-buttons and studs, while she wrapped the latter up in a bag and never saw them again.

Quite a number of cases of petty thieving occurred. A drug store, shortly before the fire came to it, was filled with a gang of roughs and pickpockets, who insisted on helping the proprietor to save a few things. They were saving them with a vengeance; opening every box and package that came in their way, and taking a dip out of each. One young man, whose face bore the picture of health, had managed to save, when detected, enough Blood Mixture to cure the scrofula in his family for the next fifteen years. Boys, who should have stolen soap, were going in for that excellent capillary restorer, Mrs. Allen's Zylobalsamum, and a man, hobbling along with a wooden leg, was filling his pockets with bunion and corn plasters. The boxes had a neat look, and he thought he would see the next day what the contents were good for. Everyone wanted to help, and one could not but admire the zeal with which these gentry emptied drawers and boxes on the floor, and scrambled for the contents. One young gentleman in his anxiety to save a mirror-stand, which certainly could never be of any use to him, cut it in two and hastened away, leaving a drawer full of toothpicks, and a bottle of rat poison behind him, which he might have had just as well as not. A citizen, who said he felt dry after working so hard all day, regaled himself with a pint bottle of Ipecacuanha wine, and left immediately after it was down, to see how the fire was getting along in another place. One can never forget these little acts of kindness. It is the performance of deeds like these which exalts a nation, and makes us feel that the world is not altogether a fleeting show or a snare.

The cry of incendiarism was raised during the first

THE GREAT FIRE IN ST. JOHN. N. B. 159

days of the fire, and a good deal of alarm prevailed. Special constables patrolled the city, volunteer soldiers were placed on guard, and the policemen were ordered to be vigilant. Several arrests were made; but the greater portion of these were unnecessary, and, in nearly all cases, the persons arrested turned out to be noisy, drunken men, whose actions were misinterpreted by the officers. Some cases of incendiarism did really occur, however, and it was just as well that the city should be guarded, and the rougher element closely looked after. There is no doubt but that the fire at half-past two in the morning, in J. and T. Robinson's brick building, York Point Slip, was caused by the torch of the incendiary; and on Monday afternoon, a man was actually caught in the act of setting fire to Mrs. David Tapley's house in Indiantown. A good deal of talk about lynching was indulged in, but no one was lynched, though rumours came thick and fast, that one man had been shot, another hanged, and any number of people, according to the fertility of the narrator's imagination, were thrown into the sea. Drunkenness was rampant, and all saw how necessary it was that this evil should be stopped short. The licenses to the sellers could not be taken away, and it was optional with them whether they would listen to the appeals of the citizens or not. A committee, at a meeting of the people was appointed to ask the bar-tenders to close their bars for one week. To the credit of these gentlemen, be it said, they acceded to the request at once, and the bars were closed. This had a salutary effect on the morals of the community.

For days after the fire, stolen goods were being constantly recovered by the police and special constables. Large quantities were found concealed in houses situate a little distance away from the city, while even in the city limits, the officers met with a good deal of success in tracing articles that had been surreptitiously carried off. Some outward-bound schooners arrived at their places of destination along the New Brunswick and Nova Scotia coasts, laden with spoils from the fire, but in most cases these were got back.

H. M. S. Argus arrived from Halifax with the Marine Artillery and some soldiers. A number of the sailors did patrol duty in Carleton, and the artillery spent several days blowing down the walls of the buildings, and doing other work entrusted to their care. A number of soldiers of the 97th Regiment also arrived from Halifax, and these together with a company of the 62nd Battalion of volunteers, and some men of the volunteer artillery under command of Lieutenant-Colonel Foster, the senior Lieutenant-Colonel of the Dominion, performed guard and other duty until the 6th of July, when the volunteers were disbanded, and the regulars were continued for a time. The men behaved excellently and did good service. They were all encamped in King's Square.

The **U. S. Revenue** Cutter "Gallatin" **made** two trips **from Boston laden** with supplies from the generous people there, for the **relief** of the sufferers **by the fire.**

With commendable enterprise, many of the merchants who were burned out, and could not secure premises in which to carry on their business, by permission of the authorities, erected shanties on King and Market Squares, which they promise to pull down before the first of May, 1878. The city now looks quite primitive. Turn where you will, shanties of various sizes and styles meet the eye.

Some very good work was done at the ferry floats by the employes of the boat. Through their exertions the fire was kept away for a considerable time from the handsome new Magee Block, which stood on the corner of Water and Princess Streets. This building will be put up again at once.

The newspaper men were heavy losers, but nothing daunted, they went to work at once and lost no time. The *Telegraph*, through the courtesy of Mr. George W. Day, printer, was out on the very morning after the fire, with a smaller, but very spicy and interesting little sheet. The *Telegraph* proprietor and editor, Mr. Elder, did not save even his fyles. The *Globe* also did not lose an issue, and on Thursday evening it was as bright and attractive as usual, and contained an excellent account of the fire. The *Daily News* lost its issue on Thursday, but on Sunday, the proprietors, Messrs. Willis & Mott, issued a very interesting paper, and so made up for what it lost on Thursday. The resume of the work of spoliation in this number of the *News* was very graphic. The *Freeman** did not issue a

---

* The *Freeman* will be issued shortly as a daily.

paper. The three principal papers immediately set to work buying type, paper, and presses, and in a fortnight after the fire, the *News* was issued full size from a new press on the site of its old office. The *Globe* and *Telegraph* followed with new presses, &c., a day or two after. The *News* and *Globe* were issued after the fire for a few days from the *Weekly Herald* office, Germain Street.

At the blowing down of the walls of the Post Office, an act of valour was performed by some men belonging to the volunteer Battery of Artillery, which deserves prominent mention. Major Cunard, Captain A. J. Armstrong, and Lieutenants Inch and Ewing, together with a detachment of the Brigade of New Brunswick Artillery, under the command of Lieutenant-Colonel S. K. Foster, marched to Prince William Street, and proceeded to blow down the walls of the Post Office. Sentries were posted all round a circle of nearly two hundred yards, and everything being in readiness the work was begun. Two bags of powder were placed against the building with the length of spouting which would contain the port fire fuse that was to connect with the powder. Two charges went off and the effect on the walls was slight. The men thought of the expediency of placing a charge against the inside as well as one on the outside of the building. The trains were laid and the fuses lit, but some loose powder igniting in a moment with the train, it exploded with a deafening crash before the men could get away, and half of the wall facing Prince William Street, came down as if a thunderbolt had struck it. Gunner John Nixon, of No. 2 Battery, was covered with the debris, but escaped uninjured, save a few scratches on the arm and a cut or two. Gunner Walter Lamb, of No. 10 Battery, was stricken down and every one deemed him dead, the smoke and debris completely hiding him. The second 70lb blast was still burning and was momentarily expected to go off, when Lamb's hand was observed to rise over his head and touch his cap. In a moment five men, unmindful of the terrible fate which threatened them, rushed in and bravely dragged from the mass of ruins, their fallen comrade. He was borne away just as the second charge went off with a roar, carrying away at a bound the remainder of the wall. Stones and bricks flew in every direction and John Anderson, who was standing in Germain Street, but whose presence there was unknown, fell badly wounded. He was conveyed to the hospital and died in a few days. The names of the five artillery men who behaved so bravely are, Lieutenant Inch, No. 10; Lieutenant Wm. King, No. 10; Corporal J. R. Andrews, No. 3; Corporal Anderson, No. 1; and Gunner R. McJunkin, No. 10. Captain Ring, of Carleton Battery, was standing within three paces of Gunner Lamb when he fell. His escape was certainly miraculous.

The pulling down of the walls has been attended by a good many accidents, some of them terminating seriously. A week after the fire some men were engaged in taking down the walls of the building in Dock Street, belonging to the Johnston estate. Two men were cleaning out the foundation at the same time. The wall trembled in the breeze, and the men looking up fled for their lives. One of them,

James Wilkins escaped, but Thomas Sullivan was caught by the pile of bricks and his head was badly cut and his limbs bruised. A day or so after this accident, another one occurred which ended fatally. Some workmen were removing the rubbish from a building, when a wall that enclosed a vault of some seven or eight feet in height fell, and George Gallagher was buried in the ruins. He was taken to the Hospital (Dr. E. B. C. Hanington, resident physician), and it was found that his spine was broken, his thigh fractured, and he had sustained serious injuries internally. He died in a few hours.

The Sunday after the fire, the ministers referred in their sermons to the very general conflagration, and its lessons. At St. Paul's Church, in the morning, Rev. Mr. De Veber preached. In the afternoon, the Rev. Mr. Mather, and in the evening, Rev. Mr. Brigstocke, of Trinity, officiated. Rev. Mr. Windeyer preached both morning and evening in his church, the Reformed Episcopal. Rev. S. P. Fay, a Bangor clergyman, preached in the Union Street Congregational Church, morning and evening. Rev. James Bennet preached in St. John's Presbyterian in the morning, and Rev. A. McL. Stavely in the afternoon. Rev. Dr. D. Maclise, in the morning preached in Calvin Church; and in the evening, Rev. Mr. Mitchell, of St. Andrew's Kirk, preached. The Exmouth Street Church held three services, Rev. Mr. Duke in the morning, Rev. Howard Sprague in the afternoon, and in the evening Revs. Messrs. Hartt and Sprague addressed the congregation. Rev. Mr. Fowler preached in

Carleton Presbyterian Church in the morning, and there was no service in the evening. The Baptist pulpit was occupied by Rev. Mr. Hickson, the pastor, both morning and evening. Rev. Theodore Dowling preached in St. George's Church. At the Free Christian Church, Rev. George Hartley preached in the afternoon. At the Portland Baptist Church, Rev. Mr. McLellan, the pastor, preached morning and evening. The Portland Methodist Church had Rev. Mr. Barrett in the morning, and Rev Mr. Teed in the evening. St. Luke's, Portland, had sermons from Rev. Mr. Almon, the rector. Brussels Street Church had Rev. Mr. Alexander. At the Roman Catholic Cathedral, at nine o'clock mass, Bishop Sweeny addressed the congregation, and at eleven, Bishop Power, of Newfoundland, preached. Rev. Mr. Wills delivered a sermon at the Unitarian Hall; and in the St. Stephen Presbyterian Church, Rev. D. Macrae preached in the morning, and the Rev. Mr. Donald, of Port Hope, in the evening.* p 166.

Thirty-nine orphans were kindly taken care of by Mr. R. B. Graham, the visiting agent of the Baldwin Place Home for Little Wanderers, who carried them to Boston, Massachusetts.

Some months ago a clever poem in several books, entitled "On the Hills," from the pen of a Nova Scotia lady of excellent reputation as a writer, Mrs. Morton, née Irene S. Elder, was placed in the hands of Wm. Elder, Esq., of the St. John's *Daily Telegraph*, to read. On the day of the fire, he put this manuscript in his safe, for protection. When the safe was opened, the manuscript was found quite legible. The scene of the poem is laid in our sister province, and it is said to contain some genuine touches of true poetry.

Apropos of manuscripts, it may be said that Prof. Wm. Lyall, of Halifax, lost a very valuable treatise "On the Emotions," which was burned in Mr. Stewart's safe, King street. Mr. W. P. Dole lost all his sonnets, and his late paper "On Definitions," upon which he had expended a good deal of time.

* Rev. Geo. M. Armstrong preached in Stone Church, (built 1824) and on the Sabbath following the Bishop of Fredericton preached in the same church.

CHAPTER XIV.

"I went againe to the ruines, for it was no longer a citty," the Drive by Moonlight—Through the Ruins—After the Fire—A City of Ashes—The Buried Silver—The Sentinel Chimneys—The Home of Luxuriance—A Recollection—The Moon and the Church—Back Again.

SHELLEY'S white-orbed maiden sits in the sky, and already her pale torch is silvering the peaks of the ruins. Let us take a carriage, and drive round the desolate city, slowly and softly, and view the giant wreck which the fire has made. There is no better time than the present The moon is up, and quietness reigns. It is as light as day. We will drive first to the barrack-ground, and look up the long hills. Three days have passed, and the first excitement is now over. A thousand weary pilgrims have made the journey to this desert of desolation a hundred times since the fire, and vainly dug on the site where their homes once were, for relics, or perhaps something more. Why, look there! it is past midnight, and those three men you see working by that blackened wall, seem so wrapped up in their occupation, that they scarcely speak to one another, or note the presence of any one but themselves. See, they are carrying away the still hot bricks, and throwing into the street bits of iron and charred wood. Look, watch them for a moment—witness how they—

> "Dig, dig, dig, amid earth, and mortar, and stone,
> And dig, dig, dig, among ruins overthrown;
> Spade, and basket, and pick, the toiling Arabs ply."

How monotonous the work appears, and how strangely weird everything looks. To speak now, and hail these men, would break the charm—would interrupt the gaunt and gloomy silence of the place. But the presence of these excavators, at such an hour as this, arouses our curiosity. We know that the standard authorities tell us, that no matter how deeply men may dig for the pirate's buried treasure, if any one speaks during the performance of the work, the spell becomes broken, the enchantment passes away, and the iron box of doubloons vanishes. We have no means of disputing this, and wouldn't if we could. We have no desire to attempt to prove the contrary, but rather incline to the belief that the authorities are right, for we have it on the word of a gentleman who once owned a mineral rod, and whose word is undoubted, that a certain Miss Pitts, who was engaged all her life in digging about the gardens of her neighbours, and who never found anything up to the day of her death, confessed to him during her last illness, that her tongue had spoiled all. Had she but kept quiet when her spade struck the iron-box, all would have been well. But her joy was so great at the sight of the treasure, that she couldn't contain herself longer, and giving utterance to her feelings she spoke, and the box of course, immediately sank. The truth of this narrative can be established by excellent witnesses, and Miss Pitts, whatever her other

VIEW FROM QUEEN SQUARE.

WENTWORTH STREET.

faults might be, had always a splendid reputation for veracity. She made and sold mineral rods too, and, in explaining their miraculous properties, gave out the advice that, by a judicious and constant use of her peculiar make of mineral rod, the whole world might speedily become rich, and at very trifling cost, thus exhibiting a vein of disinterestedness, as generous as it was rare. We say then, in the face of all this, and at the risk of destroying what happiness yet remained in the minds of the men who were thus toiling through the ghostly hour of twelve, we drew rein and hailed them. We couldn't help it. Our curiosity got the better of us, and we asked them what they were digging for. They were hunting for treasures, truly, not the pirate's though, but their own. During the fire, and unable to hire a team at any price, they had dug a deep hole in the cellar of the house and buried there, what jewelry and silver-ware they could scrape together. They were now hunting for it, and eventually they found it, in not even a discoloured state.

But let us go on. A very pleasant wind is fanning our foreheads, and there is a charm about this drive which we never experienced before. A grim charm truly, but nevertheless, a charm after all. Are we not going to see the ruins. The ruins which came to us in a night—the heritage of the fire. We have a Dunga and a Dugga, and a Carthage of our own. In a few brief hours we had a desolation here, which, in other lands it took great centuries to create. We have crumbling ruins, and shapeless masses of stone in the very heart of a community which boasted, but a short time before, of a civilization and an enterprise unsurpassed the world over. Let the eye wander as we pass along the deserted streets, and take in the full view as it appears. What a fascination there is about this district of sorrow. Why is it we pause, and wonder if Troy ever looked like this; or the ruins of Sodom stood out against the sky like that house there, this edifice here or that once noble structure beyond. All, all is desolation, all blackness, despair, decay and misery. Look at those ponderous walls, which defied the flames to the last. See they are still standing, broken it is true, but standing proudly and defiantly for all that. See, the moon is throwing her light upon that church yonder. See how she dances, now high, now low, look, she disappears behind the tall wall, and all we see for a moment is a dark shadow. Now there she is again. Here comes the glittering Cynthia with her robes of white. She is coming along up, up, up by that angle there. Now she is soaring along the sky. Now she seems to stand right over our heads. How light it is. How bright and beautiful the moon is to-night. How playful the mad thing is, how merrily and joyously she disports herself in the heavens, and yet how kindly she turns her sympathetic face on the vale below. She sails along, casting lingering and tearful glances on the havoc-stricken land.

We will drive over to that eminence there and look at the squares of ruins, and notice the fragments of columns which remain. Turn your head round, and look at those sentinel chimneys standing so erect, and so regularly in line. Ah, that is where the old barrack stood, and those chimneys, no doubt, heard many a well-told tale of the bivouac and the battle-field. Could they but speak tonight, what reminiscence would they relate of Lucknow and Cawnpore, of the Heights of Alma, and bloody plain of Inkerman. What stories would they tell you of the gallant fellows who on bleak winter nights gathered round their base, and chatted and talked of battles fought and won, and the great deeds of bravery they had seen. These high chimneys have many bits of history locked within them which the world shall never know. They stood there when the city was almost as bare of houses as it is now. They have seen the busy workman, and heard the sound of his axe and saw; they have seen the city grow more and more strong and beautiful; they have watched its growth from a mere hamlet to a metropolis; they have witnessed the erection of noble structures on sites where trees and bushes flourished before; they have seen St. John on the morning of the 20th June prosperous, enterprising, and full of energy and life; and they have seen her again before the sun went down, stricken to the earth, with her buildings in ruins, and the work of almost a hundred years in ashes. The old sentries keep guard tonight, blackened and bared.

Turn the horse a little this way. Now look up the street. Do you see that pile of bricks and mortar and those heavy stones lying near? That *debris* is all that is left of a house where in my youth, I spent many happy hours. I must take you into my confidence and tell you that the owner of that house is to-day a poor man. The day before the fire he was comparatively comfortable, rich I should call it, but the way wealth is computed now-a-days, I will content myself with saying that he was comfortably off. He had his carriage and horses—such splendid drivers, and how well he kept them—he had a library, and such books, and he knew what was in them too. History, belles-lettres, biography, science, all departments were here. You could read if you chose on an idle afternoon, in that alcove off the library, over there, a few feet from those bricks, anything your fancy dictated. I used to love to sit there and pull down his books—not to read them always, but merely to skim the cream off a dozen or so of them of an afternoon. He had some charming old books which he always kept in the extreme corner of his case. I remember with what awe I used to approach this section, and take down from the shelf his luxuriant copy of Milton, printed early in the eighteenth century, and illustrated with a grand old portrait of the blind bard. I read Pope's Homer here for the first time, and actually waded through the Chesterfield Letters. I used to sit over towards the left of where we are now, just close to that old stove-pipe which you can just see peeping through the bricks. I may live many years, or I may pass away to-night, but I shall never forget that dear old house, and the many happy, happy hours I spent there. Come away. Something seems to choke me, and one wants all his strength these days. Continue along in this direction. We shall see all that is left of many beautiful houses from here. There's the Wiggins' Orphan Asylum. The tower and the walls are there. What exquisite ruins they are. Let us look at them awhile. One can almost fancy he has seen somewhere a picture of the remains of an edifice that looked like this. I can almost hear the guide tapping his cane on the walls, and telling me to note how excellently preserved the building is, and how admirably the builders put it up. See how solid and strong it is, and hardly a discoloration marks its handsome front. That dingy and dismal-looking old wooden building near at hand is the Marine Hospital—that was saved all right.

Did you notice the jagged, fringe-like edges of that building which we passed just now, in that bend near the road? How intense the heat must have been there to wear it down like that. And did you observe that wooden door lying in the vestibule scarcely touched by the flames, while everything around it was burned to a crisp? What odd freaks the fire takes sometimes. Drive a little faster keep well to the left. The streets are full of stones and broken brick yet. We are now coming past Queen Square, and let us look in a moment on Mecklenburg Street. What a beautiful sight those burning coals make in Mr. Vaughan's house. You can see better by the loft, there, now stop. See the pale light is above, the deep blood-red light is below. What a curious meeting. You can scarcely see the dividing line between them. Drive through the street to Carmarthen, take in on the way Mr. Nicholson's

Castle, and the houses of Messrs. Magee on the left, and before you turn up the street look at that immense mass of burning coals belonging to the Gas Company, blazing away like some volcano in a state of eruption. There are smouldering fires all round the city, and ruins upon ruins meet us at every turn. My heart sickens at the sight. Let us drive home. We have visited the ruins by moonlight.

CHAPTER XV.

Aid for St. John—The First Days—How the Poor were Fed—Organization of the St. John Relief and Aid Society—Its System—How it Operates—The Rink—The Car-shed—List of Moneys and Supplies Received—The Noble Contributions.

No sooner was it known abroad that a great fire had swept away the principal portion of St. John, and that thousands of people walked the streets, homeless and hungry, than, with wonderful unanimity, generous offers of aid came pouring in from all sides, for the relief of the ruined city. Large sums of money, cargoes of supplies, and carloads of breadstuffs, furniture, and clothing arrived; and committees of citizens, notwithstanding that they were burned out themselves, and had suffered severely, forgot everything in the desire to do good, and instantly proceeded to take charge of this relief, and administer it to the needy. The spacious skating rink was at their disposal, and this splendid building soon became the house of refuge for over three hundred homeless persons. These men, women, and children lived, slept, and ate here day after day, for a week and more after the fire. The rink was also converted into a provision storehouse, and from its centre the poor, daily, received the necessaries of life. The ladies' dressing-room was thrown into a clothes department, and from this place the wants of applicants were attended to. Of course the system employed at first was very loose, and while many deserving persons received aid, others, again, who had no claims on the fund, fared equally as well. The committee took the ground that it was better a few impositions should occur than that one deserving person should "go empty away," and accordingly none were refused alms and other assistance. The greatest credit is due to these gentlemen for their kindly and disinterested labours. While in office they did much good, and the generous donors of the material which was so freely sent, can rest assured that their bounty was not misapplied. Everything passed through the hands of His Worship, Mayor Earle, the chief civic officer, and was by him placed immediately after its receipt, in the possession of the proper ones who were delegated to receive it. But this committee could not be expected to distribute the relief, after the first week or two. The sums of money, and the immense quantity of supplies, which continued, and still continue, to come, and the large increase of applicants who only now began to realize their loss, caused the work to grow more and more arduous and cumbersome. Some regularly organized system of administering aid must be devised, and a proper board of workmen selected, who would be paid fairly for their services. This was what was done in Chicago, during the days of her calamity, and our people wisely considered that a leaf out of her book would answer the purpose. A meeting was called, and though some dissatisfaction existed at the precise *manner* in which the thing was done, yet, after all, the error in such times as these should not be accounted as anything very serious. The movers meant well, and every one could not have a place on the board of directors.

Mr. C. G. Trusdell, the General Superintendent of the Chicago Relief and Aid Society, was sent down to St. John to give what counsel he could, and relate his experience to the people, and point out to them the beauties of the organization which obtained in Chicago during her troubles. He counselled the instant formation of a similar society here. He knew its workings intimately. It was thorough; it was business-like. No one, after the system was in full working order, could impose on the managers, and order would come out of chaos, and confusion no longer exist. His words had weight, for he had passed through the fire himself; and steps were at once inaugurated for the establishment of "The St. John Relief and Aid Society," with full control of the funds and supplies. The men who were selected for the task are those in whom the citizens have every confidence. The Directors are:—

> S. Z. Earle, Mayor, *President.*
> W. H. Tuck, Recorder, *Vice-President.*
> Chas. H. Fairweather, *Treasurer.*

James A. Harding.	H. J. Leonard.
Hon. Geo. E. King.	James I. Fellows.
Harris Allan.	Wm. Magee.
Fred A. King.	Chas. N. Skinner.
Andre Cushing.	Ezekiel McLeod.
James Reynolds.	Gen. D. B. Warner.

A. Chipman Smith.   E. Fisher.
John H. Parks.

Aldermen Maher, Peters, Ferguson, Kerr, Adams, Duffell, Brittain, Glasgow, and Wilson, with L. R. Harrison, *Secretary*.

These gentlemen then organized the St. John Relief and Aid Society, and assumed charge at once. The moneys were deposited in the bank, to the credit of Chas. H. Fairweather, the Treasurer; and General D. B. Warner, U.S. Consul, entered upon his duties as General Superintendent, and opened his office at the rink.

The sufferers by the fire, who had lived in the rink up to this time, were housed in tents on the barrack green. The rink was thrown into compartments. Fully two-thirds were placed at the service of the store-keeper, who dealt out the provisions, the manager of the furniture department, and the overseer of the space allotted to clothing. The space directly in front of the door-way is occupied by the different officers who perform the preliminary work. The gentlemen's dressing-room is devoted to the use of the visitors, and the other dressing-room is where the General Superintendent is to be found. No more admirable system of giving out help to those whose wants require it, could be formed. It is perfection itself, and though mistakes may occur occasionally, on the whole it moves like a piece of well-appointed machinery. The reader must understand that thousands of applications are made daily, and all sorts of tricks are resorted to by those whose necessities require no help, and every dollar given away to the undeserving, is so much carried from the mouths of the honest and honourable, for whom this magnificent donation was made. The greatest care must be exercised, and it is the business of quite a staff of officers to see that these impositions are checked, and no one is served twice on the same order. No one has been refused aid, if he was legitimately entitled to it.

The actual working of the system is an interesting study. Everything is done regularly and methodically. There is a substantial reason for every movement, and it is surprising how quickly the officers can detect an informality, or notice any attempt at deception. A brief account of the system as it works will be interesting to many. Upon entering through the main entrance, the visitor will notice, in stepping down to the floor of the rink, a number of benches. On these the applicants sit, each awaiting his or her turn, as the case may be. Before them are the interviewers, six or seven in number, seated at convenient desks. The applicant steps up and answers the questions propounded on a sheet of paper. This document is signed, and one of Mr. G. B. Hegan's (the chief of the clerks' staff) clerks numbers it. It then goes before Mr. Peter Campbell, the superintendent of visitors. He allots it to the visitor of the district to which the applicant belongs, for his name and address are on this paper. The next day this house is visited, and the wants of the residents being made known are entered on the paper, if in the opinion of the visitor, after thorough examination, they come under the proper head for relief. The applicant is told to call at the rink, where he receives orders for furniture, clothing or provisions, or all three if he needs them. After that has been gone through, it is only the question of a few minutes when he gets what he wants. He presents each ticket to the department of the various supplies, and after receiving his quota he passes out. The process is very simple, though it appears at first sight a little involved. It is the only way, however, by which a complete check may be put on what goes out or by which every dollar's worth of supplies can be strictly accounted for. Cases calling for immediate aid often come before the managers. The applicant's needs are urgent, and he cannot wait two days. He must have something now and at once. Even here the wheels of the system are not clogged. In half an hour or less he goes off with a day or two's full supply. An interim ticket is furnished for just such cases as his, and he gets enough on that "Immediate Relief" card, in advance of visitation to keep him from actual suffering, until his regular supply can come to him in due course. The plan adopted to prevent fraud works excellently, and without the remotest possibility of a mistake. This is the famous vowel index system and there is no better way than it. This is in charge of the book-keepers under W. H. Stanley, the Chief Book-keeper, whose fine ability has full scope in the management of this department. A complete registration is made of the name and number and residence of every applicant. The vouchers bearing these statements are fyled away in packages of a hundred, and it is only the work of a few seconds to find out all about the applicant as soon as he presents himself. In this department only the "issued" documents are kept. Before they pass into the book-keeper's hands they are retained by another set of clerks who hold them until the supplies are issued; when this is done the words "issued to ———" are written down on the face of the voucher in red ink and at once recorded at the book-keeper's desk and fyled as before mentioned. Mr. Hegan, whose desk faces the door, performs his functions with excellent executive skill, and the other gentlemen in charge of the different departments have the system at their fingers' end and already show much familiarity with the work. It is the duty of the visitors who call on the people named in the circulars handed them, to make every legitimate enquiry and strive to learn the fullest particulars of the applicants, as much depends on their report to headquarters. This duty is entrusted to persons of discernment and reliability, and few complaints have reached the General Superintendent of negligence and incompetency. As soon as they occur, however, the offenders are promptly dismissed. The Provision Department is in charge of Mr. Geo. Swett, formerly Manager of the Victoria Hotel. He has an efficient staff of clerks, and his store-room reminds one of a well regulated wholesale grocery store. The meat is cut up into convenient pieces by butchers, and the whole management here is reduced to a system; Mr. Swett is always courteous and looks carefully after those under him. Mr. Kerrison is chief of the Clothing Department, and

Mr. P. Gleason, is the principal officer of the Furniture Room. Miss Rowley is Superintendent of the Ladies' Clothing Department. The heads of the different departments are held responsible for the doings of their subordinates, and the utmost vigilance is accordingly exercised.

The large car-shed immediately adjoining the rink, has been converted into a store-room and receiving office. Here, Messrs. Wm. Magee and James Reynolds receive the supplies as they come to the very doors of the shed by rail, and are brought from the steamers by carts. As most of the relief comes by train there is no cartage or expense attached, and this besides being very convenient is wholly inexpensive. Not an article can leave here to go to the various departments in the rink, unless an order comes for it from some chief of a department. The supplies are usually ordered in large quantities in the morning and in sufficient amounts to last one day. The warehouse is kept well, and the goods therein are carefully looked after and subject to constant examination. Everything here, as well as in the other rooms, is done by check, and nothing can go astray.

The Directors are husbanding their resources and looking further ahead than the present hour. Care is taken to render judiciously the relief which has come from the generous friends abroad. It is likely that the St. John Relief and Aid Society will continue several years in active operation. They will have much to do, and the trials which will come with the winter will be very trying.

LIST OF BUSINESS HOUSES BURNT OUT.

Academy of Music ...A. M. Ring, Pres. ....Germain Street.
Adams, James & Co...Drygoods ....King Street.
Allan, Harris........Brass-founder ....Water Street.
Allan Bros...........Foundrymen ....   "   "
Allan, J. Howe......Provisions ....South Mkt. Whf.
Allan, John ....Tinsmith............Canterbury Street.
Allen, Geo. Em.......Commercial agent....Prince William Street.
Ames, Horace T. ....Ship chandlery ......Walker's Whf.
Albert Mining Co. .....Albertite............Pr. William Street.
Armstrong, Aaron.....Bonded warehouse ...   "   "
Armstrong, Bros. ....Founders ....Main Street.
Armstrong, John & Co.Dry goods ....Prince William Street
Austin, W. H. ......Livery Stable........Princess Street.
Andrews, Wm. Mountain, & Co.........Manuf. Agents.......Prince William Street.
Arrowsmith, J. E. ....Victualler ....Germain.
Abel, Mrs. ....Boarding-house .....   "
Aitken, Allen & Co...Machinists ....Sydney Street.
Anglin, Hon. T. W. .." Freeman " ....Prince William Street.
Almon, L. J..........Insurance............Princess Street.

Brown, Silas H.......Builder ....Pitt St.
Ballantine, J. E. & Co.Boots and shoes (retail)King St.
Barbour Bros. ....Provisions ....South Mkt. Whf.
Barbour, M. C. .....Dry goods (retail)....Prince William St.
Barbour, Robt.......Painter ....
Bardsley, Bros. .....Hats ....King St.
Butt, W. F. ....Bonded warehouse.....Nelson St.
Brennan, Henry .....Oyster saloon........Water St.
Barnes, A. B. & Co. ..Hotel-keepers ....Prince William St.
Barnes & Co.........Booksellers..........   "   "
Benn, J. C. ....Insurance ....Germain St.

Barnes, Jos. **W.** & Co. Dry goods (retail) .... Market Square.
Betts Azor, W. T. ..... Comm .... Ward St.
Bridgeo, D. .... Boarding-house ...... Prince William St.
Bartsch, A. J. H. .... Watches and Chrono-
   meters .... "   "
Beard & Venning .... Dry goods .... "   "
Benson, John .... Millinery .... "   "
Beek, Henry S. ...... Bookbinder .... "   "
Bell, Joseph .... Painter .... Duke St.
Bellony, John .... Pictures .... Dock St.
Bent, Geo. R. .... Musical instruments,
   organs .... Main St.
Bent, Gilbert .... Provisions .... South Mkt. Whf.
Bertain, G. W. E. ... Ship-owner .... Prince William St.
Berton Bros. .... Groceries .... Dock St.
Berryman, Drs. J. &
   D. E. .... Physicians .... Charlotte St.
Best, Norris .... Metals .... Water St.
Bose, Peter .... Liquors .... Smyth St.
Birmingham, Michael "   .... Dock St.
Biddington, George ... "   .... Canterbury St.
Black, Wm. .... Ship chandler .... Ward St.
Blackall, Michael ... Coaches .... Prince William St.
Blanchard, **W. E.** .... Women's wear ..... Germain St.
Blizard, S. **G.** .... Lumber yard ...... Britain St.
Blizzard, Wm. .... Fish packer .... Prince William St.
Bostwick, C. M. .... Provisions .... Water St.
Bourke, T. L. .... Groceries and liquors Dock St.
Bowes & Evans...... Tinsmiths and stoves Canterbury St.
Bradley, Bros. .... Block **& pump** makers
Breeze, Dudne ...... Liquors and groceries,
   bonded warehouse
   burned ....
Brims, A. & Son...... Brewers .... Wentworth St.

WESTERN SIDE OF CITY, TAKEN FROM LOWER COVE, SHOWING RUINS OF GAS WORKS.
Photo. by Simonson.

THE GREAT FIRE IN ST. JOHN, N. B.

Bruce, J. ....Boots and Shoes .....Sydney St.
Brockington, H. & Co.Tailors...............Germain St.
Brown, John C. .....Commission & W. I.
         goods.............Brown's Wharf.
Brown & Nugent ....Liquors ....Dock St.
Burns, G. M.........Boarding-house ..... "
Bruckhof, Wm. ......Mouldings,..........Germain St.
Bullock, Jos. ....Oils................Nelson St.
Baillie, Chas.........Fly tyer............Prince William St.
Burnham, C. E.,& Co.Furniture...........Germain St.
Burpee, I. & F. & Co.Iron and hardware....North wharf.
Butt, John H........Tailor..............Germain St.
Buist, A............Liquors ....Water St.
Buxton, Thos. B......Liquors.............Dock St.
Brundage, Thos......Sail maker.........Merritt's wharf.
Brennan, B..........Liquors.............Canterbury St.
Bank New Brunswick,Hon.J. D. Lewin,Pres.Princess St.
Bank Nova Scotia,..J. M. Robinson, AgentMarket Square.
Bank Montreal,......E. C. Jones, Agent.... " "
Brown, Miss.........Milliner...........Germain St.
Bustin, A. T........Circulating Library...Germain St.
Bayard, Dr. Wm.....Physician........... " "
Brewster, E. E.......Bottler.............Dock St.
Burke, John........Undertaker..........Princess St.
Bryden, Bros. & Co..Bakers..............
Bertaux, Geo. E......Ships...............Prince William Street.

Cain, Antony........Liquors & groceries...Mill St.
Callaghan, John...... " " Reed's Point.
Cameron J. R. & Co.,Oils and lamps........Prince William St.
Campbell, P. & J....Blacksmiths..........Union St.
Campbell, Thos......Gas fitter...........Germain St.
Carleton, Robt......Blockmaker..........Wood St.
Carroll, David........Plumber............Princess St.

THE GREAT FIRE IN ST. JOHN, N. B.

Carvill, Geo..........Iron................Nelson St.
Carvill, McKean & Co.Merchants...........Office, Walker's wharf.
Chubb, H. & Co.....Stationers............Prince William St.
Churchill, David....Fancy goods.........Prince William St.
Clarke, Alfred T.....W. I. goods.........Smyth St.
Clarke, James........Flour Inspector......
Clarke, G. H.........Auctioneer..........Prince William St.
Clementson, F. & Co..Crockery............Dock St.
Climo, J. S..........Photographs & framesGermain St.
Coholane, John......Grocer..............Dock St.
Collins, Francis.....Commission..........Dock St.
Connolly, Capt.......Nautical school.....Water St.
Colpitts, Thos. R.....Photographer........Germain St.
Conroy, H. & Son....Hair goods..........Canterbury St.
Corbitt, John.........Block & pumpmaker.Ward St.
Corbitt, Samuel......Furniture...........Prince William St.
Cornwall, Ira, jr.,...Insurance Agent.....Princess St.
Cotter, W. & Sons..Victuallers..........Prince William St.
Coughlan Daniel.....Clothing............Dock St.
Coughlan, R..........Liquors.............Ward St.
Coughlan, Thos. L...Jewelry.............King St.
Cox, Joseph..........Stone cutter.........
Crawford, W. K.....Books...............King St.
Cruickshank, James F.Ship owner..........Office Maritime Bank
Cushing, Andre & Co.Lumber..............Office Prince Wm. St.
Cotter, B............Fruit................Dock St.
Cochrane, F. J......Drugs...............Charlotte St.

Daniel & Boyd.......Dry goods, wholesaleMarket Square.
Davidson, Wm........Lumber..............Office Water St.
Davidson, Wm. J.....Tug boats........... "   "   "
Dun, Wiman & Co...Mercantile Agency..... "   Maritime Bank.
Dearborn & Co........Spices...............Nelson St.
De Forest, Geo. S...Provisions & W I goods. South wharf.

THE GREAT FIRE IN ST. JOHN, N. B. 187

Della Torre C. & W.
 & Co...............Toys................King St.
Deveber, L. H. & Sons Merchants...........Prince William St.
Devine, George F......Sheet Music......... "   "   "
Dalzell, J. W.........Furniture ....Germain St.
Devoe, John D..........Liquors & groceries...Water St.
Daniel, Dr. J. W.......Physician..............Germain St.
Dodge, Isaac A......Blacksmith.............
Doherty, Wm. & Co...Clothiers ....Market Square.
Domville, Jas. & Co...Merchants...............North Wharf.
Donovan, Jeremiah...Boots and Shoes........Dock St.
Driscoll Bros.........Ship-owners............Water St.
Driscoll, M...............Ship-chandler......... "
Duff, Alexander.......Tug Boats............... "
Duffell, Henry.......Lumber..................Charlotte St.
Dunham & Clarke......Architects............Prince William St.
Dunn, J. E..........Insurance..............Ritchie's Building.
Dunn, Jas. L., & Co...Iron and Ship-owners. Smyth St.
Dyall, James............Gas-fitter.............Water St.
DeBlois, T. M........News Room...........Prince William St.
Doody & Tole..........Plumbers............ "   "
Driscoll, Daniel.......Liquors ....Carmarthen.

Eastern Express Co...Jos. R. Stone, Agent..Prince William St.
Eaton, Geo..........Commission.............Nelson St.
Emerson, R. B.......Tinsmith...............Germain St.
Emery, Oliver & Co...Provisions and Ships..South Wharf.
Erb & Bowman.......Flour....................North Wharf.
Everitt & Butler.....Wholesale Dry Goods. Canterbury.
Everett, C. & E.......Hatters.................Prince William St.
Everett, Geo. F. & Co.Drugs...............King St.
Elder, Wm..........*Daily Telegraph*......Prince William St.
Ellis & Armstrong.....*Evening Globe*........ "   "

Finlay, Hugh........*Printer's Miscellany*..Prince William St.

Finnegan, H..............Liquors................Prince William St.
Flinn, Geo...............Saloon.................Canterbury St.
Fairweather, H. H.....Coal....................York Point Slip.
Fairweather, A. C. &
   G. E..................Insurance.............Princess St.
Fairall & Smith........Dry Goods, Retail.....Prince William St.
Fairbanks & Co.........Gilders................King St.
Farrell, Michael.......Clothing...............Prince William St.
Ferguson, John C......Grocer and Auctioneer South Wharf.
Flood, Michael.........Builder................Wentworth St.
Finn, M. A.............Wines..................Water St.
Fisher, Samuel.........Shoemaker..............Charlotte St.
Flewelling, G. & G....Matches................Water St.
Foley, H. T............Notions................Duke St.
Foster, John...........Grocers and Liquors...Prince William St.
Foster, S. K...........Shoes..................Germain Street.
Foster, S. R. & Son...Tacks..................North St.
Fleming, J. W..........Liquors................Britain St.
Francis, Manuel........Shoes..................Prince William St.
Furlong, Thos..........Wines..................Water St.
Fiske, Dr. J. M. C.....Dentist................King St.
Fitch, Dr. Simon.......Physician..............Princess St.
Firth, Wm. M. B.......Wharfinger.............Walker's Wharf.
Frith, Henry W........Clerk of the Peace.....Princess St.
Fitzpatrick, F. G. S...Bonded Warehouse....Nelson St.
Ferguson, Miss.........Gordon House...........King St.
Gabel, Z. G............Rubber Goods...........Prince William St.
Gallagher & Young.....Coopers................Ward St.
Gard, W. T.............Manu. Jeweller.........Germain St.
Gerow, Geo. W........Ship-owner.............Prince William St.
Gibbon, W. H..........Coal...................Mill St.
Gibson, W. C..........Watch materials........King St.
Gilbert, & Co..........Merchants..............Prince William St.
Griffith, Dr. Jas. E.   Dentist................Germain St.

Gilmour, A. & T. ....Tailors... ....Germain St.
Gleeson, Patk. ......Provisions ....South Mkt. Whf.
Griffin, Bros. ....Fish.. ....   "   "
Godard, J. W. ......Ship chandler.........North Whf.
Gorman, Thos. ......Provisions ....Ward St.
Grant, J. Macgregor...Insurance ....Robertson Place.
Green, Nathan ......Cigars ....Prince William St.
Greenough, A. R. ....Saloon................   "   "
Gould Bros. ....Dyers......... ......   "   "
Gunn, Thos. ....Tailor................   "   "
Guthrie & Hevenor ..Bakers ....Charlotte St.
Gale, E. W. ....Insurance ....Prince William St.
Guy, Stewart & Co....Lumber ....Office, Water St.
Gardner Sewing Machine Co. ....Princess St.
Gregory, Hugh S. ......Stevedore ....North Mk. Whf.
Grace, R. ....Umbrellas, etc. ....Princess St.
Gorrie, Henry ....Tailor ....   "   "
Gavin, P. ....Liquors ....Water St.

Hall, David H. ......Sewing Machines .....Germain St.
Hill, Rowland & Co...Crockery............Mkt. Square.
Hall & Fairweather ..Flour ,..............South Whf.
Hall, Thos. H. ......Books ....King St.
Hamilton, Lounsbury
 & Co. ....Manufacturer's agents Germain St.
Hammond, E. P. ....Sewing machines .....King St.
Holden, Chas. ......Physician ....Princess St.
Hanford, Bros. ....Commission ....Nelson St.
Health Lift Co..........R. J. Moffatt, agent..Germain St.
Hanington, Bros. .....Drugs ....King St.
Hanington, Thos. B. Auctioneer..........Princess St.
Harding, Chas. E. ...Lumber yard ....Reed's Pt.
Harding, John H. ...Mining agent........Prince William St.

Harrison, J. & W. F. Flour............ ....North Mk. Whf.
Harrison, Matthew ...Boots and shoes..... Prince William St.
Hart, S. H............Cigars ....   "   "
Hammond, John ....Shoemaker..........   "   "
Hatfield & Gregory ..Ship chandlers. .....North Whf.
Hatheway, Dr. J. C...Dentist ....Germain St.
Hatheway, Dr. Can.... "   "
Hatheway, W. H......Fish...................
Hawker, W. ....Drugs ....Prince William St.
Hay, A. & J..........Jewellers............King St.
Hayes, Edw. ....Baker.................Mill St.
Hayward, S. & Co.,...Hardware ....Prince William St.
Hamilton & Gray ....Barbers......... ......   "   "
Hayward, W. H......Crockery...............   "   "
Hegan J. & J. & Co. Dry goods ....   "   "
Hevenor & Co..........Brass-founders ....Water St.
Hillman, W. H.......Silver-plater ....Charlotte St.
Hilyard, C. E. ....Commission ....North Whf.
Holstead & Co. ......Trunks ....,.........Water St.
Holstead, John S. ....Stevedore ....   "
Horn, John ....Liquors ....   "
Hubbard, W. D. W...Auctioneer ....Canterbury St.
Hughes, John E. ......Custom House broker Prince William St.
Hunter, James ...... Locksmith ....Princess St.
Hunter, Roger ....Printer ....Dock St.
Hutchings & Co .....Mattresses .... Germain St
Hutchinson, Geo Jr...Jeweller ....   "   "
Hyke, R S ....International Hotel ..Prince William St
Hinch, James ....United States Hotel...Charlotte St
Henderson, Jas D....Fruit, etc. ... .Princess St
Hancock, F M ......Fish...................St James's St

Isbister, O R S . .....Painter ....Dock St
Inches, Dr. P R ....Physician ....Germain St

Isaacs, Joseph ....Tobacco ....Mill St
Irvine, Bros. ....Grocers ....Germain St

James, S K F.........Ship broker ....Walker's Whf
Jardine & Co.........Wholesale and retail
                       grocers ....Prince William St
Jarvis, C E L .... ..Insurance ....Princess St
Jarvis, Wm M ......   "   "   "
Jack, Henry ....   "   Canterbury St
Jewellers' Hall ......   King St
Jewett Bros ....Lumber ....Office, Water St
Jewett, E D & Co..... "   "   "
Johnston, James J.....Tailor ....King St
Jones, Simeon, & Co. Bankers ....Prince William St
Jones, Thos R & Co...Dry goods (wholesale) Canterbury St
Jones, Wm..........Tailor ....King Square
Jones, Mrs.Wm......Florist...............Germain St
Jordan, Jas G ....Ship broker ....Lawton's Whf
Jordan, W W ....Dry goods ....Mkt Square

Kivenear, Wm ......Liquors ....North St
Kearns, A G .... "   ....Dock St
Kennedy, Jas ....Grocer................South Whf
Kennay, E E.........Organs, etc..........Germain St
Keohan, Thos H .....Gilder .... "   "
Kerr & Scott.........Dry goods ....Mkt Square
Kilnapp, Geo ....Shoemaker ....Germain St
King Bros ....Groceries ....Princess St
Kinnear Bros........Commission ....Nelson St
Kirk, J T & Co......Clothing ....Mkt Square
Kirkpatrick, Hugh .. "   ....King St
Knowles, S N........Trunks ....Germain St
Kavanagh, M ......Liquors...............Dock St
Knox & Thompson....Furniture.............Princess St
Knodell Geo A........Printer...............Church St

Kaye J J & J S .....Insurance...........Princess St
Kain Mrs...........Green grocer..........Prince William St

Lumber Exchange......H J Leonard, Sec...Market Square
Larter, S............Shoemaker..........Carmarthen St
Landry & Co........Organs...............King St
Lantalum, E & Co....Junk ....Union St
Lauckner, S J.......Baker..............Sydney St
Lawton, A G ....Drugs..............King St
Lawton, Edmund .... "   Prince William St
Lawton, James ....Wharfinger.........Lawton's whf
Lawton, J. Fred .....Saw manuf.........North St
Lawton, W G ....Dry goods..........King St
Livingston, John.....Watchman office.....Canterbury St
Leach, Danl E.......Billiard saloon.......Charlotte St
Lee J W............Stoves.............Princess St
Lee Mrs............Intelligence office....   "   "
Lee & Logan,.......Grocers.............Dock St
Leonard, R J........Ship broker.........Water St
Leonard S & Co......Fish & ships.........Water St
Leonard, Robt.......Sail maker..........Water St
Lester, E H ....Auctioneer ....King St
Lewin & Allingham...Hardware..........Market Square
Leitch John & Co....Woodenware........Germain St
Lewis Wm B........Ship smiths.........Britain St
Lipman S & Son.....Cigars ....King St
Littlejohn Thos......Liquors ....North wharf
Lloyd & Co.........Coal................Lloyd's wharf
Lockhart, W A ......Auctioneer ....North wharf
Logan, Lindsay & Co.Grocers.............King St
Lordly, Howe & Co..Furniture ....Germain St
Lorimer, J B.........Grocer..............Carmarthen St
Lorimer, Wm.... ...   "   South wharf
Lunney, Thos........Clothier............Dock St

Lunt, Enoch & Sons..Steamboats...........Dock St
Lyman, C E............Machinery agent.....Market square
Lear, James..........Manufacturer's agent.King St
Lyons, Ann...........Second-hand store....Germain St
Lawton, Benj.........Boat builder........Nelson St
Lordly, Mrs..........Brunswick Hotel....Prince William St

McAllister, James....Dentist..............Germain St
MacIntyre, R & Co...Paint manufacturers..Sydney St
Maclellan & Co......Bankers..............Prince William St
Magee & Co J T ....Tinware..............   "   "   "
Magee Bros..............Dry goods...........   "   "   "
Malcolm, Andrew.....Grocer..............South wharf
Manson, Jas. ....Dry goods..........King St
Maritime Warehous-
   ing & Dock Co............................Office, North Whf
Maritime Bank.......Jas Domville, M.P.,
                 President ....Mkt Square
Maritime Insurance..Office...............Pr. Wm. St.
  Co................Wm. Pugsley, Jr., Sec.
Maritime Sewing Ma-
   chine Co ....F S Sharpe..........Charlotte St
Marshall, Robt. ......Insurance agent ......Pr Wm St
Marsters, John F.....Custom-house broker.. " " "
Martin, Wm..........Clothier ....Dock
Masters, A W.......Oils, &c...........Nelson
Masters & Patterson..Provisions ....South Wh.
Maxwell, Elliott &
   Barclay ....Shipsmiths.........Nelson
Maxwell, H & Sons...Lumber ....Britain
May Jas S ....Tailor..............Pr Wm St
McAndrews, Robt....Shoemaker..........Germain St
McAndrews, R jr....Grocer..............King St
McArdle, Patk ...... "   Pr Wm St

Macfee, **Wm** ....Blacksmith............Ward St
McAvity, Thos & Son..Hardware ....Water St
McCafferty, Hugh ..Liquors ....North Whf
McAvenney, Dr A F.Dentist ....Germain St
McCourt, Patrick....Merchant ....North St
McCarthy, Timothy...Coal.................Water St
McSweeney, John....Shipowner ....Office, Union St
McClure, Jas & Co..Photographers........King St
McConnell, Jas......Boots and shoes........   "
McCormack, Jas ....Clothing ....Ward St
McCulloch, H & H A..Dry goods ....Mkt Sqr
McDonough, M.......Tailor ....Germain St
McDougall, John....Cabinet-maker........Mill St
McFarlane, John R...Soap and candles....   "
McFeeters, W W ....Clothier ....Mkt Sqr
McGivern, R P .... Coal...... ....North Whf
McGill, L .... Shoes ....Mill St
McCoskery, C A.....Liquors ....Pr Wm St
McGovern, W F........Hatter................King St
McInnes, J A.........Tailor ....Princess St
McKenzie & Scott ..Stone cutters..........Charlotte St
McLachlan, D & Sons..Boiler makers.......York Point Slip
McLauchlan, Chas &
  Son................Ship-brokers ....Office, North Wharf
McLaughlan, D J....Commission ...   .North Whf
McLean, Wm M ....Ship-broker ....Office, Peter's Whf
McLaren, L ....Physician ....Charlotte St
McLeod, Geo.........Merchant ....Water St
McMann, L & Sons..W I goods... ....Smyth St
McManus, J N ....Clothing.................Mkt Sqr
McMillan, J & A ....Booksellers & station·
                      ers ....Prince Wm St
Masonic Hall.........Ritchie's build .. ...Princess St
McSorley, J ....Groceries & liquors ..Duke St

THE GREAT FIRE IN ST. JOHN, N. B. 195

Melick, John..........Ship-broker ....Water St
Meneley, W ....Blockmaker ....Ward St
Merritt, E M........Liquors ....Dock St
Merritt, Chas........Capitalist... ....Water St
Miller, J O ....Confectioner ....Charlotte St
Milligan, J & R ...Marble-cutters ....King Sq
Mills, Alf ....Chronometers ....Pr Wm St
Mitchell, John ....Carver................
Mitchell, John ....Boots & shoes ....Pr Wm St
Moore, Wm ....Painter ....Germain St
Moore, Robt ....Auctioneer.......... King St
Moore, Ellen..........Milliner ....King St
Morrisey, W C ....Undertaker ....Charlotte St
Morrisey, Patk ....Liquors ....Duke St
Morrison, Geo jr ......Grocer................South Whf
Moulson, Jas ....Grocer ....Water St
Moynehan, Daniel....Clothing ....Dock St
Mullin, Bros .... " ....Dock St
Mullin, J J .... " ....Prince William St
Mullin, John ....Boots and shoes.........King St
 " " ....Liquors ....Dock St
Munroe, John J ......Trunks ....Princess St
McGinley, W..........Barber..............Canterbury St
McKillop & Johnston Printers .... " "
McKillop, John, & Co Geo Em Allen, agent..Prince William St
McLeod, Ezekiel ......Official Assignee ....Princess St
McAvity, John D....Grocer................. " "
Muldoon, E ....Liquors ....Duke St
McDonald & Hatfield Clothiers......,.........Dock St
McAleer, Mrs........Liquors ....Duke St
Michaels, M ....Tobacconist ....Prince William St
Major, Wm ....Toys .... " "

Nash, Thos............Ærated waters ....Dock St

New Brunswick Paper
    Co .... T P Davies, manager Canterbury St
Nicholson, J W .... Wines .... Robertson Place
Nicoud, Simon .... Jeweller .... Germain St
Nixon, Geo .... Glass and paper hang-
                       ings .... King St
Noble, Geo A .... Boot-maker .... Canterbury St
Notman, W & J .... Photographers .... Germain St
Normansell, H S ...... Victualler .... Duke St

O'Brien, Richard ..... Liquors .... Germain St
O'Gorman, John ... Groceries and liquors Dock St
Olive, W H .... Ticket agent .... Office, Prince Wm St.
O'Regan, Chas ...... Ship broker .... Office, South Whf
O'Connor, T J ...... Boarding-house .... South Whf
Osgood, S P .... Marble-worker .... King Square
Oulton, Bros .... Ship-broker .... Office, Water St
Oddfellows' Hall ....   Germain St
Odell, Mrs .... Fancy boxes .... King St
O'Hara, Chas .... Barber .... Mill St

Provincial Building
    Society ... . C W Wetmore, Pres... Prince William St
Paddock, M V .... Drugs .... Mill St
Partelow, C J ...... Liquors .... South Whf
Partelow, G L .... " .... Ward St
Patterson, W H .... Jeweller .... King St
Patton Bros .... Liquors .... Water St
Patton, Danl .... Liquors .... Dock St
Peiler, E & Bro ..... Piano dealers .... Prince William St
Pengilly, T M .... Drugs .... " " "
Pengilly, ... Oil-clothes .... " " "
Percival, Purchase &
    Co .... Fancy goods .... King St

Peters, Albert......Tanner ....Britain St
Peters, Thos W......Capitalist...........Prince William St
Phillips, Miss S......Hair worker.........Germain St
Philps, Geo.........Banker..............Prince William St
Potter, C E..........Painter..............Germain St
Potts, J W..........Grocer..............Water St
Powers, M N........Undertaker ....Princess St
Powers, Stephen.....Liquor..............Mill St
Price, James.........Tailor...............Princess St
Prichard & Son......Iron................Merritt's wharf
Pullen, James H.....Painter..............Charlotte St
Purchase, Wm......Watchmaker.........Dock St
Provincial Ins Co....H H Reeve, agent...Princess St
Pattison, Geo.......Tinsmith............Church St
Purdy, Wm H......Shipowner...........Maritime Bank

Quick, Augustus.....Ship Chandler......Water St
Quinn, P J..........Dry goods..........Market Square
Quinn, Wm..........Blocks......... ....Britain St

Rankine, Thos & Sons. Bakery.............Mill St
Ranney, H R........Insurance............Prince William St
Reeve, H H.........   "   Princess St
Ray, Chas R........Agent ....Market Square
Raymond, Thos F....Royal Hotel.........Prince William St
Redmond, P C......Clothier ....Market Square
Reid, Miss Kate.....Boarding.... ....
Reed, J & R........Shipowners..........Water St
Reed, Thos. M .....Drugs...............Market Square
Richardson, Alex & Co. Saw manufacturers...Union St
Ring, Z............Shipowner..........Maritime Bank
Ring, Allan M......Homœopathic Phys...Germain St
Rising, Wm........Grocer.... ....South wharf
Risk, John..........Broker......... ...Nelson St

Richards, John......Liquors...............Prince William St
Roberts, D V........Ship chandler............Water St
Robertson, C A......Livery Stables........King's Square
Rodgers, James......Liquors.............Charlotte St
Robertson & Corbett..Grocers, retl... .....King St
Robertson, D D & Co.Ship brokers.........Smyth St
Robertson, Geo......Whs grocer..........Water St
Robertson, Le Baron..Cigars ....Prince William St
Robertson, R & Son...Sailmakers, &c........Water St
Robinson, C & Co.....Undertakers.........Princess St
Robinson, C E.......Shipbroker ....Reed's Point
Robinson, T. W......Salt, W I Goods.......Union St
Roop, John..........Sailmaker............Water St
Ross, John...........Saloon....................Prince William St
Rogers, John........Tailor ....Prince William St
Ring, G Fred ....Commission ....Maritime Bank
Rowan, Archd ....Gasfitter ....Water St
Ruggles, St Clair ....Grocer.................Charlotte St
Runciman, John .....Gasfitter ....Water St
Rural Cemetery Co ...G Sidney Smith, Sec Princess St
Russell, J H ....Hotel ....King St
Rolph, A P.... .....Agent ....Duke St

St John Gas Light Co A Blair, Pres...........Carmarthen St
 "   Halifax Lith-
    ograph Co ....L D Clark, Manager...Church St
 "   Mutual Ins Co O D Wetmore, Sec ...Princess St
 "   Building Soc C N Skinner, Pres ...Prince William St
 "   Board of TradeS J King, Sec............Market Square
Salmon, Geo ....Variety ....King St
Sancton, G F........Tugboats..............Office, Water St
Salmon & Cameron ...Photos.................King St
Scammell Bros   ....Ship-brokers ....Water St
Scammell, C E, & Co Ship chandlers .... "   "

THE GREAT FIRE IN ST. JOHN, N. B.

Schofield & Beer .....Produce ....Walker's Whf
Schofield, Samuel ....Ship owner.............Office, Prince William
                                                                St
Scott & Binning ....Dry Goods.............King St
Scott, Geo A ....Provisions & groceries Prince William St
Scott, T A ....Saloon................Charlotte St
Seely, A McL ......Merchant ....Germain St
Seely, D J ....Comm, etc...........Water St
Sharkey, P & Son ......Clothiers............King St
Sharp & Co ....Dry Goods...........   "
Sharp, Laban L ....Jeweller ....   "
Sheraton & Skinner...Carpets ....Prince William St
Skinner, F S ....Grocer..............King St
Small & Hatheway ...Steamboats...........Office, Dock St
Small's Hall ....   Dock St
Smith, A Chipman ...Drugs ....Market Square
Smith, Geo F & Co ..Ship chandlers ......North Whf
Smith, H R ....Bookseller ....King St
Smith, Wm...........Ship-smith ....
Snider, G E ....Auctioneer...........Robertson Place
Sparrow, Geo.........Saloon...............King St
Spence, W A ....Hay..................York Point Slip
Stafford, Jno W........Liquors ....Ward St
Spring Hill Mining Co Coal................Office, Water St
Starr, R P & W F..... " ....Smyth St
Steeves Bros ....Merchants ....Prince William St
Stephens & Figgures...Grocers ....Dock St
Stephenson & McGib-
    bon ....Lumber ....Office, North Whf
Stephenson & McLean Provisions, etc ....North Whf
Stephenson, Robt....Boots and shoes.......Prince William St
Stewart, Geo, jr.......Chemist ....King St
Spencer & Wortman...Patent Medicines ....Church St

Stewart, John..........Grocer..............Carmarthen St
Stewart, Luke......Shipbroker..........North wharf
Stewart, Robt..........Toys................Germain St
Stewart & White....Furniture and Auc-
                    tioners............Prince William St
Storey, J K........Dry Goods..........King St
Strang, Saml........Commission...........South wharf
Street, A L B........Wines..................Princess St
Suffren, Geo.........Jewelry ....King St
Sweeney, John......Boots & Shoes......Prince William St
Swift & Johnson....Painters ....Church St
Saunders, James......Boots and shoes.........King St
Street, W W........Stadacona Ins Co...Prince William St

Temperance Hall....   King St
Talbert, A J.........Dry Goods............Dock St
Taylor Bros..........Shipowners.............Prince William St
Taylor & Dockrill....Grocers ....King St
Taylor J M...........Commission ....North wharf
Tennant, R H B....Shirt mfr................Prince William St
Thomas, Geo........Shipbroker............Water St
Thomas, Geo E......Adjuster...............   "   "
Thompson, G F & Sons Paint mfrs............Princess St
Thompson, Richd....Fancy goods..........Market Square
Thomson, Wm & Co...Shipbrokers ....Smyth Street
Thorne, W H & Co...Hardware ....Canterbury St
Thurgar & Russell...Liquors ....North wharf
Tippett, A P.........Manufacturers' agent.Water St
Toll, James..........Fisherman............Water St
Troop & McLauchlan.Ship chandlers........Water St
Troop & Son........Ship owners ....Water St
Trueman, James....Grocer................South wharf
Tufts, Francis.......Provisions, &c........   "   "
Tufts, H K..........Boots & shoes........Prince William St

RUINS OF CUSTOM HOUSE FROM NORTH END AND EAST SIDE.

Tufts, Samuel ......Grocer................Germain St
Turnbull & Co. ......Flour, &c.............Ward St
Turnbull, J E...... Sash factory.........Main St
Turner, James D....Oysters................ ...Water St
Turner, Joshua S....Fruit .... "   "
Thompson, Mrs Annie Boarding house........Germain St
Travers, B...........Physician ....Sydney St

Valpey, J H.........Shoe mfr...............Prince William St
Vassie, Jno & Co....Dry Goods whs........Canterbury St
Vaughan & Donovan Boots & shoes.......Princess St
Vaughan, J R......Boots & shoes........Prince William St
Venning, J H.......Engraver............. ..Germain St
Vroom & Arnold.......Ship-brokers ....Water St

Ward, Wm M......Liquors ....Charlotte St
Walker, Jno & Co...Ship chandlers........Walker's wharf
Walton, Wm.........Crockery...................King St
Waterbury, Wm.....Hardware ....King St
Waterhouse, L H....Coal....................North wharf
Watson, A C........Fruit ....Water St
Watson, W C........Shipbroker....... ......Nelson St
Watson, W H.........Groceries & liquors...King St
Watson & Co.........Books .... "   "
Watts & Turner......Dry Goods..........Market Square
Webb, W E........Cordage ....Smyth St
Welch, Richd........Tailor ....Germain St
Wetzell, R......... ...Ice-dealer ....Prince William St
Walsh, M & Son........Boots & shoes.......Reed's Pt
Wetmore C W......Broker..................Prince William St
White, G & V S....Merchants ....North wharf
White, James E......Stock broker............Prince William St
White, Thos........Confectioner ....Germain St
White & Slipp.......Flour ....North wharf

N

Wheeler, Miss........Boarding.................Charlotte St
White & Titus ....Flour, etc ....North Whf
Whiting, G H...........Agent ....Canterbury St
Whiting, W J ....Flour, etc ....South Whf
Warn, Wm & Son....Barbers ....King St
Willis, E, & Co.........Paper Collar Manufs..Canterbury St
Willis & Mott ...." Morning News".....   "   "
Wilson, Gilmour & Co Mantels ....Prince William **St**
Wilson, J N ....Liquors ....Church St
Wisdom & Fish..... ..Machinery ....Prince William St
Wishart, John ....Merchant ....Walker's Whf
Wetmore, E J ....Flock Manuf ....North St
Wills & Rubins.......Ship-smiths ....Water St
Woodworth, J L......Agent Mispeck Mills...   "
Weiscoff, Jacob......Liquors ....Prince William St
Walker, Thos........Physician ....Princess St.

Young, Adam .....Stoves................Water St
Yeats, A, & Sons ...Iron..................Union St

CHAPTER XVI.

The Oddfellows and the Fire—Relief Committee at Work—Searching out the Destitute Brethren—Helping the Sufferers—The Secret Distribution of Aid—List of Donations.

THE Society of Oddfellows is a Mutual Relief Association, one of the first duties of its members being to search out worthy and distressed brethren, and relieve their necessities. The member who neglects to carry out this noble principle, violates his obligation. The order has obtained a strong foothold in the city, and many benevolent men have joined it that they might thereby be actively instrumental in doing good to their fellowmen. The brother who suffers, and whose family requires assistance meets with no obstacle in his way, for a liberal hand almost as unseen as those blessings which come to us disguised, is near, he receives the offerings of his companions, not as charity, but as his due He is an Oddfellow, and that talismanic word is all sufficient. In *his* time he had helped many. When his turn comes the same rule is observed. The mode of giving relief is twice blessed. It is done in secret, and without ostentatious parade. No member ever deems his spirit crushed when he takes aid like this to his family. And no widow, however proud, thinks for a moment that she is accepting alms, when her immediate and other wants are supplied from the "Widows' and Orphans'" Fund. So anxious are the members to have it thoroughly understood that the aid that is given is not that which is known as charity by the outside world, but is the legitimate due of the Oddfellow, that it is expressly laid down, that no member, however well circumstanced he may be, can refuse the sums which are from time to time placed at his disposal. If he be sick he receives weekly a sick benefit allowance. This he is bound to take. He may if he choose, it is true, donate it back to any fund he likes, but it is preferred that this should not occur. In addition to money benefits the order provides something else which is more enduring than money, and which cannot be bought at any price. The member is no sooner sick than he finds a warm-hearted brother by his side, eagerly trying to interpret his wants, and perform some little act of kindness that may perhaps assuage his pain for a time. In a hundred ways this excellent society does good. The distressed are relieved, the sick are watched over, and the dead are buried. Where it is necessary, the brethren sit up during the night with the patient, and in a thousand ways the good work goes on.

Up to the present time no calamity has disturbed the prosperity of the Order in the Province. Indeed, on the contrary, its career has been wonderfully successful. The different lodges have grown prosperous, and the two principal funds, the "Widows' and Orphans'," and the "sick benefit," have for some time had quite a respectable balance at their banker's. These still remain intact, and are held strictly in trust to enable the ends of the society to be carried out when required. The recent fire, of course, destroyed a considerable amount of the property belonging to the organization; but the actual suffering was confined to the private members of the order. Many of these endured great hardships, and met with reverses of no ordinary kind. Men who had all their lives helped others, now found themselves in a moment dependent on their friends for relief for pressing needs. They had saved nothing from the burning, and some of them who were insured had trusted to offices which went down with the general crash. The result was immediately apparent. Something had to be done and at once. Their distressed and harassed members must be relieved. The whole tenets of the order demanded this. The common humanity which dwells in the hearts of so many members cried out to the afflicted ones, "Your loss is ours; we are ready to divide with you." A meeting of the leading members was had on the 22nd June, at the Oddfellow's Hall, Town of Portland, and steps were taken for the administration of immediate relief. The same spirit which actuated the brethren here seemed to prompt the members abroad to deeds which can never be forgotten while a Lodge or an Encampment exists. The chairman of the meeting, D. D G.M. Murdoch, on the evening of Friday, announced to the assembly that the Lodge in Moncton had generously contributed $25, and asked to be drawn on to the extent of one hundred dollars, and Brother White, of Bangor, had forwarded the handsome sum of three hundred dollars, and offered more if needed. Offers of assistance came from Boston, Chicago and elsewhere. These tidings were received with great joy by the members. They knew now of the sympathy which was felt for them abroad, and their first duty was the organization of an Executive Committee. This was done on motion of Bro. Vradenburgh and one member from each Lodge, and the Encampment were appointed such Committee. These were N. G. McClure, of "Siloam," N. G., Court of "Peerless," N. G., Torrance, of "Beacon," N. G., Hea, of "Pioneer," and Henry Hilyard, chairman of Portland Town Council, of the Encampment, together with Bros. Gilbert Murdoch, and Rev. G. M. W. Carey. A sub-committee was subsequently appointed on the recommendation of Bros. Vradenburgh and Kilpatrick, whose duties it would be to seek out and report to the Executive Committee any brother they found to be in distress. This Committee was very judiciously selected, and comprised the following gentlemen: R. R. Barnes, James Byers and J. Rubbins, for Beacon Lodge; H. A. Vradenburgh, W. A. Moore, and Alex. Duff, for Peerless Lodge; F. Barnes, Hamon and A. J. Smith, for Siloam Lodge; and John E. Hughes, J. A. Paul, and Jos. Wilson, for Pioneer Lodge. Action was then taken on the telegrams received, and a committee was appointed to attend to the replying of the same, and the transmission of the thanks of the St. John Oddfellows to their brethren in the United States and Canada.

The Executive and sub-Committees held a meeting immediately after the session of the General Body, and the following officers were appointed: D. D. G. M. Gilbert

THE GREAT FIRE IN ST. JOHN, N. B. 207

Murdoch, Chairman; R. Radford Barnes, Treasurer; and John E. Hughes, Secretary. The meeting then adjourned, and all future sessions of committee were ordered to take place in Room No. 9, Park Hotel, where the three heads of the Department of Relief would hold daily meetings, receive reports, and supply all assistance needed by the brethren. The system has worked admirably. The greatest secrecy has been observed, and no one outside of the Committee know even the names of the brethren who are being helped in the hour of need. The greatest care is being exercised in searching out distress, and no one can ever tell the immense amount of good which this society is doing. Relief from Lodges and brethren continue to come in rapidly, and all moneys are deposited in Maclellan & Co.'s banking house, and subject to withdrawal by check. Up to this time, Aug. 20th, the following sums have been received:—

Moncton, N.B., Prince Albert Lodge	$100 00
Bangor, Maine, Oddfellows	400 00
Boston, Mass, Howard Lodge	100 00
Charlottetown, P. E. I.	250 00
Summerside, P. E. I., Prince Edward Lodge	100 00
Fredericton, N.B., Victoria Lodge	320 00
Ontario, Grand Lodge, per J. B. King	400 00
Cannington, Ontario, Peaceful Hope Lodge	50 00
Pictou, N.S., Eastern Star Lodge	200 00
Memphis, Tenn.	300 00
Chicago, Ill.	500 00

Montreal, Quebec, Mizpah Lodge $50 00
Haverhill, Maine, Mutual Relief Lodge........... 100 00
Oldtown, Maine, Torratine Lodge 115 00
Dover, Maine, Kineo Lodge..................... 50 00
Brampton, Ontario, Golden Star Lodge.......... 50 00
Portland, Maine, Oddfellows 487 00
Oshawa, Ontario, Corinthian Lodge 50 00
Chicago, Ill., Northern Light Lodge 10 00
Portland, N.B., Peerless Lodge 140 00
Stratford, Ontario, Aaron Lodge............... 25 00
Granville Ferry, N.S., Guiding Star Lodge 30 00
Goderich, Ontario, Huron Lodge................ 80 00
Spring Hill, N.S., Eureka Lodge.... .... 50 00
Petitcodiac, N.B., E. J. Ritchie................... 1 00
Woonsocket, R. I. , Palestine Encampment....... 10 00
Lewiston, Maine, Golden Rule Lodge........... 125 00
Belleville, Ontario, Belleville Lodge............ 50 00
Stellarton, N.S., Fuller Lodge..................... 50 00
Vale Colliery, N.S., Moore Lodge 50 00
Staynor, Ontario, North Star Lodge 30 00
Eureka, California, Humboldt Lodge............ 50 00
Toronto, Canada Lodge 50 00
Rhode Island, per J. F. Driscoll 200 00
St. Catharines, Ont., Union Lodge.............. 100 00

SUPPLIES.

Charlottetown, P. E. I., Bedding and Provisions.
Portland, Maine, 4 cases Clothing

LIST OF DONATIONS.

MONEY RECEIVED.

Amherst, N S $500 00

Augusta, Me	$1000 00
Annapolis, N S	554 00
Accident Ins Co, Canada	200 00
Aberfoyle, Ontario	200 00
Armstrong, Ed (New York)	5 00
Albert Mines, N B	115 00
Ayer, Ontario	200 00
Attleboro', Mass, Methodist S School	15 00
Arichat, N S	367 00
Boston	5000 00
Boston Felt-roofing Co.	100 00
Bank of British North America	2433 33
Bathurst, N B	400 00
Brantford, Ont	1000 00
Brockville, Ont	500 00
Bath, Me	1300 00
Bayside, St Andrews, N B	90 00
Brockville, Midland Counties	200 00
Brookville, N S	5 23
Bell, Mr., Dublin, Ireland	486 67
Boardman, Gorham, New York	100 00
Boynton High School Children, Eastport, Me	2 38
Bangor, Me	7000 00
Beveridge, B. & Sons, Andover, N B	100 00
Bridgetown, N S	393 92
Bridgetown, Me., Congregational Church	14 65
Bowmanville, Ont	300 00
Beder, S, New York	4 00
Bucksport, Me	320 00
Billing, W W, New London, Conn	100 00
Burt & Henshaw, Boston	50 00
Buffalo Board of Trade	332 68
Buffalo School Children	1000 00
Borgan, Capt, ship "Tros"	5 00

210 THE GREAT FIRE IN ST. JOHN, N. B.

Baltimore, Md..	$541	97
Boston, Theatre Benefit...................................	886	03
Belfast, Me	524	00
Bowman, J L, Brownsville, Penn	25	00
Blanchard, Chas, Truro, N S	10	00
Boyd, John E, Three Rivers, Quebec............	10	00
Baird, John, & Co's Employes, Alamonte........	13	00
Berlin, Ontario	300	00
Chicago Union Stock Yards	1200	00
Chicago Clearing House................................	1000	00
Chicago Produce Exchange	1000	00
Chicago Board of Trade................................	5274	10
Chicago City...	10,000	00
Charlottetown, P E I.....................................	5000	00
Canning, N S	279	90
Clarke, Dodge & Co, N Y..............................	250	00
Canada Screw Co, Dundas, Ont	200	00
Canada Life Ins Co	500	00
Crerar, Capt W G, Pictou, N S	50	00
Carleton County Council, N B.......................	1000	00
Clarke, Ontario, Municipality of....................	400	00
Campbell, J W, Chicago, Ill...........................	50	00
Commercial Union Ins Co.............................	2500	00
Citizen's Hose Co, St Catharines, Ont	200	00
Carmody, Rev Canon, Windsor, N S.............	10	00
Caton, Judge, Ottawa, Ill..............................	50	00
Campbellton, N B	147	00
Clifton, Ont...	300	00
Chatham, N B..	700	00
Crain, Marshall, Brunswick, Me.....................	25	00
Chatham, Ont...	500	00
Chatham, Ont, Masonic Concert....................	169	18
Clinton, Me, Masonic Service	53	00
Cornwall, Ont..	300	00

THE GREAT FIRE IN ST. JOHN, N. B. 211

Dominion Government	$20,000 00
Dorchester, N B	615 00
Digby, N S	700 00
Dalhousie, N B	200 00
Dublin, Lord Mayor of	486 67
Dover, Me	245 75
Detroit, Mich	1000 00
Dominion Organ Co, Bowmanville, Ont	102 00
Dungannon, Ont., Orangemen	29 10
Elliot National Bank, Boston	647 00
Elcon, Ont	500 00
Fredericton, N B	8000 00
Fuller & Fuller, Chicago	50 00
Flanagan, R J, Newcastle, N B	5 00
Fredericton Lime Rock Church	24 00
Fowler J & G, Charlottetown, P E I	100 00
Fox J J, Magdalen Islands, per J V Ellis	25 00
Galt, Ont	500 00
Guelph, Ont	1000 00
Garringe, Wm, Chicago	4 25
Glasgow, Scotland	14,600 00
Grand Rapids "friend"	1 00
Guysborough, N S	121 00
Grace Church, Detroit, Mich	97 42
Gloucester, Mass	100 00
Grey County Council, Ont	500 00
Galt Churches	674 17
Grant, Capt I I F, Bermuda	5 00
Halifax, N S Bay	1 08
Halifax, N S	10,000 00
Hawson, John Gloucester	5 00
Ha lowell	500 00
Hamilton, Ont	13,900 00
Hamilton, C C, Cornwallis, N S	5 00

Harvey N B	$15 00
Halifax Garrison	564 71
House of Commons, Ottawa	1000 00
House of Commons Clerks	150 00
Harrington Methodist E C, Me	20 00
Howe Scale Co	250 00
Hillsboro, N B	60 00
Haldimand	200 00
Hartford, Conn	42 00
Imperial Fire Ins Co	2433 33
Johnson, John C,	250 00
International Mines, N S	100 00
Kingston, Ont	1584 00
Knox Church, Hamilton Ont	100 00
Knox Church, Woodstock, N B	185 25
Liverpool, England	14,600 00
London, Ont	5000 00
Lawrence, Mass	500 00
Liverpool, N S	819 27
Lynn, Ont, Presbyterian Church	20 20
Londonderry, N S	15 00
Lincoln Methodist E Church	5 00
Lincoln, Me	500 00
Louisburg, C B	27 00
Lawrencetown, "from a friend"	10 00
Lewiston, Me	500 00
Meahan, T, Boston	5 00
Moncton, N B	1300 00
Mount Vernon, Iowa, "friend"	1 00
Malden, Mass Congregational Church,	15 26
Maritime Association, New York	6800 00
Manchester, England	3660 00
Magee, Thos, Baie Verte	50 00
Mongaup Valley N Y, per Rev. W Ferrie	33 30

McIntosh, J S, Boston	$50 00
McLean, Rev. James, Londonderry, N S	2 00
New York, Providence and Stonington Line	500 00
New York	8500 00
Newcastle and Douglastown, N B	1000 00
North Sydney	400 00
New Haven Chamber of Commerce	823 76
Nutting, G. S. Newton Mass	1 00
New Glasgow, N S	1000 00
North British and Mercantile Ins Co	2433 33
New Bedford, Mass	500 00
New York Stock Exchange	772 50
Norwich, Ontario	100 00
Nantucket Women	50 00
Odell, D S, Eastport, Me	10 00
Ottawa Custom House Officials	180 00
Orilia, St James' Church	20 00
Oak Park, Chicago, Ill	100 00
Philadelphia	5500 00
Parrsboro, N S	100 00
Portland, Maine	6000 00
Peterboro', Ontario	3124 00
Palmer & Embury, New York	50 00
Paris, Ontario	600 00
Pictou, N S	1232 46
Port Hope, Ontario	1034 20
Port Latour, N S	68 27
Portsmouth, N.H	697 00
Peel County Council, Ontario	1000 00
Rogers, J H, Boston	100 00
Rice, N W & Co, Boston	100 00
Richibucto, N B	410 00
Rosmond Woollen Co	50 00
Raymond, Percy J, Hebron, Yarmouth	1 00

Harvey N B	$15 00
Halifax Garrison	564 71
House of Commons, Ottawa	1000 00
House of Commons Clerks	150 00
Harrington Methodist E C, Me	20 00
Howe Scale Co	250 00
Hillsboro, N B	60 00
Haldimand	200 00
Hartford, Conn	42 00
Imperial Fire Ins Co	2433 33
Johnson, John C,	250 00
International Mines, N S	100 00
Kingston, Ont	1584 00
Knox Church, Hamilton Ont	100 00
Knox Church, Woodstock, N B	185 25
Liverpool, England	14,600 00
London, Ont	5000 00
Lawrence, Mass	500 00
Liverpool, N S	819 27
Lynn, Ont, Presbyterian Church	20 20
Londonderry, N S	15 00
Lincoln Methodist E Church	5 00
Lincoln, Me	500 00
Louisburg, C B	27 00
Lawrencetown, "from a friend"	10 00
Lewiston, Me	500 00
Meahan, T, Boston	5 00
Moncton, N B	1300 00
Mount Vernon, Iowa, "friend"	1 00
Malden, Mass Congregational Church,	15 26
Maritime Association, New York	6800 00
Manchester, England	3660 00
Magee, Thos, Baie Verte	50 00
Mongaup Valley N Y, per Rev. W Ferrie	33 30

THE GREAT FIRE IN ST. JOHN, N. B.

McIntosh, J S, Boston	$50 00
McLean, Rev. James, Londonderry, N S	2 00
New York, Providence and Stonington Line	500 00
New York	8500 00
Newcastle and Douglastown, N B	1000 00
North Sydney	400 00
New Haven Chamber of Commerce	823 76
Nutting, G. S. Newton Mass	1 00
New Glasgow, N S	1000 00
North British and Mercantile Ins Co	2433 33
New Bedford, Mass	500 00
New York Stock Exchange	772 50
Norwich, Ontario	100 00
Nantucket Women	50 00
Odell, D S, Eastport, Me	10 00
Ottawa Custom House Officials	180 00
Orillia, St James' Church	20 00
Oak Park, Chicago, Ill	100 00
Philadelphia	5500 00
Parrsboro, N S	100 00
Portland, Maine	6000 00
Peterboro', Ontario	3124 00
Palmer & Embury, New York	50 00
Paris, Ontario	600 00
Pictou, N S	1232 46
Port Hope, Ontario	1034 20
Port Latour, N S	68 27
Portsmouth, N.H	697 00
Peel County Council, Ontario	1000 00
Rogers, J H, Boston	100 00
Rice, N W & Co, Boston	100 00
Richibucto, N B	410 00
Rosamond Woollen Co	50 00
Raymond, Percy J, Hebron, Yarmouth	1 00

River John, Pictou Co, N S	$381 50
Rogers' Hill, N S	40 36
Sarnia, Ontario	1050 00
St Andrews, N B	650 00
Sayer & Co, Cognac, France	200 00
Sackville, N B	312 58
Smith, Mrs M W, Ipswich, Mass	25 00
Sherbrooke, Ont	1000 00
St George, N B	200 00
Summerside, P E I	1500 00
St Thomas, Ontario	500 00
San Francisco, " Caledonia Club "	500 00
San Francisco	5600 00
Salem, Mass	770 00
St Catharines, Ont	500 00
Sargent Ignatius, Machias, Me	25 00
Springhill Mines	200 00
Sternberg, J H, Penn	25 00
Shediac, N B, Amateur Comedy Club	11 00
St Martin's, N B	302 62
St Clements, Annapolis	20 00
Springfield, Mass, Children	14 00
Storer & Son, Glasgow, Scotland	121 76
St Matthew's Church, Quebec	100 00
Stratford, Ontario	564 00
Sons of Temperance, Detroit, Michigan	300 00
Toronto, Ontario	20,000 00
Truro, N S	2000 00
Todd, Edw & Co, per J & A McMillan	25 00
Trites, J S, Sussex, N B	8 00
Thurlow F, per A O Smith	85 00
Titus, Erastus	25 00
Telegraph Operator, St John	5 00
Thamesville	2 00

THE GREAT FIRE IN ST. JOHN, N. B. 215

Uniacke, R J, Annapolis, N S	$36 20
Victoria Municipality, N B	200 00
"Valley City" Lodge I O O F, Dundas, Ontario	105 00
Whitby, Ontario	200 00
Williston, Edward, Newcastle, N B	50 00
Windsor, N S	4287 32
Woodstock, N B	200 00
" " Methodist Church	30 00
W C B & G H F, Custom House, Ottawa	2 00
Weymouth East, N S Congregational Sunday School	20 00
Welland Co, Ontario	600 00
Westmoreland Coal Company, Philadelphia	100 00
Walker, J & Co, Montreal	250 00
Wilkins, Judge, of Nova Scotia	80 00
Wentworth Co, Ontario	1000 00
Waterloo Council	200 00
Walker & Sons, Hiram	200 00
Yarmouth, N S	836 73
York County Council, Ontario	3000 00

SENT TO MESSRS. DANIEL & BOYD FOR DISTRIBUTION.

W W Turnbull, Esq, St John,	$200
G N Vanwart, Esq, Woodstock	100
Daniel Hawkesworth, Esq, Digby	20
B Rosamond, Esq, Almonte, Ont	50
Messrs. Loch & Co., New York	50
Messrs. James McLaren Nephews, Manchester	£100 Stg
Messrs. Marshall & Aston, Manchester	50 Stg

SENT TO JOHN BOYD, ESQ, FOR DISTRIBUTION.

James H Moran, Esq, St John,	$100
Hon. Isaac Burpee,	100
Thos. Furlong, Esq,	50
Canada Life Assurance Co.	500

Thomas Nelson & Son, Edinburgh.............. .... £50 Stg
This last through Dr. Rand, for teachers
Clothing from St Andrews Church, Montreal, by Rev.
   Gavin Lang, value... $280
George Sloane, Esq, New York........................U S C 50
Sent to Thos. Maclellan, Esq, from the Upper Canada
   Bible Society, the Scriptures to the value of.......... 500
Liberal offers of books were sent to J & A McMillan, to
   form the nucleus of a public library, from the publish-
   ing houses of Belford Bros, Toronto ; Harper & Bros,
   New York.
I Atwood Barnes, of New Haven, Conn, sends through
   Gen. Warner... 29
Capt. Ezekiel Jones, of Baltimore, sends by Thos S Adams, 50
From Charlotte Co, N B, Bocabec, $41 75, Elmville,
   Dig'deguash, $21 40, Bay Side, $41 10, Waweig, $16. 120
W & T Spink, Duffin's Creek, Ont, send through Hall &
   Fairweather 50
Mrs A Robinson, of Fredericton Junction, on behalf of
   the ladies of that place sends, through Everitt & But-
   ler, a parcel of children's underclothing.

SUPPLIES RECEIVED.

Amherst, N S, Supplies to value of.................... $600 00
Annapolis, N S, Supplies............................... 742 37
" Argus " H M S, by order of Admiral, provisions
Adams, Mrs Robt, Fall River, N Y, clothing
Alberton, P E I, supplies
Andover, N B, provisions
Andrews, A A, clothing
Avard, Wm, Botsford, N B, pork
Boston, Per " Gallatin " 2 cargoes supplies

RUINS OF BANK OF NEW BRUNSWICK.
Photo. by G. F. Simonson.

Boston, Per W S MacFarlane, supplies
"   Per Schr "G. G. Jewett," supplies, clothing, blankets.
Burnham & Morrill, Portland, Me, provisions
Barnard, E A & Sons, Calais, Me, provisions
Burns & Murray, Halifax, N S, supplies
Bridgetown, N S, clothing
Bangor, Me, supplies
Beals, Thos P, Portland, Me, spring-beds
Beer, E & W, Charlottetown, P E I, clothing
Boston, Y M C A, supplies
Billings & Wetmore, tea
Blouchard, Chas, Truro, N S, supplies
Bowmanville Ladies, clothing
Baird, John & Co, Almonte, clothing
Bowmanville, Ontario, 1 case clothing

Chicago Union Stockyards supplies to amount............ $3000 00
Charlottetown, P E I, supplies and clothing
Charlottetown, P E I, ladies, 2 cases clothing
Cummings, Wm & Sons, Truro, N S, supplies
Calkin, B H, Kentville, N S, clothing
Christian Temperance Union, Moncton, N B, three cases clothing
Cowdry, E T & Co, Boston, Mass, supplies
County Line, P E I, supplies
Christie, Brown & Co, Toronto, supplies
Campbellton, N B, supplies
Coats, J P, Chicago, clothing
Chatham, N B, supplies
Cambridge Queen's Co, N B, 47 Blankets
Crawford, Jas, & Co, Toronto, supplies

Dorchester, N B supplies
Derring, Milliken & Co, Portland, Me, two cases blankets
Digby, N S, supplies
Darling, Adam, Montreal, supplies

Dover, Me, supplies
Ellsworth, Me, ladies seven packages clothing
Fredericton, N B, two cases cooked provisions
Fredericton, ladies, five cases clothing
Fredericton, N B, large quantities supplies
Fletcher & Co, Portland, Me, provisions

Galbraith, Christie & Co, Toronto, supplies

Halifax, N S, 2525 blankets
Halifax, N S, large quantities supplies
Halifax, N S, 50 stoves
Halifax, N S, ladies' committee, supplies
Humphreys, N, Petitcodiac, N B, supplies
Herritt, T,   "   "   supplies
Heney, A, New York, supplies
Hampton, N B, supplies
Hallowell, clothing
Harris, J & C, Moncton, supplies
Hay, R & Co, Toronto, carload bedsteads
Hillsborough, N B, supplies
Harvey, N B, supplies
Howe Spring Bed Co, New York, 50 beds
Jennings & Clay, Halifax, clothing
Jones, D F, & Co, Gananoque, Ont, supplies
Jodoin & Co, Montreal, 15 stoves
Kentville, N S, supplies
Lockport, N S, clothing
Lewis, J T, & Co, Portland, Me, clothing
Lawrencetown, N S, 29 packages clothing
Lawrencetown, N S, J W James, clothing
Leavitt, F A, Portland, Me, one tent
Leath & Gore, Portland, Me, 16 boxes soap
Londonderry, N S, supplies

Lewis, W N, Boston, one gross liniment
Lukeman, John R, Salem, Mass, supplies
Lugsden, J & J, Toronto, 25 straw hats
Moncton, N B, supplies
Montreal, per Hon P Mitchell, 17 carloads supplies
Montreal, large quantity supplies
Montreal, 36 packages clothing
Milltown, N B, provisions
Moss, S H & J, Montreal, 2 cases clothing
Malone Bay, clothing
McGuiness, P, & Co, Montreal, one bale blankets
McLean & Blaikie, Londonderry, N S, supplies
New York, supplies
Newcastle & Donglastown, N B, supplies
North Sydney, cargo of coal
New Haven United Workers, clothing
Norcross, Miller & Lee, Boston, clothing
Ottawa Ladies' Committee, supplies
O'Brien, James, Montreal, clothing
Portland, Maine, large quantities supplies
Primrose & Co, J W M, Halifax, 5 barrels flour
Power, J F & Co, Montreal, 50 barrels flour
Paul, M L, Syracuse, supplies
Pierce, E, and Co, per "Gallatin," furniture
Piper, Henry, Toronto, supplies
Philadelphia Maritime Exchange, clothing
Quebec, supplies
Quincy, Ill, 50 barrels meal and 50 barrels flour
Riddell, John, Montreal, clothing
St. Andrews, N B, supplies
Sackville, N B, supplies
" " stoves
Shaw Bros, St John, N B, bread
Scotch Bakery, St John, N B, bread

Sussex, N B, 1 carload provisions
Smith, Mrs. M W, Ipswich, Mass, supplies
Saratoga, N Y, supplies
Salem, Mass, supplies and clothing
Salem, Mass, "Fraternity," clothing
Salem Y M C A, supplies
Shediac, N B, supplies
Stewart, C J, Amherst, N S, supplies
St Clements, Annapolis, N S, supplies
Saratoga Springs, N Y, clothing
Toronto, Ontario, large quantity of supplies
Toronto Ladies' Committee, quantity of supplies
Tupper, Hon Chas, C B, Toronto, supplies
Toronto Coal Mining Co, 250 tons coal
Temple, Mrs, Fredericton, N B, clothing
True, Geo W, Portland, Me, 5 barrels flour and 5 barrels meal
Thompson & Bligh, Halifax, N S, supplies
Truro, N S, supplies
Thurston, Hall & Co, Cambridgeport, Mass, 5 bls flour
Unitarian Parish, Portsmouth, N H, clothing
Upper Canada Furniture Co, Bowmanville, 50 bedsteads
Upper Clarence, N S, Supplies
Unitarian Society of Dedham, Mass, supplies
Upper Canada Trundle Bed Co, beds
Vincent & McFate, St John, shoes and slippers
Wetmore Bros, London, Ontario, 20 bls oil
Wilson Packing Co, New York, 50 cases beef
Woodstock, N B, per Connell & Hay, supplies
Woodstock, N B, supplies
Wolfville, N S, clothing and supplies
Warman Bros, London, Ontario, 20 bls flour
Waterman, Bros., London, Ont., 20 bbls. oil
Woodcock, A, Toronto, supplies

Yarmouth, N S, supplies
Y. M. C. Union, Boston, 6 cases clothing

THE PROPERTY OWNERS.

The following is a list of persons whose properties were destroyed. Where the number of houses owned by each is more than one, it is so stated:

NORTH MARKET SLIP.

Heirs Dougald McLauchlin
G Sidney Smith

Heirs R L Hazen
G W Gerow

ORTH STREET.

Wm Kievenar (2)

SMYTH STREET.

Geo Moore
Heirs P McManus
P McCourt
P McDevitt
Thos Sheehan
Peter Bone
Mrs Kievenar

Maloney
D Rooney
J Dunlop
J C Brown estate
Heirs Chas Brown
Margaret S Robertson (6)
Mrs Espy

DRURY LANE.

Mrs Ann Leonard
Heirs John Ansborough
John Allen
Wm County
Jas Morrow
John Donovan
Heirs Henry Graham (2)
Heirs Thos Daley

Heirs Helen O'Leary
Thos Hourihan
Ed Mullin (2)
John Holland
Catherine Healy
Margaret McCarron
Heirs John Bryden

MILL STREET.

Mrs Mary Ann Carleton
W Finn
Robert Grace (2)
John Lloyd (2)
Heirs John Frost
Heirs E Lawrence
Thos A Rankine
Thos A and Alex Rankine
John Bellony

Thos A Peters (2)
Mrs Ann Leonard
A G Kearns
John Allen
J Brittain
James Morrow
John Ryan
Ed Hayes

GEORGES STREET.

Heirs Peter Sinclair
Thos A and Alex Rankine
Michael Burke

S R Foster
Michael Dineen
Heirs Wm Sullivan (2)

DOCK STREET.

John McSweeney (2)
John O'Gorman
Heirs B Ferguson
Johanna R Ritchie
Heirs F W Hatheway
Heirs Wm Hammond
James Dever
Heirs John Stanton
Henry Melick
Heirs John Melick
Robt Robertson
Heirs Hugh Johnston

Thomas Parks (2)
Heirs —— Robertson
W F Butt
Otis Small
J W & G H Lawrence
Trustees Varley School
R Grace (2)
S J & W D Berton
Heirs Elijah Barker
D Moynehan
Joshua Corkery
John Gallivan

HARE'S WHARF.

Margaret Hare.

ROBERTSON PLACE.

Mary Allan Almon.

FIRE PROOF ALLEY.

Heirs of Benjamin Smith. | Wm Carvill.

THE GREAT FIRE IN ST. JOHN, N. B.

NORTH MARKET WHARF.

Eliza Robertson.
John Kirk.
D. J. McLaughlin.
J. Hendrick.
R. P. McGivern.
Heirs of John Duncan.

George F. Smith.
Heirs of D. J. McLaughlin.
J. V. Thurgar.
Hannah A. Bates.
Diocesan Church Society.
Heirs of George Bonsall.

NELSON STREET.

Jane Inches
Jos R Stone
James Lawton
Eliza Robertson
John Fitzpatrick
B R Lawrence
Mrs William Hammond
Ed T B Lawton

Wm Scovil
W H Brown
Chas Lawton
Heirs of B Smith
Heirs of D J McLaughlin
Fred Fitzpatrick
George Carvill
Benj Lawton

SOUTH WHARF.

Heirs H W Wilson
Heirs of Thos Merritt
J H Allen
Jas Trueman
G C Wiggins
W Scovil
Barbour Bros

Heirs T Gilbert
G S DeForest
H & B S Gilbert
J E Masters
Heirs I L Bedell
J & R Reed
Heirs of B Smith (2)

WARD STREET AND WALKER'S WHARF.

Heirs of B Smith
W B Smith
G S DeForest
Mrs Catherine McNamara,
M Lawrence
John Mitchell
Gallagher Young

Turnbull & Co
Heirs of J Walker
H & B S Gilbert
B R Lawrence
Wm Breeze
Wm M B Firth (3)
William Meneally
W T Betts

JOHNSON'S WHARF.

Hall & Fairweather
Heirs John Walker

John Wishart
W A Robertson

DISBROW'S WHARF.

Magee Bros.

WATER STREET.

Sarah A and Jane Tisdale
Wm B Jack
W W Turnbull
James Harris & Co
G Carvill
The City (3)
Henry Brennan
W A Robertson
Mrs Louisa Hanford (2)
Alex Keith (2)
James E Holstead
Henry Vaughan
Archibald Rowan
Bank of New Brunswick
Heirs E Stephens (2)
Heirs Richard Sands
Heirs Andrew Hastings

B R Lawrence
B S & H Gilbert
Allan Brothers
James Ferrie
Heirs John Walker, (3)
Magee Bros
Chas Merritt (4)
J & R Reed (2)
Geo McLeod
Heirs Wm McKay
Norris Best
Heirs G L Lovitt
Geo G and Thos Chubb,
Thos Furlong
Stephen Whittaker
Heirs Wm Parks
Heirs J M Robinson

MARKET SQUARE.

Heirs J M Walker
Heirs John Wilmot
Daniel & Boyd

Heirs Thomas Merritt
J N McManus
J. Melick
Richard Thompson

PRINCE WILLIAM STREET.

Ed Sears
The City (4)
Henry McCullough
Maritime Bank
Heirs John Gillis
Mrs. John Kinnear
Isaac Burpee
Heirs John Ennis
Heirs Noah Disbrow
Heirs S Nichols (2)
John Armstrong
L H Vaughan
J L Dunn
John Anderson
J & A McMillan
Heirs of J M Walker
F A Wiggins
Heirs Jane Boyd

Bank of Nova Scotia
Maria S Bayard
A B Barnes
Heirs Geo. L. Lovitt
Hugh Davidson
Nathan Green
Susan and Phœbe Purdy
Mrs John McIntyre
Patrick McArdle
Wm Cotter (2)
Heirs F Ferguson
T F Raymond
Thos McAvity
Heirs Thomas Pettingill
Heirs James Pettingill
Heirs Ed Finnegan
Robt S Hyke
John Foster (2)

John McCoskery
Moses Lawrence
Chas King
Geo A Freeze
Robt Pengilly
Heirs Thomas Reed
Heirs Wm McFadden
C E Robinson
C E Harding
Joggins Coal Mining Association
W H Hatheway
Wm Blizzard
Heirs Wm McKay
Rev Wm Scovil
J J Kaye
Dominion of Canada (2)
Hanford Estate (2)
P Morrissey
Wm Finn
Ann Thomas

John Tilton
Henry Vaughan and heirs Simonds & Vaughan
Ellis & Armstrong
Chas Merritt (3)
Charlotte Gibbons
Bank of New Brunswick
Heirs H Chubb (4)
Heirs Ambrose Perkins
Heirs Wm Major
Heirs J M Walker
Rich S & J S Boes DeVeber
Jessie H Nickerson
Alex Jardine
Heirs Richard Sands
John Hegan
Heirs John Hastings
Robt Douglas
Heirs Benjamin Longmuir
Daniel & Boyd

CANTERBURY STREET.

W G Lawton
John Vassie
A G Bowes
Jas O'Connor
Heirs W H Owens
Sarah Owens
A R Wetmore
Jas Walker

Willis & Mott
North British and Mercantile Insurance Co
Thos R Jones (3)
Geo V Nowlin
Geo. Moore
Heirs D J McLaughlin

GERMAIN STREET.

Heirs John Ward (2)
Heirs W Tisdale
Jas E White
Rector and **Wardens Trinity** Church
John A Anderson
D J McLaughlin, Jr (2)
Ed Sears (2)
Trustees Wesleyan Methodist Church (2)
Trustees St John Grammar School (2)

Trustees St Andrew's Kirk
Victoria Hotel
Otis Small and Moses Lawrence
Heirs Edwin Bayard
H R Ranney
John McMillan (2)
Heirs Robertson Bayard
Heirs Sam'l Seeds (3)
Trustees Home for the Aged
Trustees Germain Street Baptist Church (2)
John Harding (2)

John Chaloner
Mrs Duncan Robertson
Heirs Wm Hammond (3)
Wm Thomas
W C Perley
Chas Phillips
Heirs G E S Keator
Jas Miller (2)
Caleb Larkins
Heirs Donald Cameron
Wm J Stevens
Heirs Alex Balloch
Mrs Samuel Seeds
J W Climo
Chas R Ray
J R Ruel
Mrs H Johnston
Heirs Thos Parks (2)

Heirs Ed Ketchum
Heirs Lachlan Donaldson (2)
Wm Bayard
Alex Sime
Jos Bullock
Jas Lawton
Wm Davidson
Academy of Music Co
Wm Breeze
J C Hatheway
Geo V Nowlin (3)
Heirs Dan Leavitt
James H Peters (4)
Trustees Mrs Alexander
Robt Robertson
Heirs D J McLaughlin
S K Foster (3)

CHARLOTTE STREET.

Chas Merritt
John Holden
James Vernon
Dr L McLaren
Dr John Berryman
Mary L Wheeler
P Doherty
James Mason
Mrs T Coughlan
S Corbitt
S Hayward
Mary A and heirs Samuel Crawford
Eliza Chapman
Johannah Dacey and heirs
Timothy Dacey
Thos Welly
John Farren
Heirs Benj Longmuir
Heirs Francis McAvenney
Heirs Wm Potts
C E Harding
Pugsley, Crawford & Pugsley
Wm Breeze

R P McGivern
Jas Vernon
Agnes Stewart (2 houses)
John Marvin
S Smith
John Watson
Charlotte Stevens
T McAvity (2)
W McDermott
Alexander and heirs R Jardine
Maritime Sewing Machine Co
A McDermott
J Fisher, Sr
J McGivern
Dominion of Canada
John Sandall
J D McAvity
H Duffell
Mary and heirs Peter Fleming (2)
M Flood
Kate Mulherrin
H Maxwell (3)
Wm White
W H Harrison

THE GREAT FIRE IN ST. JOHN, N. B. 227

John Fielders
Wm McAuley
Jane Murray
Eliza McLaughlin
Louisa Hanford
John D Devoe (3)
Nancy Hazen
Ann D Thompson
James Williams
Wm Davidson
Mary Earley
Mrs Fred James
P Besnard Sr
Geo Stockford

John Lawson
John Nugent
D Mullin
Rev A Wood
James H Pullen
John Berryman Sr (3)
J O Miller
Jas Langell
Corporation Trinity Church (3)
G Prescott (3)
J Guthrie and B Hevenor
G Williams
J D Gaynor (2)
John Winters (2)

SYDNEY STREET.

Dr Travers
W J B Marter (2)
T C Humbert
John McBrine
Roman Catholic Bishop (3)
Geo V Nowlin (2)
Ed McAleer
E Kinsman
Trustees Reformed Presbyterian
    Church
W S Marvin
William Davidson
John Anderson
Susan Dobson
William Meneally
George J Coster
R Gregory
M Flood
J E Armstrong
Wm Wedderburn
N Best
H Thomas
John Murray
J Knox
Wm Burns (2)
Robt McKay
E M S Stewart (3)
Wm Vassie
T W Peters

E L Perkins
R Rolston
Sarah McRory
John Carney
Alex Kearns
Ellen Mooney
Coldwell Howard
Jas Lemon
Sarah Taylor
Elizabeth Robbins (2)
J D Vanwart
Ann Wane (2)
Dominion of Canada
John McAnulty
Alex McDermott
Mary Clark and heirs
John Clark
C Longstroth
R W Crookshanks
E L Perkins
Chas Hillan
S K F James
Margt Maloney
W Morrison
M McAleer (2)
S J Lauckner
J Milligan (2)
John Gray
Trustees St David's Church

E Richey
Rebecca Schoular and heirs
David Marshall
L S Currie
James Vernon (2)

Wm B Aitkin
Robt McIntyre & Co
J L Taylor
D J Laughlan
Henry Jack

HORSFIELD STREET.

J H Pullen
Mrs W McKay (2)
P Besnard (2)
John Lowe (2)
Ellen McAvenney
John Nugent (2)
Sophia McLean

Mary Durant
Thos Bedell
Catherine Noyes
M Perry
Knox & Thompson
W Breeze

HARDING STREET.

R Carleton
Mary Donahey
Sarah Gillis (2)
John Wilson (2)
Mary Richard

Neil Morrison
Geo Henderson
James O'Connor (3)
Wm McDermott (2)
Heirs J W Young (2)

PAGAN PLACE.

Joseph Sulis
Louisa Donald
Mrs Emma Allison
A L Palmer

Moses Lawrence (2)
R Leonard
Chas S Taylor
S G Blizard

ST. ANDREW'S STREET.

T W Peters (2)
R Gaskin
H Aldbone
John Kee (2)
James Gilmour
James Ritchey
John Ritchie

James Sterling (2)
John Wishart
Margaret Suffren
E Woodley
John McCaffery
Robert Wetsell

CARMARTHEN STREET.

Ann Cronin
Elizabeth and Samuel Gardner
Heirs Aaron Eaton (3)
H A Austin
George E King

Charles **Barnes**
Mary A Ward
E E Lockhart
James Adams (3)
J D Lorimer

Samuel Ferguson (2)
Geo P Johnston (3)
Hugh Bell
Catherine Bonnell
James Hill (2)
W D Carron
James Muldoon
Gas Light Co.
Trustees Methodist Church
Trustees Orphan Asylum
Margaret O'Neil (2)
James McKinney
James Crockford
Mary Ann Pointer
Daniel Smith
John Kirk (2)
Samuel Dunham (two)
Alex Steen
S Scribner
Daniel Doyle
Mary Doyle
John Kirkpatrick

— Smith
H S Normansell
Jane Carson
Catherine Nagle
R Evans
John Richey
Thomas Rankine
Thomas Doyle
John Wilson
Chas McLean
J Henderson
H Henderson
Rev J R Narraway
Andrew Kenney
L H Waterhouse
Wm Nixon
D Driscoll
R Wetsell
George Sparrow & J S Richardson
Wm Finley

WENTWORTH STREET.

E E Lockhart
Thos Dobson
G Sparrow
George Blatch
C Sparrow (2)
J W Fleming
H Whiteside
John Fitzpatrick
H Coffey
M Barnes
C Flaherty
C E Sulis

B P Price (3)
James Moulson (2)
John A Anderson
B McDermott
R B Emerson
J T Barnes
George Doherty (2)
C Cathers (2)
Alex Steen
William Hill (2)
Knox and Thompson (4)
John Carr

MAIN STREET.

John E Turnbull (4)
John Woodley
J G Jordan
A Steen (2)
J Tole
James O'Brien
Wm Bowden

Wm Coxetter & Michael Tucker
T M Reed
Sarah L Collins (2)
D McDermott
P Vanhorn
James Mahoney (3)
James Moulson

E Richey
Rebecca Schoular and heirs
David Marshall
L S Currie
James Vernon (2)

Wm B Aitkin
Robt McIntyre & Co
J L Taylor
D J Laughlan
Henry Jack

HORSFIELD STREET.

J H Pullen
Mrs W McKay (2)
P Besnard (2)
John Lowe (2)
Ellen McAvenney
John Nugent (2)
Sophia McLean

Mary Durant
Thos Bedell
Catherine Noyes
M Perry
Knox & Thompson
W Breeze

HARDING STREET.

R Carleton
Mary Donahey
Sarah Gillis (2)
John Wilson (2)
Mary Richard

Neil Morrison
Geo Henderson
James O'Connor (3)
Wm McDermott (2)
Heirs J W Young (2)

PAGAN PLACE.

Joseph Sulis
Louisa Donald
Mrs Emma Allison
A L Palmer

Moses Lawrence (2)
R Leonard
Chas S Taylor
S G Blizard

ST. ANDREW'S STREET.

T W Peters (2)
R Gaskin
H Aldbone
John Kee (2)
James Gilmour
James Ritchey
John Ritchie

James Sterling (2)
John Wishart
Margaret Suffren
E Woodley
John McCaffery
Robert Wetsell

CARMARTHEN STREET.

Ann Cronin
Elizabeth and Samuel Gardner
Heirs Aaron Eaton (3)
H A Austin
George E King

Charles Barnes
Mary A Ward
E E Lockhart
James Adams (3)
J D Lorimer

Samuel Ferguson (2)
Geo P Johnston (3)
Hugh Bell
Catherine Bonnell
James Hill (2)
W D Carron
James Muldoon
Gas Light Co.
Trustees Methodist Church
Trustees Orphan Asylum
Margaret O'Neil (2)
James McKinney
James Crockford
Mary Ann Pointer
Daniel Smith
John Kirk (2)
Samuel Dunham (two)
Alex Steen
S Scribner
Daniel Doyle
Mary Doyle
John Kirkpatrick

— Smith
H S Normansell
Jane Carson
Catherine Nagle
R Evans
John Richey
Thomas Rankine
Thomas Doyle
John Wilson
Chas McLean
J Henderson
H Henderson
Rev J R Narraway
Andrew Kenney
L H Waterhouse
Wm Nixon
D Driscoll
R Wetsell
George Sparrow & J S Richardson
Wm Finley

WENTWORTH STREET.

E E Lockhart
Thos Dobson
G Sparrow
George Blatch
C Sparrow (2)
J W Fleming
H Whiteside
John Fitzpatrick
H Coffey
M Barnes
C Flaherty
C E Salis

B P Price (3)
James Moulson (2)
John A Anderson
B McDermott
R B Emerson
J T Barnes
George Doherty (2)
C Cathers (2)
Alex Steen
William Hill (2)
Knox and Thompson (4)
John Carr

MAIN STREET.

John E Turnbull (4)
John Woodley
J G Jordan
A Steen (2)
J Toly
James O'Brien
Wm Bowden

Wm Coxetter & Michael Tucker
T M Reed
Sarah L Collins (2)
D McDermott
P Vanhorn
James Mahoney (3)
James Moulson

Jane Halcrow
L Markie
G J Sulis (2)
Wm Lewis
J & R Magee
J W Nicholson
G R Bent (2)
A L Rawlins
D Knight
F Mahoney
Ed Thurmott

Wm McKinney
Archibald Dibblee
George Thomas
John Guthrie
Mary Ann Ratcliff
James McKinney
O V Troop
Rector and Wardens St James' Church
C Langstroth
Andrew Armstrong

BRITAIN STREET.

Sarah McFadden
Jane Barbour
John Collins
John Scott
H Spears
Thos Miller
Thos McCullough
Thos Crozier
Jas Price
Wm J Colson
P McGonagle
C Larkins
H W Purdy
E Murray
Heirs D Hatfield
Jas McAvity
Wm Furlong
John Abbott
John Bartlett
Albert Peters
Mrs O'Keefe
Geo Garraty
B Coxetter
E Thompson
Margaret McPartland
F Stewart
D Jordan (2)
Wm Ennis
Jas Nicholson
Robt Barbour
Albert Betts
W H Purdy

C Merritt (3)
Geo W Belyea
J Jardine
Jas Gorman
J Moore (2)
Lawrence McMann (2)
J Packthall
F M Hancock
C J Ward
Mrs Jas Bell
W H Hatheway
John Hutchinson
Peter Besnard, Sr (3)
R Johnston (2)
J Hayes
Neil Hoyt
N Carroll
M Barnes
Heirs L H DeVeber (2)
F Pheasant
A Doyle
R Dalton
W J Pratt
D Robinson
W A Magee
S McGarvey
Bridget Murphy
Thos Bisset
Bridget Farren
J George
Ed Duffy
J E Turnbull (2)

E Thompson (2)
John Moran (2)
John Crowley
W H Quinn (3)
F S Williams (2)
John Wishart

D J Schurman
Mary McCurdy
H Maxwell
S G Blizard
Thos Robinson

ST. JAMES STREET.

O Cline
R Cline
J Kemp
John Bridges
W I Whiting
J McLarren
E Thompson
Park McManus
Wm Leahy
S Rutherford
John Doody
John Sherrard
John Knowles
John Sears (3)
C Cain
Wm Furlong (2)
Bridget Murphy
John Watson
Thomas Viall
Geo Young
Jas Ellis
E D Perkins (2)
Wm Simpson
Alice McKean
P McGonagal
M Burk
Mrs Thos Hanlon
Samuel Fisher
Eliza Wilson
John Wilson, jr
Jas A Campbell
D Sullivan
R Holmes
C Moriarty
John Runciman
Robt J Caldwell
W Casey

School Trustees
Rev William Scovil
John Fisher
John Cain
Rev Wm Scovil and Trustees of
  Wiggins' Orphan Asylum
J Drake
Wm Duffell
Thos White
Thos Pike
F P Robinson
John Winters
Jas Price
Wm Gilfillan
Jane White (2)
Wm Russell
Mrs David Millar
Heirs Thos King
P Condon
Jos Akroyd
David Stewart
Patrick Ferrie
Chas Osburn
Elizabeth Spence
Rev M Ritchey
Thos Kedey
Wm Lewis (3)
M Flood
John Wishart
John S Mullin
John Littler
Heirs Daniel Hatfield
Heirs F Dibblee
Purdy heirs
B Coxetter
T G Merritt
Heirs R Sands

Caleb Larkins
T F Raymond
Mrs Francis Clementson
D J Schurman

Thos Littlejohn
Chas Sinclair
John Callaghan
T M Reed

PITT STREET.

Silas H Brown
Henry Lawlor
James Cummings
F Jordan
Rebecca Fisher

Ed K Fisher
D S Robinson
James Hewitt
C Lawton (2)

SHEFFIELD STREET.

Gilbert estate
Matthew Thompson (2)
James Carr
E Vanhorn
James Brown
Heirs Geo McKelvie (2)
John A Anderson
R Robertson
Margaret Hennigar
Joseph Kimpson
Ferguson & Rankine (2)
Y M C Association
M McVane (2)
Robert Cunniff
John Kirk
Alex Harvey
Jane Wasson
Mrs. P. Riley
J H Anthony
John McCabe (2)
John Woodburn
C O'Keefe
Richd McCluskey

John Fisher
A McDermott
Purves & Moore
J Drake
E Magee
John Porter
Rector and Wardens St James' Church
Stephen & James Oakes
S Dunham
Mary Ann Pointer
Catherine O'Neal (2)
Daniel Smith
Joseph McCullough
McKelvey heirs
Trustees Methodist Church
David Dodge
Elizabeth Nixon
Lewis Wheaton
Geo Anning
Joseph Sulis
Jas Vanhorn

QUEEN SQUARE.

Thos Furlong
Isaac Woodward
John Boyd
Geo B Cushing
R Cruikshanks

A L Palmer
Jas Manson (2)
W B Smith
John Horn
J W Barnes

VIEW FROM QUEEN SQUARE.

GERMAIN STREET, SHOWING VICTORIA HOTEL.

THE GREAT FIRE IN ST. JOHN, N. B.   233

D Robertson (2)
Mrs Charles Brown and heirs of Chas Brown
John Stewart

F. Tufts
John Tucker
H. Jack
E. L. Jewett.

QUEEN STREET.

John Foster
R Longmaid
Thos P Davies
H. Hawkins
Jessie Day
Mrs Alex Dalsell
J H Harding
J U Thomas
Joseph Sulis
Geo Riley and heirs
Robt Riley (2)
J O'Connell
Wm Davis and heirs
John McNichol
Mary Bersay
John R McFarlane
James McCart (2)
Ed Edson
Mrs Jane McPherson
Heirs John Thomas
Hugh Kelly
S Benterell
John Hamilton
Margaret Homer,
Heirs John Roberts
Geo S Fisher
Robt Turner
John McBrine (2)
R Cassidy (2)
Thos Jordan
D. S. Kerr
John Pettingill
C Flood (2)
Geo Suffren
Chas E Raymond

John Fitzpatrick
James Gallagher
Geo J. Nixon
A. Quick
Heirs R Bayard
R J Leonard
G F Soley (2)
Alex Steen
Hugh Carswell
Mrs John Millidge
H S Normansell
Heirs John Whitne
John Wilson, jr
John Wilson (2)
Margaret and heirs Joseph Hanley (2)
Thos Doyle
Andrew Evans
Robt Marshall
Wm Black
F M Hancock
Alex McKelvy
Wm Pike (2)
Heirs D J McLaughlin,
J McFarlane
Thomas McAvity, jr
Robt Hickson
M Francis
D Brown
Mary Crothers and heirs John Crothers
Ann Thomas
Andrew Keohan
Mary Williams
John Scallon (2)
Simon Leonard

MECKLENBURG STREET.

Jas Hutchinson and heirs Jos Stevenson (2)

Richard Longmaid
H Vaughan

P

John Vassie
Chas Maclean
Heirs James Whitney
Margaret Hillman
C McIver
Chas Whitney
John Dyers
Mary Dockrill
W M Jordan
Jas Emerson
Jas McNicholl
Heirs Joseph Atkins
Mary Ann McLean
S L Lewin
T W Seeds
Benj Dodge
John Ennis
John Dick
James Woodstock

Phœbe Bookhout
Martin Burns
Edward Purchase
Thos Dobson
Ann Atkins
Jas Knox
Francis Gallagher
Mathew Steen
Wm Causey
Geo V Nowlin
Andrew Armstrong
W McVay
Wm McKeel
Heirs Aaron Eaton
John Magee
William Magee
J. W Nicholson
J R Armstrong

DUKE STREET.

P McArdle
Peter Flannigan
Mrs Francis Ferguson (2)
Joseph Bell
John McSorley (3)
Heirs R Bayard (2)
A Blain
Peter Besnard (3)
Mrs Livingstone
Mrs W Fraser
John Marven
S Tufts
J Shannon
O Bailey
Trustees Madras School
Seely & Besnard
R W Crookshank
Susan Stephenson
B Brennan (2)
Robt Thomson (2)
Samuel Gardner
Andrew Gilmour
R Robertson, **jr**
S K Brundage

Joseph Henderson
H Henderson
Wm H Randall
Wm McBay
J Wilkins, sen
J Wilkins, jr
Wm Francis
James Adams
Mrs Gilchrist
James Saunders
Wm Whitney
Sarah Partelow
Ed Purchase (2)
Robt S Jones
Geo Sparrow
Mary Ann McLean (2)
M Morrison
Charlotte Jones
Michael Burns
P Bushfan
William Wright
Heirs William Melody
Margaret Hartness
E Burnside

THE GREAT FIRE IN ST. JOHN, N. B. 235

Howard D. Troop
John Marven
John Cook
James Adams
Sarah Ferguson
Heirs Edward Brundage (2)
W Stephens
Jacob Seely
Trustees Christian Church
John Wishart
L A Waterhouse
James Milligan
Sarah Jane Ferguson
George A Thompson
John Richards

W F Butt
Arthur Daniel (2)
Heirs Daniel Culbert
James Vernon
Mrs. Earley
Sarah Gillis
J. O'Connell
Peter Dearness
Heirs Michael McGuirk (2)
Ann Jane Ritchie
Geo Stockford
Caroline Wood
Hugh Davidson
Susan Chittick (2)
J & R Reed

ORANGE STREET.

Wm Meneally
John Smith
Andrew Gray
M. Hennigar (2)
Andrew Kinney (2)
Jas Adams
W R MacKenzie
D G MacKenzie
W E Vroom
G E King
H D Troop
C W Weldon
A C Smith
R R Sneden
E J Barteaux
Joseph Prichard (4)
Jane Cook
James McLean
Catherine Allen

Thomas Johnston
Henry Lawlor
B Murphy
James E Whittaker
J R Woodburn
Z G Gabel
James Estey
Charles Drury
Emma J Daley
John Sweeney
J W Hall
G McLeod
J A Venning
R Blair
Margaret Sinnott
Heirs R McAfee
Heirs Wm Bailey
James Morrison
Heirs P Williams

PRINCESS STREET.

Alexander Barnhill
W J Ritchie
E Thompson
Patrick Bradley
J C Hatheway

E Sears
P Fitzpatrick
Wm Burtis
A Buist
Jas Hunter

Knox & Thompson
John Burk
J H Lee,
Thos Rogers
John Anderson (2)
John Murphy
B Bustin
G Bent
Margaret Hunter
John Nugent
Mary Craig
James H Bartlett
Mrs David Miller
Thos Miller
James Bustin
Fred Dorman
O Doherty
Adam Young
C E Robinson
John Healey
John Gardner
Mrs Mary A & E E Lockhart (2)
Heirs of Geo A Lockhart
R W Thorne
H Williams
W Sandall
Robert McAndrews
James Robinson
Susan and heirs J Johnston
Ann Hamilton and heirs Clara Dean
William Fogg
Mary Ann Ellsworth
J V Troop
Simeon Jones
Alex Lockhart
Trustees Centenary Church (2)
Heirs John Mason
Heirs Thomas P Williams
W C Drury
J A Godsoe
D W Scammell
G Henderson
A W Whitney
T D Wilson

Mrs Ellen Smith
John Doherty
Trustees J S Turner
Thomas Bustin
P Halpin
B Paterson
Barbara Clark
W C Godsoe
James Trueman
Ed Willis
Joseph Miller
Robert Law
Geo Thomas
Judge Watters
Benj Lowe
H A Hatheway (2)
Harriet Trueman
W Walton
Geo Mathews (2)
S A Dixon
E M Merritt
Michael Thompson (2)
Rev Alex McL Stavely
H S Gregory
Helen York and Captain Thos York
John Anderson
Jas Sullivan
Geo F Thompson
J J Munro
J E Ganong
T G Merritt
Jane Woods
John Burke
Mrs Jas Drake
G C Wiggins
W H Hayward
M. N Powers
Catherine and heirs Michael Donnelly
F A Wiggins
Rev Mr McCarty
Trustees James Leitch
Charles Patton

LEINSTER STREET.

F Cassidy
James Milligan
Lydia Gardner (2)
Joseph Edgar
Mrs Wallace
Mrs Samuel Bustin
Trustees of Baptist Church
Jane Rutherford
H L Francis
Mary Murray
Francis McDevitt
Trustees Varley School
Mrs E Lunt and heirs
Jos Lunt
A W Masters
Silas H Brown
James Sullivan
Mrs Lydia J Calhoun

Joseph Reed
W H & D Hayward
A H Eaton
John Corr
S K Foster
John Gallagher
Dennis Sullivan
Heirs Wm Bailey
Francis Hewitt (2)
John Roop (2)
Geo W Masters
G V Nowlin
Chas H Dearborn
G Merritt
Gilbert Murdoch
T C Humbert
John McBrine (2)

CHURCH STREET.

G A Knodell
M Thompson
Geo Pattison
Thos S Wetmore
James H Peters

Mrs Jane Disbrow
Ellen Mahoney
Ed Maher
A Bowes
R T Clinch and heirs E Barlow

KING SQUARE.

C M Bostwick
C Merritt
Trustees Irish Friendly Society

Heirs B Ansley
R Milligan
C A Robertson

KING STREET.

Mrs John Gillis
Heirs John Gillis
James Manson
R T Clinch and heirs E Barlow
D J McLaughlin and heirs Daniel McLaughlin
S E Whittaker
James E Whittaker

Geo A Barker
Mrs Geo Taylor
John Dougherty
Heirs Wm Melick
Mrs John Hay
John Fisher
Wm Kennedy
Corporation of Trinity Church

Thos H Hall (2)
Samuel Schofield
Thomas Seely
Ann Howe
John Mitchell
Mary Piddler
Wm Peters

Heirs H Chubb
Joseph Nichols
James R Ruel & Robert Light
Mrs Chas C Macdonald (3)
Jos W Hall (2)
W H Scovil
R T Clinch and heirs E Barlow

UNION STREET.

J C Brown estate
Peter and John Campbell
Daniel Donovan
Mrs Lantalum (2)
J W Hall (2)
John Gallivan
John McSweeny (3)
Heirs D J McLaughlin
C Lawton
James Dever

J Fred Lawton
L Burns
J Hegan
John Lloyd
Hare heirs
Mrs John Bryden
John Higgins
A Richardson
A Yeats & Sons (3)
J & T Robinson (2)

CHAPTER XVII.

The losses of the Masonic Fraternity.—Great Destruction of Masonic Regalia and Paraphernalia.—Organization of the General Masonic Board of Relief.—Amount received in Aid of the Suffering Brethren.

THE losses of the Masonic fraternity have been computed, and found to be much greater than was at first supposed. The private lodges saved nothing, and all their warrants, banners, jewels, clothing, and other paraphernalia were lost. Some of them even did not rescue their seals; and Hibernia, Union Lodge of Portland, and New Brunswick Lodge, lost their records. The Union Lodge of Portland was a heavy loser. Her loss amounts to $1,250: Albion, No. 1, $850; St. John's, No. 2, about $600; Leinster, No. 9, and New Brunswick, No. 22, foot up to $750 each; and Hibernia, No. 3, to $850.

The Chapters have also fared badly. Carleton Royal Arch Chapter, formed in 1802, lost the seal and $1,150 worth of property; while New Brunswick Chapter meets with a loss of $1,475.

There were two Encampments which met in Masonic Hall. St. John Encampment not only lost $2,300 worth of property, which included the rich regalia of the order, the jewels, banners, charters, and general paraphernalia, but also the seal of the Encampment, and the regalia in the armory, which was owned by the private members. This latter consisted for the most part, of the chapeaux, swords, belts, gauntlets, baldrics, aprons, etc., **usually** worn by the Sir Knights when on parade and other duty. Hardly a member of the organization saved his masonic clothing. The regalia of this body was especially gorgeous in character, and no better dressed organization, before the fire, existed anywhere. The Union De Molay Encampment experienced the same loss of general wardrobe and appliances. Their loss reaches upwards of two thousand dollars. The bodies of the Ancient and Accepted Rite **lost** everything but the records. The Royal Order of Scotland—a very select body,—saved their records only; the entire paraphernalia and regalia were lost. All the furniture and furnishings, the organ, etc., belonging to the General Hall Committee of the body, with all the paintings, photographs, and engravings, were destroyed with the rest.

Only the regalia and records, and full register of members belonging to the Grand Lodge were saved. The magnificent library of over four hundred volumes, many of them rare and scarce, and the most complete thing of the kind **in** the Dominion, was burned. In the work of collecting these books, the Grand Secretary, W. F. Bunting, Esq., spent many years; and the destruction of the noble volumes is a serious and irreparable loss to Freemasonry; many of the books destroyed can never be replaced. Besides this, a good many were **of** incalculable value, on account **of** certain associations connected with them, and each **one** had a little history of its own. Some **of** them were presentation volumes, others again were out of print, and not a few were high-priced modern text-books, especially valuable to the masonic student. All the blank forms and certificates, fyles of documents and books of constitutions, and all copies of printed proceedings, were swept away in the common ruin. Grand Lodge has suffered severely, and her total loss above insurance cannot be less than one thousand dollars; while the loss she has met with which money cannot replace is enormous. Even Carleton Union Lodge, which met on the other side of the harbour, did not escape. Her beautiful banners, which she had lent St. John Encampment at the time of the late ball, were in the lodge room when the fire was sweeping all before it, and they were consequently burned.

The walls of the Lodge-room were always tastefully decorated with well executed engravings on Masonic subjects. These all perished, as well as the handsome autotype of H. R. H. the Prince of Wales in full Masonic regalia, which was presented to the craft last year, by Thomas Furlong, Esq., and which was greatly admired. An oil painting of P. G. M. Balloch, by Holman, in full Masonic clothing, which hung near the Master's Chair, and a fine picture in oil of "The Ascension," by Dr. T. A. D. Forster, formerly of St. John, were burned along with everything else. Indeed the fraternity will find it impossible to replace a tithe of the useful and ornamental things with which it was surrounded. The order in this city was well equipped, and amply provided with everything.

Notwithstanding, however, that they had suffered so largely themselves, publicly and privately, as individuals and as masons, the leading members of the fraternity at once organized a board of relief and proceeded to care for the wants of the brethren who had met with reverses. The general masonic board of relief is a special organization which grew out of the present calamity, and is separate and distinct from the regular or ordinary relief board of the city. It is composed of city members of the Board of General Purposes of the Grand Lodge, and the presiding officers of all the Masonic bodies of the city. Grand Master R. T. Clinch is Chairman, Grand Treasurer Jas McNichol, Jr., is Treasurer, and Grand Secretary William F. Bunting is Secretary of the board. R. W. Bro. Edwin J. Wetmore is clerk, and has charge of the office and attends daily from three to five o'clock in the afternoon, to receive applications from brethren in distress. The board meets every day, in the office rented for the purpose, from four to five o'clock to consider applications and grant such relief as they deem advisable. In the administration of the fund at their disposal the board exercises great discretion and discrimination. Not only are brethren of the craft helped, but the hearts of their widows and orphans are made glad. Often the board does not wait for a distressed brother to make application for relief, but other means are taken to find out his necessities and aid is sent to him whenever this can be ascertained. All benefits are granted in money, and range from sums of twenty to fifty dollars, payable by check signed always by the treasurer, and one other officer of the board. As soon as money is received it is deposited in the Bank of British North America, in the names of the Chairman, Treasurer and Secretary. The system works admirably and already a great amount of good, in really necessitous cases, has been done. The gentlemen at the head of the board are men of sterling character and reputation, and any funds placed in their hands are judiciously and properly disbursed. Every provision is being made for the coming winter months, when it is expected that sore distress will prevail in the city, and with this in view the board feel the necessity of having a good fund at their disposal to meet the wants of worthy but unfortunate members of the fraternity. Thus far the craft abroad have responded to the needs of the suffering brethren quite liberally. Up to late date these sums have been received:

From	Craft in Chicago, Ill.	$930 00
"	Grand Lodge of Canada	1,000 00
"	" " Illinois	237 75
"	Craft in Charlottetown, P.E.I.	300 00
"	" Newfoundland	336 44
"	Masonic Relief Board, Memphis, Tenn.	94 75
"	St. Andrew's Lodge, Bangor, Me.	95 00
"	St. John's Lodge, Bathurst, N.B.	50 00
"	Star in the East Lodge, Oldtown, Me.	66 50
"	Alexandria Lodge, St. Mary's, York Co., N. B.	20 00

CHAPTER XVIII.

The Destruction—The Loss—Estimates—The Acreage and Streetage—
Has the Land Decreased in Value ?—Incomes swept away—What is
Left—Hope !—The Insurance—The Corporation Loss—The Dominion
Loss—Additional Deaths—The Wounded—The Orange Body.

IN forming an estimate of the destruction which the fire has caused great care has been exercised. I have been careful to verify every statement I advance. Thoroughly competent engineers have, at my request, re-surveyed the area through which the fire raged, and I am therefore in a position to give reliable information on a subject which has given rise to much speculation and doubt. The acreage has been taken and the streetage made and the result has shown that the fire destroyed two hundred acres of territory and nine and six-tenths miles of streets. To be more exact the acreage is not quite two hundred acres but so very near it that it may be accepted at that estimate. Not more than two-fifths of the city have been burned and the reader will see the truth of this when he comes to consider that Carleton which forms a part of this city has been untouched by the flames, and all the upper portion of the city has escaped. While the acreage and streetage shew that the city is not totally destroyed, yet what has been burned represented enormous value. The fire penetrated to the very heart of the great commercial centre of St. John. It laid waste the fairest portion of the city. It swept away the palace-houses of our wealthy people and destroyed nearly every public building in the place. When one considers all these circumstances and begins to realize the situation, he is apt to form too high an estimate of the loss. He looks around him while going about surveying the ruins, and on every side he sees the great waste and the figures forming in his head grow larger and larger as he proceeds to sum up the result of the sad fire. Every man has his own opinion, and it is curious to observe how widely diversified these opinions are. The cautious man places it at fifteen millions, and his hot blooded and visionary friend with equal show of reason estimates the loss at nearly fifty millions. The estimate ranges widely and wildly. The books of the assessors on examination show a loss to property of much less value than even the owners put upon it before the fire. But one can see how fallacious these results are, when the reader learns that in making up the assessments the assessors value a merchant's stock at not what it is, but what in their opinion they think it should be. For instance, a man has three hundred thousand dollars worth of stock in warehouse. He really owns about fifty thousand dollars worth and owes for the balance. He is not taxed on his debts but on what he is worth. Yet the fire carried away the sum total of the goods in his possession. The assessors' books show hardly a tithe of the actual value of the loss. It can only be correctly stated after a thorough examination, and as nearly as can be ascertained the entire destruction throughout the city reaches upwards of twenty-seven millions of dollars. This is the loss in solid **value**. But that much money will not replace the goods thus destroyed. There were many things burned which were of what might be called fancy value, and which money can in no way replace. And in making our estimate these things have been valued only nominally. The loss, therefore, in round figures, is not a whit below the amount we have given, $27,000,000. The talk about taxable property is all nonsense. Every man who says so, knows that he is talking nonsense. Hardly a man lives to-day who is taxed in the proportion that he should be. **The** richer a man is, the more easily he can hide his wealth, and **an** examination of the assessment books will enable any reader to find a hundred examples in proof of this. Another argument is brought forward. We are told that the land is not burned up, and in that land there is great value. That is true enough, every word of it. The land is not burned out of existence. It is still where it was, but it is by no means as valuable as it was before the fire. A thousand circumstances were brought to bear on it, locality, desirability, and necessity, and all these had an influence in enhancing its value. Most of these reasons, and cogent reasons they were too at the time, have now gone out with the fire. Men who thought they must have a piece of land because it was in a good situation, and because it was located near their own lots, were ready to buy what they wanted at a good price, often merely to carry out some hobby or idea paramount in their minds. But these ideas have vanished. This hobby can be ridden no longer. He can have the lot now if he wants it, at a good deal lower rate than he offered for it, but he can't afford it. The owner's means are swept away, and he cannot afford to build again, and is anxious to sell his land, that he can go and rent a house to live in. The land in almost every part of the burnt district will drop, and has already dropped, in value. It is still there, and so it was there a hundred years ago. It is more valuable now than it was then. I don't pretend to say that we are no better off than when the loyalists landed, for we are. Our roads are laid out; our people are thrifty, enterprising, and skilful. The greater portion of the city is still intact. We have a splendid system of water supply and sewerage. We have, or, will have very soon, gas burning again. We will have comforts once more. But what I do mean to say is, that it will take very many years to build the city up again as it was before the fire. It will take very many years to enable the land-owner to realize anything like the price he once commanded for his property. Of course, in the leading business streets there will be but little difference, though it will be felt in a good many quarters. Take some portions of King and Prince William streets, for example. Some men realized a snug income from the rental of the shanties which were erected on good business sites in these streets. They owned the land, and the shanties were theirs. Their whole income came from this source. Their wooden buildings yielded them a far more handsome return for their outlay than many of the massive brick buildings near them did to their owners. Why was this? Simply because they were in a good locality. These shanties are now level with the earth. The revenue is swept away. hese men own the land, but their means are gone. They cannot rebuild. If they did, the rent they would receive would be far less than the rookeries yielded, and they must sell their property or mortgage it. The land has lost a great deal of its value, and it will take a long time for it to regain that loss. We must look these things boldly and seriously in the face. No reflection is made on the people when these statements are advanced. No more enterprising populace lives than the people of St. John. Many are used to hard work. They have hewn out of the solid rock one of the most beautiful cities in the Dominion. They have met a thousand obstacles in their path, and they have swept them all aside. And they will ride over their calamity and begin again the hard road upward. They will rebuild the city once more, and plant bright things where ruin and despair now stand, but we must not flatter ourselves that we have lost nothing, and that our land has not deteriorated in value. It is as wrong to be over sanguine as it is to give way to gloom and do nothing to better our misfortunes. We must work with determination and lose no time. We must show the world—that kind world which has fed the mouths of our poor and clothed the unfortunate—that there is backbone and muscle still left in the city, and that while we have men to work we have no women to weep. It might have been worse. We have lost lives, we have lost all our buildings—we have lost everything that goes to make home happy cheerful and bright—we have lost our stores and shops—

SKATING RINK.

THE TEMPORARY W. U. TEL. OFFICE.

THE GREAT FIRE IN ST. JOHN, N. B.

we have lost a hundred comforts—but, thank God, we have not lost our glorious hope in the future. In that hope is our salvation. It is that hope which stirs us on, which quickens our energy, which tells us that it might truly have been worse. It is the one beautiful thing that is left to us. It is the angel which smiles back to us when we raise our eyes upward. It is the figure in the cloud which says to prostrate man, " Rouse, rouse yourself! all is not lost, there is a future for you all." Ah, yes, it might have been worse. There is desolation all around—there is death in many households—there is mourning and crying and moaning—but hope still sailing grandly near us, so near that we can almost touch her, still smiling sweetly on us tells us all will yet be well and bids us be of good cheer.

The number of houses burned on the several streets in the city, is sixteen hundred and twelve. They were located as follows:—

Georges Street	10
Mill Street	20
Drury Lane	17
Smyth Street	20
North Street	5
North Market Slip	8
Hare's Wharf	1
Robertson Place	1
Fire Proof Alley	2
North Market Wharf	11
Nelson Street	18
Dock Street	26
Market Square	6

South Market Wharf	16
Ward Street	10
Peters' Wharf	11
Johnston's Wharf	2
Lovett's Slip	1
St. John, "Water" Street	51
Canterbury Street	19
Prince William Street	95
Germain Street	87
Charlotte Street	84
Sydney Street	75
Carmarthen Street	59
Wentworth Street	34
Pitt Street	38
Sheffield Street	52
Main Street	58
Britain Street	101
St James Street	98
Pagan Place	9
Harding Street	15
Queen Square, south side	10
Queen Square, north side	10
St Andrew Street	17
Queen Street	80
Mecklenburg Street	44
Duke Street	105
Horsfield Street	17
Orange Street	42
Princess Street	106
Church Street	10
Leinster Street	45
King Square, south side	6
King Street	60
Total	1612

The number of people rendered homeless foot up to about thirteen thousand, and the number of families to about twenty-seven hundred. As near as can be got, the insurance on merchandise, furniture and buildings, is placed as follows. This is not quite correct but at this hour it is as nearly correct as can be ascertained. It will average this at all events, and amounts in the aggregate to about seven millions of dollars.

Queen	$700,000
North British & Mercantile	800,000
Lancashire	500,000
Provincial	100,000
Liverpool, London & Globe	480,000
Guardian	420,000
Canada Fire & Marine	50,000
Citizens	200,000
National	140,000
Royal	520,000
Commercial Union	420,000
Royal Canadian	350,000
Western	90,000
Imperial	480,000
Ætna	246,000
Hartford	148,000
Phenix of Brooklyn	60,000
British America	27,000
Stadacona	320,000
Central, of Fredericton	60,000
St John Mutual	75,000
Northern	500,000
Canada Agricultural	8,000

Most of the Insurance Companies paid up at once

"The Stadacona" pays its liabilities within a year. The "Provincial" has suspended but promises to pay in time and the condition of the "St. John Mutual" is quite hopeless, and will pay scarcely anything. The "Central" of Fredericton, N.B., will pay in a short time, it is said.

The loss to the shipping will amount to about fifty thousand dollars. The St. John Corporation loses heavily, and the insurance which was held on some properties is exceedingly light. The City Hall cost, at the time of its purchase from the directors of the old Commercial Bank, the sum of $23,000. Since then a good deal of money has been expended on it. The insurance was only $15,000. The Police Court and station on Chipman's Hill, which were both burned, the one a wooden building and the other of brick, had insurance to the small amount of $2,000. The Fish Market, useful and by no means ornamental, was insured for $600. The Lower Cove Market, the upper or second story of which contained a public hall, and was used by temperance societies sometimes, was insured for $1,200. In the rear of the first floor of this building, a lock-up was situate, for the accommodation of delinquents and law-breakers in that portion of the city. The city stables on Carmarthen street were uninsured, as was also the toll house at the Carleton ferry landing. The building occupied by Mr. May at Reed's point, and which was owned by the corporation, was insured for 1,000. Two cottages on Orange street were insured for $3,000. These were occupied by Mr. A. J. H. Bartsch, the watch-maker, and by Mr. Chas. Parker. Mr.

Samuel Phillips' residence, on Duke street, and which belonged to the corporation, was insured for $400. The warehouses on Pettingill's Wharf had insurance to the amount of $5,000. The barrack and sheds belonging to the city were uninsured. Two-thirds of the fire alarm was destroyed, and all the watering-carts, slovens, hose, &c., belonging to the corporation, were burned. No. 1 engine-house was destroyed. No. 2 experienced a little damage after Dr. Travers' house caught fire. The sidewalks can only be replaced at a heavy cost, and the damage to the wharf property is enormously large.

The Dominion Government loses about half a million dollars. The Custom House and Post Office will be rebuilt at once, and plans are already prepared. All the Government military stores were burned, and the three hundred rifles belonging to the 62nd battalion were lost. Most of the new uniforms belonging to the corps perished likewise. None of the Dominion Government's property was insured, and the loss will therefore be complete.

The list of callings has been carefully gone over, and shows a return of the following, who have been burned out :—

Architects	4
Auctioneers	7
Bakers	11
Banks	5
Bankers, Private	4
Barristers	80
Blacksmiths	10
Block and pump makers	8

Boarding-houses 55
Boat builders 5
Bookbinders 5
Book stores 7
Boot and shoemakers 38
Boot and shoe stores 14
Brass founders 6
Builders 27
Cabinet makers 9
Clothiers 29
Commission merchants 93
Confectioners 6
Dentists 9
Druggists 8
Dry goods (wholesale) 14
Dry goods (retail) 22
Dining and oyster saloons 10
Flour dealers 32
Fruit dealers 7
Grocers (wholesale) 40
Grocers (retail) 102
Gasfitters and plumbers 9
Hair dressers 13
Hardware stores 8
Hotels 14
Insurance agents 29
Iron merchants 8
Liquor dealers (wholesale) 27
Liquor dealers (retail) 116
Livery stables 8
Lumber merchants 12
Marble works 6
Merchant tailors 36
Newspapers 7

Painters 13
Photographers 6
Physicians and surgeons 15
Printers (job work) 10
Riggers 7
Sailmakers 5
Ship chandlers 14
Ship smiths 8
Stove dealers 8
Tobacconists 7
Undertakers 4
Watchmakers and jewellers 12

The following list shows the manufacturing establishments, using steam power, which were destroyed, and gives the number of hands employed in each :—

Name.	Business.	No. of hands employed.
Jeremiah Drake	Block maker	5
John E. Turnbull	Sash factory	18
Armstrong Bros	Foundry	10
T. Rankine & Sons	Bakery	30
S. R. Foster & Son	Tack manufacturers	50
W. D. Aitken	Machinist	10
John Norris	Auger maker	2
R. A. Saunders	Pattern maker	2
Wm. Lowe	Wood turner	1
Wm. Smith & Co.	Ship-smith	8
H. Allan	Brass foundry	8
Maxwell, Elliot & Bradley	Ship smiths	4
Dearborn & Co.	Coffee and spices	10
J. Akroyd	Machinist	1
J. Smith	Foundry	4
Geo. F. Thompson	White lead man'r	7

D. McLaughlin & Sons....Boiler makers.......... 15
T. McAvity & Sons........Brass manufacturers.... 16
Bradley Bros...............Block makers............
Geo. R. Bent..............Organs................. —

This, and the list above, I use through the permission of Mr. Elder, of *The Telegraph*, who had them carefully made up from reliable sources.

In addition to the number of deaths mentioned in one of the earlier chapters of this book, very large addenda must be made. Since that chapter was written, a good many more persons are known to have perished. The list on the death-roll is very large. Mr. Garret Cotter, a young man, working in the tailoring establishment of Mr. James S. May, as a cutter, and an old man named Peter McGovern, who lived on Straight Shore, met their deaths at the same time and at the same place. A cornice fell from the Adam's building and killed them. Young Cotter lived in Crown Street with his mother. His father met with a violent death some years since, having been killed on the railway. Two young men were drowned in the harbour before the very eyes of horror-stricken spectators. James Kemp, aged 21, formerly a clerk in Michael Farrel's clothing store, and Thomas Holmes, a lad of seventeen years, and who resided in Harding Street with his mother, put out to sea in a small boat laden with what little property they could get into it. The bottom of the boat broke, and the craft filling at once, both men were drowned in a second. The people on vessels in the harbour lying close by the ill-fated boat, were so excited at what they saw, and the men sank so rapidly, that nothing could be done to save them, and they perished in full view of those on board. Kemp leaves a wife and one child. Mrs. Cohalan, wife of Wm. Cohalan, was lost in Smyth Street. Her body was never recovered, but it is established beyond all doubt that she fell an early victim. All that was left of Mrs. Bradley, who once lived in Princess Street, were some human bones which were found on her door-step after the fire. The remains of Richard Thomas, an employé in Fred. Fitzpatrick's warehouse in Nelson Street, were found on the site of Richard O'Brien's saloon in Germain Street. Robert Fox, who belonged about the Marsh Road, has been pronounced dead.

The accidents were very numerous, and were of various degrees of importance. In the hurry, the names of all persons who suffered by the fire, and had experienced bruises and fractures, could not be obtained. Some were sent at once to the Public Hospital, and even here there was not time to fully record the names of all who were brought in. The physician in charge, Dr. Hanington, did all in his power to make the unfortunates comfortable and easy. The matron of the establishment and other assistants also rendered efficient and prompt aid. The names of those who were for a while in the Hospital, and received injuries at the fire are Daniel Dooley, John Ross, Patrick Brady, William Coxetter, William Donohoe, Helen Davidson, Bayard Thompson, **Walter** Lamb (injured at the explosion), Andrew Donovan, Michael **Barrett**, William

Porter, Jeremiah Sullivan, Thomas Sullivan, Richard Powers, John Anderson and George Gallagher. The last two men died in the Hospital from the effects of their wounds.

The thanks of the people of St. John are largely due to C. J. Brydges, Esq., and R. Luttrell, Esq., of the Intercolonial Railway, who promptly placed fast trains at the service of the Relief Committee, and forwarded free passengers and supplies. Excellent service was thus performed, and Mr. Luttrell lost no time in meeting the emergency. Indeed he spent several days in relieving the wants of the sufferers. Few will forget these kindly acts.

In concluding this chapter I might add that the Orange Lodges which met in Mr. Thos. H. Hall's building, King street, lost quite heavily. Their regalia was, for the most part, entirely consumed, but the banners were saved. The insurance on the hall and furniture was only five hundred dollars. The members had gone to a great deal of expense lately in fitting up their lodge-room, which was one of the tastiest in the city. The decorations were very handsome. The loss will reach at least two thousand dollars. A relief organization has been formed by leading brethren of the order, and the wants of sufferers by the fire are being looked after. The Grand Master, Edward Willis, and Messrs. A. G. Blakslee, John A. Kane, J. B. Andrews, Walter McFate, W. A. King, W. Roxorough, James Elliott, and Samuel Devenne, comprise the Relief Committee.

CHAPTER XIX.

The Books we have Lost—"The Lost Arts"—The Libraries of St. **John**
which were Burned—The Pictures which were Lost—The Few that were
Saved—A Talk about Books and Pictures—The Future—What St. John
men must Do—Acknowledgments—Conclusion of the Story of the Fire.

It is only when we come to look around us that we can discover how much we have lost. In one's lifetime a thousand little things are gathered and put away, and we find ourselves turning to them every now and then. Money cannot supply these. Many of them are endeared to us through association. Some are the gifts of **friends** who have since passed away, never to return, **and** others again came into our possession in various ways. We may supply, with a portion of our insurance money, a few books, copies of the ones which we have lost, but these will not be the same. They will not be our copies. We love to read our own books. No Suckling can be the same as the one we lost the other day. It was not a rich copy, but it was a whole-souled, generous old fashioned volume, full of the old Knight's daintiest bits of melody. **We** used to love to linger over the little age-stained page, and recover lines we had lost. And dear old Shenstone, too, is gone. We can easily **get** another Shenstone, but it won't seem at all like the old copy. In our own books we know just where to find what we want, and new copies **never** seem the same. And then there **are** books we like to take up now and then, just to fill in the odd moments of our lives; books of engravings and the like, and volumes of *Punch*, and great volumes of cartoons of say forty and fifty years ago. These are all gone now and few can be replaced.

What great inroads the fire has caused among our private libraries, what a wreck it has made of those precious books we all loved so dearly. And those pamphlets, too, upon which we placed so much value, and the thousand little odds and ends of literature which we so tenderly gathered year in and year out. And our scrap-books— great, good-natured fellows, with broad sides and liberal pages, ready to take in all sorts of matter. These are no more. And whole hosts of unbound magazines, which we had tied together, and expected every day to send off to the binders. These are ashes too. We hesitate before we turn over the books we rescued from the burning, lest we discover greater losses, and miss fairer treasures. How many sets of books have been destroyed, how many massive tomes have been withered by the heat, how many dainty books of poetry have been swept away!

What lovely companions books are. What glorious friends they make. How kindly they speak to us and tell us what they think. We read gruff Tom Carlyle, and pause at his estimate of Cromwell, and hunt through the histories of England to see what Smollett and Hume have to say about the same grim protector. We run through a few pages of Taine and iscover how grandly he criticises

the masters of English literature, but after all we go back
fondly to our own Arnold, and read what he has to tell
us before we quite make up our mind that the clever
Frenchman is right. We sit at the feet of Holmes and
read a chapter or two of his matchless Autocrat, and then
with our mind full of the delicious sweets, we get down
our copy of Hunt and after skimming a page or two of
his "Seer," dip into the crisp and sparkling pages of
Hazlitt's *Round Table*. Ah, yes! the fire may take all
else we have if it will only leave us our books. True, a
man, as the bard hath it—

> "May live without books—what is knowledge but grieving?
> He may live without hope—what is hope but deceiving?
> He may live without love—what is passion but pining?
> But where is the man who can live without dining?"

But after all the mind craves as much for food of its
kind, as the stomach does for meats and bread.

Though in St. John we had no public library, there
were very many private collections of books in the city.
Some of them were very large and well-selected. Dr.
Wm. Bayard's collection, not one volume of which was
saved, was beyond all question the fullest and ripest medical library in the Dominion. It was the accumulation of
many years. The collection was begun by his father and
added to largely by the Doctor himself. Some rare medical works, rich in plates, costing as high as £30 sterling
each, were to be found here, besides books covering the
whole range of medical thought and practice. The English classics, exhibiting the very cream of letters, and

some fine specimens of modern literature filled acceptably the doctors shelves. Not a volume was saved. Indeed a photograph album was the only article rescued from the burning house. Mr. James R. Ruel, the Collector of Customs had a fine library, rich in theology and literature of the higher class. Controversial works books of science, and the whole range of British Poetry, ever found a welcome on Mr. Ruel's library table. In the departments of History and Geography this library was especially rich and full, and every work of character about the Reformation in England could here be consulted. Mr. Ruel's reading in this department was extensive, and he made writings of this kind his especial study. His whole collection, rare and costly as it was, and representing the labour of many years, perished before a hand could be raised in its defence. Mr. B. Lester Peters's library showed great care and culture in its selection. It too was very complete in History, Biography, Belles-lettres and Theology. Mr. Peters's fine literary taste served him well in making his collection of books, and nearly all his volumes displayed wonderful skill in rich bindings. In old playwrights, such as Shakespeare, Jonson, Massinger, Beaumont and Fletcher, and the other famous ones of that glorious age in literature—The Elizabethan—Mr. Peters's library was ample. Indeed, in works of this class no finer collection existed in the city. And in poetry which exhibited the rarest thoughts of the bards, in the works of such poets as Milton, Chaucer, Spenser, Dryden, Pope and Clough, Mr. Peters's shelves contained a perfect mine of wealth. His collection of pamphlets, the labour of thirty years, was unique and full. He had the whole of the famous Connolly and Wilmot controversy, the scattered papers of the late Dr. Gray, the Maturin pamphlets, the Colenso pamphlets, the notes on the Lost Tribes of Israel, and a thousand others, neatly and carefully put away in cases specially prepared for them. Those are all gone, and not a fragment remains. The gorgeous library of John Boyd, Esq., of Queen Square, with its enormous collection of works belonging to modern literature, its rare list of old books, its magnificent sets of presentation volumes from the authors, its numberless volumes that came from the publishers to Mr. Boyd as gifts, were swept away in an instant. The books in Mr. Boyd's cases were a reflex of the owner's taste and judgment. He had not a poor book among the whole. The entire range of English and American essayists, the whole course of British and American poetry, the cream of historical books, the ripest thoughts of the philosopher, the most delightful gems of fiction, the works of the scientists, and the great tomes of biography, clad in the most luxuriant of luxurious bindings, were the companions of Mr. Boyd's study. His lectures, common-place books, scrap-books, in fact everything which he possessed of a literary character were burned. Even the literary notes which he made from time to time in his record books during the odd moments of his too unfrequent leisure, and the bits of criticism on new poems which he occasionally made for future use on the platform and elsewhere, perished in his desk. His entire intellectual labour vanished in an hour. Mr. A. L. Palmer's splendid library with his own valuable annotations, Mr. A. A. Stockton's voluminous and admirable library, begun by his late uncle, and Mr. Chas. W. Weldon's Law and general library were destroyed before their owners could save a single book. The Rev. Dr. Watters's library, so rich in theology and biography, was burned almost entirely. Lately large additions had been made to this delightful collection. A good many of the late Judge Chipman's best books found their way here, and the most of these were lost. Rev. Mr. Stavely's books were all burned, and not one of Rev. Mr. Carey's fine collection escaped. Some of his books were very rare and high-priced. Mr. Robert Britain's books were of general and private interest. The former embraced almost the whole range of English literature, and the latter included the best books on chemistry and science. Indeed in books belonging to the latter class, it will be difficult to find so large a collection anywhere. Mr. J. D. Underhill possessed a library of rare beauty and value. It was very large in historical works and the writings of the principal British, American and French authors. In biography and fiction of the higher order there was a a good supply. Mr. Underhill, for several years, had been a great book-buyer, and hardly a trunkfull was saved. For costly books, handsomely bound, no richer collection existed in St. John than the splendid library of Mr. Fred. R. Fairweather. He had the entire set of Balzac's works in the original, luxuriously and massively bound. His Shakespeares, for he had several editions, copiously illustrated and exquisitely finished, were bound in heavy antique morocco. His books of plates, his dramatic library, his collection of plays of the Cumberland edition, his books on costumes from the time of the Saxons to our own day, represented large value, and a refined and cultured taste. In dramatic literature alone, Mr. Fairweather's library was probably the fullest in the Dominion. Indeed his loss in this department is a positive loss to literature, and a collection such as he owned can never be again supplied. Many of the books are out of print, and cannot be purchased to-day at any price. The books lost in the city, on the day of the fire, will number many thousands of volumes. No city of the size of St. John could boast of finer private collections of books, anywhere. It will be many years before collections as rich, as unique, and as delightful can be procured again.

In pictures, the loss met with is really irreparable. We had no public gallery, because our citizens, whose means admitted it, purchased for the walls of their own houses a charming bit of colour now and then, or a delicate engraving or a drawing. A few of the masterpieces of the English and American artists found their way here from time to time, and in the way of engravings the collection was really quite large. We can only give a tithe of the pictures lost. Dr. McAvenney possessed a decided gem in water-colour, by Birket Foster, and a charming landscape in oil from the brush of Mayner, an Irish artist. The latter was a twenty pounds' picture, and one of the prizes which came to St. John last year from the Irish Art

Union. It was exceedingly vigorous, and, though small in size, every detail was perfect. In addition to these, Dr. McAvenney lost several fine engravings and one or two exquisite drawings. Dr. Wm. Bayard's loss in pictures is quite large. He owned a capital landscape, *The Vale of Strathmore*, by John Cairns, of Edinburgh. This was burned, with some others of lesser note, together with a good many engravings, chiefly London Art Union subjects. Mr. R. M. Longmaid lost all but one of his pictures. Some of these were of great value, and included, among a number of others, *Francis I. and Henry VIII. on the Field of the Cloth of Gold*, by the late G. F. Mulvany, R.H.A., and one of Cairns' Scotch subjects, showing a striking bit of Highland scenery, called *Glen Cairn*. The one picture saved was a Welsh Landscape, by A. Vickers. This had been lent to a friend in the upper part of the town, and was accordingly not burned. Mr. Charles Campbell managed to preserve a number of his pictures; among them the bold *Coast Scene*, by John Cairns, which will be remembered by many who saw it as a very striking study. Mr. W. C. Perley, among the very few articles rescued from his house, saved two very pretty little landscapes, one an Irish scene and the other a delicious specimen of C. C. Ward's art. Mr. B. Lester Peters lost nearly all of his engravings, but succeeded in rescuing a study by F. W. Hulme, and a little gem by A. Vickers. Hon. George E. King saved a few water colours by eminent British artists, which he had. Mr. Donald G. MacKenzie, who had half-a-dozen striking oil paintings, recovered them all a few days after the fire. Mr. John Sears lost heavily in the Department of Art, but saved his one great picture, a portrait which is an undoubted Rubens, and one or two family likenesses. Mr. Stephen J. King, whose treasures consist in drawings by McKewan, Philps and others, and some oil-paintings, saved them all. Mr. W. P. Dole lost a pair of very beautiful water-colour drawings of Canadian scenery, by D. Gale, and three or four excellent engravings. He was fortunate in saving however, two charming works by Hulme, two small bits by Vickers, two by G. A. Williams, one of C. C. Ward's pieces, and one of the late John T. Stanton's best works. Mr. Stanton was a New Brunswick artist of fine taste and decided skill. Mr. Dole also saved some of his water-colours, notably those by Bell Smith and Frantz. The author lost an excellent drawing illustrating an idea in Thackeray, and a number of clever caricatures from the pencil of an amateur artist, Mr. Forbes Torrance, of Como, besides several engravings of merit, and a massive bronze figure representing Painting. Mr. Henry Vaughan lost his large costly painting from the John Miller collection, of Liverpool, England. Mr. James Stewart lost his whole collection of paintings; several of these were of his own work, while a number were by foreign artists. Mr. Stewart copied a landscape painting by an English artist which came out here as a prize, some years ago, and when his work was finished and the two painings hung side by side, the owner did not know which was his own picture. This copy was for some days in Mr. Notman's studio before the fire, and it is believed that it is lost, as no trace has been had of it. The reader will see from this scanty enumeration of known losses, how great has been the destruction in art-treasures alone. We have not even hinted at the wholesale destruction of bronzes, bas reliefs and bits of sculpture and statuary. In these departments the loss has been also very severe. No money can replace these treasures. These were the things which rendered home bright and happy. It is the love of art and literature which refines and beautifies mankind. It is the book and the picture, and the figure of pale marble which rouse a thousand new delights. They take away the brutal in our nature. They lift us up as it were. We look around the room and the eye rests on something beautiful. We feed our tastes. The picture on the wall refines us, the open book fills the mind with a hundred delicate, footless fancies. We breathe a new air. The etchings on the table, the portfolio of drawings and the books of engravings give to our mind a delight as wonderful as it is delicate and delicious. Can money replace these ? Can money buy for us these pictures and books which have been for so many years our companions and friends ? Can money replace the bronze figure ? Can money bring to us again the portrait of the dear one who lies out there in the green wood buried ? Can money supply us with that precious volume of poetry which the author gave us just a year before he died ? We may make our homes bright again. We may hang pictures on the walls. We may fill to the full our book-cases and hanging-shelves once more with the great things in literature, but our thoughts will wander back to the days before the fire came and robbed us of all those delights which peop'ed and filled our homes. But we must not give way altogether to gloom and despondency. We must try and forget the past and devote all our energies, all our brains and skill to the rebuilding of the homes and workshops which have been scattered to the winds. We must never rest till the great end is accomplished; we must never cease working. As Christians, as men, as the proud descendants of a sturdy and stalwart race, we must show the world that we are not a generation of pigmies, and that from these very ashes and ruins a brighter, a more glorious and more prosperous city will arise and resume her old place as the metropolis of the Lower Provinces.

I have told the story of the great fire in St. John in my own way. I have tried to do justice to my theme. Like many others I have passed through the flames, and received as it were my first "baptism of fire." My book has many imperfections. It was necessary that it should be hastily prepared. My publishers demanded this, and gave me a fortnight to write it in. I can therefore claim nothing in favour of the book from a literary point of view, but this I can claim—the history is reliable in every particular. Not a statement within its pages was committed to paper until it was thoroughly and reliably avouched for. I have verified every word which this volume contains; and while the haste in which it was prepared precluded my paying much attention to style, the book is a complete record of the fire as it was, and not as a lively imagination might like it to be. Before taking leave of my readers, I must publicly thank Mr. Joseph W. Lawrence for the splendid aid which he gave me in furnishing the data and historical information about our old churches and other edifices. I had full access to his records and commonplace books, and through these means was enabled to verify much that had come to me in an imperfect condition. To Mr. Gilbert Murdoch, C.E., and Mr. Wm. Murdoch, C.E., of the Water Works and Sewerage Departments, I must also return my thanks, for valuable information about the water supply, for the capital map which accompanies this volume, and for facts connected with the acreage and streetage of the district burned. General Warner, Mayor Earle, Mr. A. C. Smith, Mr. John Boyd, Mr. A. P. Rolph. Mr. Dole, Mr. Hiram Betts, Mr. Elder, Mr. J. L. Stewart, Mr. McDade, Mr. O'Brien, Mr. Stanley, Mr. G. B. Hegan and others, also largely rendered me assistance in collecting information, and to these gentlemen I return my grateful thanks.

The little picture of the ruins, by moonlight, of the Germain street Baptist Church, was very kindly supplied by Mr. John C. Miles, a St. John artist of good reputation. I have great pleasure in acknowledging his politeness here, and at this time.

In conclusion, I might add, that to Mr. E. Lantalum belongs the credit of sounding the first alarm of our great fire.

ADDITIONAL LIST OF DONATIONS.

MONEY.

A friend...	$2 00
Ailsa Craig Presbyterian Church, Ont,..........	18 60
Ayr Knox Church and Sacred Concert............	76 00
Allendale, Ont. Methodist Church..............	6 60
Augusta, Me....................................	820 40
Barrie, Ont.....................................	166 00
Baltimore, Md..................................	80 62
Bobcaygeon Orangemen.........................	15 00
Bangor, Me,....................................	5,000 00
Belfast, Ireland................................	£300 Stg
Buffalo, N. Y..................................	$179 83
Chicago Union Stock Yards.....................	105 25
Chippawa, Ont. Trinity Church.................	38 65
Chicago Apollo Musical Club, Concert..........	990 75
Chicago, Ill....................................	2,050 00
Chatham, N. B..................................	250 00
Capt. Thompson, ss. "Britannia,"..............	500 00
Charlottetown, P. E. I.........................	500 00
Charlottetown Odd Fellows' Entertainment....	208 00
Departmental Clerks, Ottawa...................	445 53
Edinburgh, Scotland............................	£100 Stg
Ed. L. Evans, Rondeau, Ont....................	2 00
E. & J. Burke, Dublin, Ireland.................	250 00
Fredericton, N. B...............................	2,000 00
Fergus, Ont....................................	20 50

Geo. M. Fowler, British Consul, Aènfuegos	$100 00
Glasgow, Scotland	£1,000 Stg
Great Western Railway Employees	$450 00
G. W. Davis, Boston, Mass	14 11
Galt, Ont., Churches	114 69
Greenville, Nova Scotia	16 00
Huron Co. Council, Ont	2,000 00
Hayden, Gere & Co., New York	25 00
Hastings Co. Council Ont	1,000 00
Jacob E. Klotz, Hamburg, Ont	25 00
Mackenzie, Flatlands, N. B	2 00
M. McLeod, Cardigan, P. E. I	18 20
Miss Logan, Orillia, Ont	10 00
Mansfield, P. E. I	55 50
New York	2,105 90
Oshawa Benevolent Society	30 00
Petrolia, Penn	200 00
Presbyterian Churches, Wentworth, N. S.	13 00
Pictou, N. S	5 00
Portland, Me	4,500 00
Philadelphia, Penn	1,109 80
Picton, Ont	300 00
P. E. I. R. R. Employees	62 45
Stewiacké	40 00
St. Luke's Episcopal Church, Chelsea, Mass	5 00
Springhill Mines, U. S	18 95
Toronto	400 00
Uxbridge, Ont	51 40
Victoria Co. Council, Ont	400 00
Wingham, Ont	15 50
Woodstock, Ont. Literary Institute	37 25
Waterloo Co. Council, Ont	1,000 00
Woodstock, N. B	151 00
Wm. Ingalls, Bolton, England	£5 Stg

THE GREAT FIRE IN ST. JOHN, N. B.

Wroxeter and Fardwick Presbyterian Churches	$55 24
Windsor, Ont..................................	500 00
Yorkville, Ont.................................	300 00

SUPPLIES.

Augusta, Me, clothing.
Brunswick, Me, clothing.
Carter & Co., Elora, Ont., potatoes.
Chicago Union Stock Yards, large quantity supplies.
C. Fawcett, Sackville, N. B., stoves.
D. Fiske, Fredericton, N. B. tracts.
D. G. Smith, Chatham, N. B. clothing.
Isaac M. Bragg, Bangor, Me., clothing.
J. Borland, Bowmanville, stoves.
James Stewart & Co., Hamilton, Ont., stoves.
J. C. Risteen, Fredericton, supplies.
James Hamilton, Port Elgin, potatoes.
J. L. Goodhue, plasterers' hair.
Milwaukee, Wis., supplies.
Montreal, supplies.
Mount Stewart, P. E. I., supplies.
Prof. John Owen, Cambridge, Mass., offers books and magazines for a library.
Salem, Mass., supplies.
Stewiacké, clothing.
Thurston Hall & Co., Cambridgeport, supplies.
Wm. Openheim & Son, New York, clothing.

ADDENDA.

SUPPLEMENTARY DONATIONS.

MONEY.

Bridgetown, Maine	$70 00
Dungannon	29 10
Cornwall, Ontario	300 00
Portsmouth, N. H.	697 00
Salem	70 00
Newfoundland Government	2,000 00
Kingston, N. B.	20 00
Stayner, Ontario	75 00
Detroit, Michigan	427 81
Baden, Ontario	2 00
Stewart Henry, Montreal	25 00
Bear River, Nova Scotia	105 00
Hughes, Thomas, London, England	£10 0 0
St. George's Church, Trenton, Ontario	$15 00
St. John County Agricultural Society	400 00
Winnipeg *Free Press*	53 05
Chesterfield, Ontario, Presbyterian Church	57 00
Bailey & Noyes, Portland, Maine	25 00
Port Hope	8 00
Sydney, C. B.	295 40
Musquodoboit	5 25
Listowel, Ontario	140 35
Coristine, James & Co., Montreal	100 00
" " Employés	71 60

ADDENDA.

Milwaukee, **Wisconsin**	$100 00
Bark "Cedar Croft," Captain and Crew	£5 3 0
Mayor of Brooklyn, New York	$50 00
Lœser & Co., Brooklyn, New York	50 00
Winnipeg	300 00
Bridgewater, Nova Scotia	128 25
Norfolk County Council, Ontario	500 00
Ward & Payne, Sheffield, England	£10 0 0
Kingston, Ontario	$340 00
Oakville Odd Fellows' Open-air Concert	75 00
Victoria, British Columbia	800 00
Caledonia Restaurant, Winnipeg	21 50
Mount Stewart, P. E. I.	25 50
Virginia **City**, Nevada	250 00
Thomas Frith & **Sons**, Sheffield, England	250 00
Nellie H. **Carleton**, St. John, N. B.	3 64
Chicago, **Illinois**	601 75
Windsor, Nova Scotia	23 00
Attleboro	15 21
Westmoreland and Botsford Parishes, New Brunswick	95 25
J. J. Ronaldson & Sons, Sheffield, England	97 76
Diocese of Huron, Ontario	2,000 00
Toronto "Sons of England," Kent Lodge	30 00
Trenton Concert	61 00
Quebec	4,558 85
Great Western Railroad Employés	300 00
Methodist and Baptist Churches of Caledonia, N. S.	3 37
Sent to G. Sidney Smith, Esq., for distribution, from Major-General and Mrs. Beauchamp Walker	£15 0 0
Mrs. A. G. Foley, Peterboro', Ontario	$5 00
Sent to Rev. Dr. Maclise for distribution :—	
From Houlton, Maine, **by John** McMaster	250 05
From Goodwill Church, **Montgomery**, New York, by Rev. **J. M.** Dickson	20 00

ADDENDA.

Sent to Oddfellows' Fund :—

Lynn, Mass., Providence Lodge....................	$50 07
Clinton, Ontario, Warriner Lodge—Per J. B. King...	75 00
Westville, Nova Scotia, Scotia Lodge................	50 00
Boston Oddfellows—Per Grand Master Perkins......	340 00
Humboldt Bay, Cal., Eureka Lodge..................	20 00
Woonsocket, Rhode Island, Woonsocket Lodge.......	20 00
Empire Lodge, St. Catharines, Ontario.............	50 00
Sarnia Lodge, Sarnia, do.	43 00
Cuyahoga Lodge, Cleveland, Ohio...................	50 00
Romeo Lodge, Stratford.............................	25 00
Monami Lodge, Mechanics' Falls, Maine.............	25 00
Crystal Wave Lodge, Pugwash, Nova Scotia.........	11 00
E. Ashley, Wilmot, C. E............................	20 00
Engineering Department I. C. Railway.............	492 67
Locomotive Do	1,281 68
Traffic and other Do	347 70
J. S. Fry & Son, Bristol, England..................	£10 Stg·
John Carruthers, Kingston, Ont..................	100 00

From returns in detail, just furnished by the Oddfellows' Lodges, the results of the fire, in relation to its effects on individual members appears to have been as follows :—

NAME OF LODGE.	Present Membership.	No. of Sufferers.	Dependents on Sufferers.	Total Sufferers and Depend's.	Approximate value of Property lost by Sufferers.
Pioneer, No. 9	198	78	182	260	$392,860 00
Beacon, No. 12........	118	36	94	130	113,550 00
Peerless, No. 19.......	83	10	34	44	26,560 00
Siloam, No. 29........	44	28	28	56	24,440 00
Totals........	443	152	338	490	$557,410 00
Less Insurance.....................................					140,052 00
Net approximate Loss...............................					$417,358 00

Many of the sufferers had *no* insurance. The supposed superiority of the fire department, and general efficiency of the water supply, having led to a false security—to a popular belief that it was impossible for St. John to be scourged by fire, as Boston and Chicago had been.

SENT TO MASONIC FUND.

Grand Lodge of Quebec	$200 00
A Brother, Newcastle, N. B.	4 00
National Lodge, Chicago	23 62
Knights Templars, Portland, Maine	117 00
Germania Lodge, Baltimore	18 93
Grand Lodge, Louisiana	189 00
Carleton Union Lodge of Carleton, N. B.	50 00
Grand Lodge of Wisconsin	94 50
St. John's Lodge, Toronto	150 00
Phœnix Lodge, Nashville, Tenn	947 00
Grand Lodge, Utah	56 70
St. Andrew's Lodge, Frederickton, N. B.	25 25
Loge des Cœurs Unis, Montreal	50 00
Rising Virtue Lodge, Mount Moriah Chapter, and St. John's Commandery, Bangor, Me.	284 25
Detroit Commandery	94 50
Springfield do.	500 00

SUPPLIES.

Halifax, N. S., 25 Stoves.
Boston Y. M. C. Union, **Clothing.**
Montreal, Clothing.
Musquodoboit, Clothing.
Toronto, Meats.
Taylor, Robert, Halifax, N. S., Boots.

Peke & Eaton, Halifax, N. S., Tea.
Hart, R. T. & Co., " Supplies.
Victoria Corner, N. B., 12 pairs Boots.
Canterbury Ladies, Bedding.
Bridgetown, N. S., Supplies.
Rev. C. McMullin, Hartland, N. B., Butter.
Norwich, Ontario, Clothing.
Philadelphia Maritime Exchange, Clothing.
Gibson, Alexander, York County, Supplies.

A BRIEF ACCOUNT

OF THE

FIRE IN THE TOWN OF PORTLAND,

SATURDAY MORNING, 20th OCTOBER, 1877.

JUST four months after the great calamity in St. John, the people of the Town of Portland were called upon to endure a hardship of almost equal dimensions. In one sense their endurance demanded even greater strength, for their trouble came, not in summer when the grass was green, and the air was soft and balmy, but in the very heart of a New Brunswick Fall, when the wind pierced the coarsest garment, and the ground was white with frost. It was in the small hours of the morning too, that men and women, half asleep and palsied by terror, rushed wildly into the street, shivering with cold and trembling with fear, as they heard the mad bell tolling the alarm. They lived in the merest tinder boxes, and in many of these were domiciled three, and sometimes four and five families. It was a fire of terrible importance, and at one time the destruction of the whole town was feared. But the lesson which the fire of June 20th taught had a salutary effect on the people, and, aided by a brave band of firemen, they made every effort to stay the onward march of the flames, and in this, success was partly attained. The fire destroyed seven blocks of buildings, and threw into the street two hundred and ninety-five families, which numbered, in the aggregate, fully three thousand persons. Of buildings swept away, there were ninety-seven dwelling houses, the Methodist Church and the Temperance Hall. The actual loss is estimated at two hundred and fifty thousand dollars, and the insurance scarcely reaches the sum of seventy thousand dollars. One man suffered a horrible death, and a number of people were injured more or less seriously. The fire was indeed a sore and bitter trial, and had it not been that the community had only a short time before experienced the horrors of the greater conflagration, the present calamity would have ranked as one of the great fires of Canada. Coming so soon after the St. John's scourge, men failed to realize at once the magnitude of destruction which it caused. But those who had twice passed through the flames knew to their cost, and realized in an instant, what it was to be burned out a second time. Seven hundred persons from the burnt district of St. John's had taken up their residence in the suburban town. They were in most cases poor in a pecuniary sense, but their hands were strong, and their hearts were not downcast. The flames had carried away all their earthly possessions, and they found themselves the day after the fire comparatively penniless. But there was work to do, and these men and women sternly resolved to do it. They removed to Portland, secured quarters there, and had just completed their arrangements for the winter, when this fresh trouble broke out, and once more they found themselves, with twenty-three hundred others, in the street without a home, and no sheltering roof over their heads. Their lot was indeed a sad one, and no wonder is it, that some of them were loud in complaint, and that many women walked down from Fort Home that day and wept bitterly at the heartrending sight which met their eyes. They saw desolation on the plain below, and tall chimneys kept watch and ward over a field of smouldering embers. The steam engines still continued to play on the dying flames, though the sixth hour of the fire had long since passed away, and men in command hurried along the streets now giving orders, and now working with the rank and file, striving to save what remnants of property yet remained unburned, and caring for the immediate needs of sufferers.

The fire broke out at a quarter to three o'clock in the morning, and originated in a wood-house in the centre of the block, between Main and High Streets. This woodhouse was in the rear of Henry Pratt's house, and as fire had been discovered in this locality twice recently, many believed that it was the fiendish work of an incendiary. The fire spread with great rapidity, though there was little wind at the time, and by three o'clock the entire block,

Main Street on the north, Chapel Street on the south, Acadia Street on the east, and Portland Street on the west, was one mass of flame. In another hour the fire raged more violently, and was extending to the lower streets. The firemen, who were early on the spot, worked with untiring energy, and displayed almost superhuman endurance and wonderful courage. Aid from the city came very soon after the fire was observed, and the new contingent also worked with admirable nerve, and exhibited splendid skill in preventing the conflagration from spreading. Members of the Town Council, with Chairman Henry Hilyard at their head, made extraordinary efforts to keep the flames back, and indeed the whole arrangements for fighting the fire were excellently conceived and well carried out.

At five o'clock the fire had reached its height. The blocks from Main Street to High Street, inclusive, were completely obliterated, and only gaunt chimneys remained. From High Street to the very water's edge the flames sped on unresisted. Camden Street was burning, the large houses on the foot of Portland Street, the houses from Temperance Hall, in Simonds Street to Thomson's slip were consumed. Rankin's wharf with immense piles of dressed lumber was threatened with immediate extinction. The steamers "Ida Whittier," "Xyphus," and "Victor," were for a time in danger. Three tug boats arrived opportunely, and the water which they threw saved the wharf and lumber. At half-past eight the fire was subdued.

FIRE IN THE TOWN OF PORTLAND.   283

The property destroyed consisted of all the houses in Main Street between Jones's corner and Orange corner; all on Chapel Street, all on Acadia Street except a small block and the greater part of Chapel Street; all along the east side and part of the west side of Portland Street, the east side of Simonds Street from High Street to the water, and both sides of Camden Street. Of course a great deal of drunkenness prevailed and numerous arrests were made. Thieving, as usual, was largely indulged in.

The saddest event of the day was the loss of life. George Baxter, a ship carpenter, who dwelt in High street, was found in a charred state in the ruins of his house. It is thought he went in to save some of his effects, and being unable to make his way out again he was smitten to the ground and suffered one of the most terrible of deaths. The other casualties were John Henry Maher, slightly injured, James Ennis badly cut on the head. Nicholas Ryan fell off Dickinson's house, Chapel Street, and sustained serious bruises. Mrs. Reed was struck by a falling ladder. John Cobalan, jr., had one of his fingers broken, and Mrs. Nowlan was slightly hurt. Wm. Carr and James Kennedy were injured slightly.

The destruction of the Methodist Church is a very serious loss. It was built in the year 1841, and succeeded the structure built in 1828, which was destroyed in the former year. The first trustees were Alex. McLeod, Samuel H. McKee, George Whittaker, William Nesbit, H. Hennigar, Robert Chestnut, Robert Robertson, G. T. Ray,

John B. Gaynor, George Lockhart, James Bustin, John Owens and Francis Jordan, Rev. Messrs. R. Williams, J. B. Story, and S. Busby were strong supporters of the church in its young days and were long identified with its interests. On the first Sunday after the fire of 1841 the congregation met in the open air and prayed and sang hymns. The Rev. Mr. Allen addressed the people from a rock. Rev. Mr. Teed was the pastor at the time of the present fire. When he came to preside over its destinies he found the church struggling with a debt, and he worked with great zeal to free it from this burden.

The Temperance Hall was one of the most useful institutions in the town, and many will deplore the destruction of this building.

The following is a complete list of the buildings burned. The first name mentioned in each case is that of the owner, the other, that of the occupants :—

Main street, south side, from Acadia street to Portland Street.—Mr. Woods, occupied by self as a boarding house, and by R. Jones as a grocery store—two families.

Andrew Pratt, by self as a dwelling ; Miss Pratt as millinery store ; Henry Pratt, as dwelling ; and by Mr. Hopkins as a book store—4.

Chas. Long, James Meally, tin shop ; Robt. Adamson, and John W. Perkins—3.

Wm. Gray, by self, Gray & Scott, meat store ; Mrs. Cotner—4.

Widow Gordon, by self as a grocery store and dwelling—1.

Widow McJunkin, by self as a boarding house, and by Robert C. Gordon, as a liquor store, and by John S. Mitchell—3.

John Bradley, by A. G. Kearns, as a grocery and liquor store—1.

Thos. McColgan, by T. M. & S. B. Corbett, groceries ; Thos. McMasters, hair-dressing saloon ; John Carlin, S. R. Lindsay, Wm. Hooper, Messrs. Kyle & Tait—7.

Portland street, east side, from Chapel to Main street.—Thomas McColgan, by self as a liquor store ; Edward Brown, Joshua Russel—3.

FIRE IN THE TOWN OF PORTLAND. 285

Chapel street, north side, east from the Pond to Portland street.—Wm. Dickson's house (damaged), by self, Robert Currie, Widow McAnulty, Arthur McCauslin—4.
Widow Farson, by self, Wm. Conway, Widow Gallagher, Geo. Kimball, Daniel Leary, John Mohan, Jas. Daley, Mrs. Daley, Mrs. Knowles, Chase & McCallum—11.
Charles Long, by self, John Law—2.
Barn belonging to Wm. Gray.
Barn belonging to Robt. Gordon.
Barn belonging to John McJunkin estate.
Barn belonging to John Bradley.
Chapel street, south side, from Portland street east to Water.—Miss Mary Long, by Mrs. McArthur, Mr. Appleby and Mrs. Gorral—3.
Chas. Long, by self and son as grocery and dwelling ; Chas. Colwell, Alex. Long, Abraham Craig—5.
Mrs. Nancy Lackey, by Local Preacher Oram, Miss McJunkin, John McJunkin—3.
Joseph Reed, by Samuel Baker, Frank Crawford—2.
Barn belonging to Sarah Irvine.
Arthur Rodgers, by self, Mrs. Clancey, Arthur Desmond and Mr. Long—4.
Widow Sullivan, by Thos. Sullivan—1.
John Damary, by self and Thos. Damary—2.
John Corrigan, by self—1.
Thos. Currie, by self and John Quinn—2.
Wm. King's house, damaged considerably.
Acadia street, east side, from High street to Main street.—Mrs. Sarah Irvine, occupied by self, Thomas Kerr, Nancy Irvine, Messrs. Campbell & Hartt—5.
Geo. McMonagle, by self as a grocery and dwelling ; Widow Nelson, William McGuire, John McGuire, David Smith—5.
Mrs. Farson, by Mrs. Gallaher, Mrs. McCacherin—2.
Geo. McMonagle, by Thomas Sharp and Patrick Bogan —2.
Alex. Duff (house damaged considerably), by Thomas McGill and Henry McCarthy—2.
Acadia street, west side, from High to Main street.—Joseph Reed, by self, Andrew Crawford, Wm. McConnell, Mrs. Wark—4.
Widow Farson, by self as grocery and liquor shop and dwelling ; Jeremiah Sullivan, James Brown, David McBurney, Jeremiah Speight, widow Marley—6.
Portland street, east side, from High street to Main street.—John Connolly, by Messrs. Smith, as a grocery store, Capt. Rawlings, of the Portland Police, and by David Speight, as a boarding house—3.
Methodist Parsonage, occupied by Rev. Mr. Teed, Pastor of the Portland Methodist Church—1.
[The houses of Mr. McColgan are mentioned in connection with buildings on Main and Chapel streets.]

High street, north side, from Portland street east to water.—John Brooks, by George Wetmore, Wm. C. Dunham—2.
Thomas Polly, by self, John Alcorn, John Humphreys—3.
George Smith (brick cottage), by self and Robert Smith—2.
George Ruddock, by self and George Brown—2.
Widow Ruddock, **by Mr.** Ellis—1.
Andrew Myles, by self, Messrs. Porter and Rogers—3.
Edward Sergeant, by self and Mr. Stantiford—2.
George Young, by self and Mrs. Upham—2.
Robert Ewing, by self, Walter Brown, R. A. H. Morrow—3.
Edward Elliot, by Geo. Jenkins, John Green, Frank Wallace—3.
Capt. Aubrey, by self and Mr. Reed—2.
Edward Elliott, by self and Mr. McAllister—2.
Portland street from Rankin's wharf to Camden street.—Alex. Ferguson, by self, Captain Buckhard, and Wm. Sleeth.
Hugh Montague, Robert and Joseph Carson—3.
John Irvine, by self and Widow Craig.
John McCachney, by self, mother and Jas. McCachney.
Geo. Carter, by self, Joseph Murphy, Geo. Carter, Jr.—3.
T. Travis, by self, as grocery and liquor store and dwelling. August Mavison, Mr. Wilson, Mrs. Riley and another—5.
Camden street, south side, from Portland street to Acadia street.—James Bartlett, by self, Henry Bartlett, Archibald Tatton, Capt. Bartlett, **James** Tubman—5.
John McJunkin, by self, Capt. Charles Harper, Harry Bassett—3.
Arthur Kyle, by self, John Cunningham, John O'Connell, Mr. Rebels, Mrs. McDormott, William John Hammond—6.
Acadia street, from Camden South to water.—Daniel O'Hara, by self, and Chas. Hara—2.
Patrick Dawson, by self, Peter Nelson, **and a** family from the City **burnt** district—3.
Mrs. Hamilton, by self—1.
Wm. Carter, by self—1.
Portland street, west side, from Camden to High street.—Wm. McIntyre, by self, Geo. Giggy, Geo. Morgan, James Power, Harry Stephens, Wm. Gillan, and a family from the City burnt district—7. [In rear house belonging to David Breen, occupied by self and N. Frizzle.]
Thomas McMasters, by self, John Boyd, Widow McJunkin, James Ryder, Messrs. Mullay, Brown and Christopher—7.
Widow Kerr, by self—1. [Mr. Murdock's house in rear, by one tenant—1.]
Wm. A. Moore, occupied by self as a dwelling, John Currie, groceries; James Pender, Joseph McIntyre, the Misses Darrah—5.
Portland street, east side, from Camden to High street.—Richard Anderson, by **self** and Samuel Devennie—2.
Richard **Anderson, by** William Hill, as a grocery store and dwelling; John Rubins, **tailor shop,** James McCord—4.

Robert McIntyre, by Bernard Gallagher, dwelling and grocery store, Samuel C. rett, Richard McIntyre—3.

Robert McIntyre, by self, Ike Munroe, Oliver Colwell, Robert Black, C. rrington—5.

Wm. McIntyre, by Wm. Maxwell and Robert McMurray—2.

Wm. McIntyre, by Jacob Brown, Misses Sharp, Duke Brown, Geo. DeLong, Levi DeLong—5. [House in rear occupied by Joseph Lee and John Mullay—2.]

Benj. Lawton, by self and brother—2.

Camden street, north side, from Simonds east to water.—Thos. W. Peters, by Thomas Mansfield, as a dwelling and a grocery store, John Nowlin, Jeremiah Sullivan and two others—5.

Thos. W. Peters, by Mr. Leonard and Edward Cutten—2.

John Higgins, by self—1.

George Grear, by self, John Ross, John Cooper, Mr. McLean—4.

ichard Anderson, by Harry Laskey, John Thompson, Miss Osborne—3.

Widow Wilson, by self, H. Brockings, Widow Bailey—4. [Unoccupied house in rear.]

Stephen Murphy, by self, Messrs. Hamilton, Ralston and Hoolahan—4.

Acadia street, west side, from Camden to High street.—Wm. Searle, by Hugh Hutchinson, Wm. Bell—2.

James Bartlett, by David Doherty, Mr. Fitzgerald—2.

Robt. McKay, by self, Messrs. Irvine and Munroe—3.

Mr. Reed, by Thomas Graham and another—2. [Rear house owned by Mr. Reed.]

Thomas Youngclaus, by Messrs. Stayhorn, Kirk and Beaton—3.

James Kyle, by self and Mr. McGee—2.

Widow Ruddock, by self and a family whose name could not be learned—2.

Wm. Elliott, by self, James Smith and John Devennie—3.

Acadia street, east side, from Camden street to High street.—John H. Crawford, by self, as a grocery and dwelling—1.

Thomas Gillespie, by Mr. Tait, Joseph Allen, Widow Garvey and Widow Boyne—4.

High street, south side, westward from water.—John McDermott, by self, Patrick Carlin and Thomas Smith—3.

Miss Daley, by Wm. Peacock, Widow Knodell and Joseph Speight—3.

George Baxter, by self as dwelling and grocery store ; and by Mr. Dunham—1.

Geo. Baxter, by Messrs. Wilson, and Kirk and another—3.

Widow Young, by self, Wm. Young, and George Easty—3.

Patrick Flynn, by Messrs. Stack and Thompson Kennedy, and Widow Logan—3.

James Scott, by self, and James Barbour—2.

Joseph Sullivan, by self—1.

Joseph Logan, by self, Widow Buchanan, Widow McDermott—3.

Temperance Hall, owned by Governor Tilley, J. C. Edwards, and Portland Division, S. of T.

Simonds street, east side, from High street to water,—Andrew Johnston's house, occupied by four families—1.

Paul Gillespie, by John Buckley, James Gillespie, and Mr. Akerley—2.

Widow, by self, James Spence, and Charles Brown, and two others—5.

Widow Crawford, by self, as dwelling and grocery shop, and by James Buckley—2.

Alex. Urquhart, **by self**—1.

Thos. W. Peters, **by Widow** Morrison, John Morrison and **Mrs** Wilson—3.

LOSSES OF INSURANCE COMPANIES.

PROVINCIAL.

Thos. McColgan,	$1600
Methodist Church,	3000
Wm. Elliott,	1200
Chas. Long,	1200
Mrs. S. J. Young,	500
R. Jones,	600
Total,	$8100

LANCASHIRE.

Capt. Aubrey,	$800
Thos. Travis,	800
Other claims about	1400
Total,	$3000

NORTHERN.

Methodist Church,	$4000
Mrs. Buchanan,	1000
Geo. Baxter,	800
Robt. McHarg,	800
Total,	$6600

NORTH BRITISH AND MERCANTILE.

Mrs. Gordon,	$900
John Connolly,	1600
T. W. Peters,	2500
Methodist Church (re-insurance),	$1000
Total,	$6000

QUEEN.

Geo. Ruddock,	$1200
Methodist Mission House,	2400
James Scott,	1700
H. Montague,	800
John McKechnie,	800
Robert Rankin,	2000
Do.,	1500
R. Ewing,	1200
E. Sargent,	800
E. Elliott,	1000
A. Johnston,	700
Jas. Pender,	500
Estate Jas. Kerr,	600
	$15,200
Partial losses,	1000
Total,	$16,200

CITIZENS'.

Messrs. Corbett,	$400
Mrs. Farson,	1200
Wm. McIntyre,	1250
Chas. Long,	1100
John Bradley,	400

FIRE IN THE TOWN OF PORTLAND.

David Breen,	$300
Wm. Gray,	200
Mary Long,	400
Thomas McMaster,	600
R. McIntyre,	700
Arthur Rodgers,	700
Thomas Youngclaus,	800
Total,	$8050

ROYAL CANADIAN.

Mary Ann Daley,	$600

CANADA FIRE AND MARINE.

Thomas Aubrey,	$100
Mary Long,	300
John McDermott,	600
Ann Leckey,	500
Margaret Curry,	200
R. C. Gordon,	1200
G. F. Smith,	800
Gertrude Farson,	1500
F. C. Dunham,	550
G. F. Jenkins,	500
John Greer,	500
John Reed,	200
Total,	$6950

ÆTNA.

G. McMonagle,	$1000
R. McIntyre,	600
James Bartlett,	300
A. R. Ferguson,	2000
Total,	$3900

HARTFORD.

Jos. Stubbs,	$500
Jas. Boyle,	400
John Brook,	1000
Geo. R. Rigby,	300
Richard Anderson,	1000
Total,	$3200

IMPERIAL.

R. A. H. Morrow,	$200
R. Flynn,	1000
Samuel Gillespie,	1200
John Brook,	1000
Wm. Ruddock, estate,	1400
Mrs. Sarah Irvine,	800
Robert Rankine,	1500
Total,	$7100

BRITISH AMERICAN.

James Bartlett,	$400
Mrs. S. Osborne,	100
Total,	$500

ISOLATED RISK.

R. Jones,	$500
Chas. Long,	400
Total,	$900
The Guardian,	$4000
The National,	500
Western,	200

At eleven o'clock the Portland Town Council met to consider the best way in which relief for the sufferers could be administered. The Mayor of St. John, Dr. Earle, the High Sheriff, and **Harris Allan**, Esq., of the Relief and

Aid Society, were present. On motion it was resolved that the council should attend to the wants of the homeless, and committees were immediately appointed to perform the various duties incumbent on them. These were Couns. Chesley and Munro, to look up school-houses; Couns. McLean and Holly, clearing engine house; Couns. Puddington and Cochran, securing cooking stoves; Couns. Purdy and Hamilton, supplying provisions; Couns. Gilbert and Austin, straw mattrasses; Chairman, H. Hilyard and Couns. Chesley, Shelter, His Lordship Bishop Sweeny, and Messrs. Robert H. Flaherty, and F. Hazen having offered the committee the use of their buildings, were publicly thanked for their kindly forethought. On the night of the fire upwards of fifty families were provided with shelter by the authorities.

On Monday, 22nd October, at a general meeting of St. John Relief Committee, it was decided that temporary relief should be at once given to the poor. This lasted one week. At the expiration of that time the Board of Directors, consisting of the whole Council of the Town of Portland were in a position to administer their own relief. The committees of the societies are as follows :—

EXECUTIVE COMMITTEE.

The Chairman, and Messrs. Chesley, Duff, Puddington, and Cochran.

SHELTER COMMITTEE.

Messrs. Gilbert, Austin, Purdy and J. H. Parks.

FIRE IN THE TOWN OF PORTLAND.

VISITING COMMITTEE.

Chairman, and Messrs. **Holly and** Maher.

SUBSCRIPTION COMMITTEE.

Messrs. Puddington, Cochran, Maher and Holly.

A very efficient ladies' committee was promptly organized, and through their noble efforts a vast deal of suffering was prevented. Mrs. Simon Baizley, Mrs. Barnhill, Mrs. D. B. Roberts, Mrs. Thomas Hilyard, Mrs. Teed, Mrs. Almon and others comprised this committee.

Up to November 28th, 1877, the following donations have been received in aid of the people who were burnt out :—

CASH.

St. John Relief Committee	$5,000 00
Hon. Isaac Burpee	100 00
Rev. Wm. Armstrong	25 00
Rev. Geo. Armstrong	20 00
George A. Schofield	10 00
A. Cochran, Halifax, N. S.	1 00
Mrs. Parnther	5 00
Rev. T. Partridge, collection taken at Rothsay	30 50
G. Sidney Smith, Esq.	10 00
Draft from Wheelright, Anderson & Co. Boston, Mass., $50 American currency	48 50

Norman Robertson................	$10 00
Wm. Wright, Esq., Liverpool, England, £100 stg.,........................	479 32
Wm. Shives Fisher................	4 00
Proceeds of entertainment at Fairville	50 70
Proceeds lectures by Bishop Fallowes of the Reformed Episcopal Church.	45 00
Collection from St. Jude's Church, S. S. Thanksgiving Day...............	12 75
George W. Roberts, Liverpool........	100 00

SUPPLIES.

P. Nase & Son, twenty barrels potatoes, one chest tea.

Vroom & Arnold, thirty barrels potatoes.

James J. Fellows, two barrels cabbages.

Chas., Fawcett, (Sackville, N. B.) four stoves.

Manchester, Robertson & Allison, goods to amount of one hundred dollars.

Geo J. Fisher, thirty rolls roofing paper.

Thomas Cusack, blankets to value of $75.

www.ingramcontent.com/pod-product-compliance
Lightning Source LLC
Chambersburg PA
CBHW022017240426
43667CB00042B/634